Autism Spectrum Disorder

in the Inclusive Classroom

Barbara Boroson

New York • Toronto • London • Auckland • Sydney
Mexico City • New Delhi • Hong Kong • Buenos Aires

Dedication

To Mom and Dad, with love forever.
Now nothing is the same.

Acknowledgments

I am lucky to have been surrounded by many steadfast supporters while writing and updating this book. Together they are a testament to how a community filled with the spirit of caring collaboration and positivity can make anything happen.

With fondness and appreciation, I thank Ann Horowitz, Jennifer Grace, Marla Levine, and Terry Dunn for keeping me writing, believing, and laughing; Leah Tahbaz and Elyse Varos-Pollack for their artful turns of phrase; Joy Nolan, Lucia Murillo, Dena Gassner, Margaret Bailey, Michael Giustino, and Daniel Pilowsky, M.D., for their expert input; Stephanie Dalbey and Carol LoCascio, Ph.D., for mentoring me way back when; Una Murray for her hard-won wit and wisdom; and especially Nancy Clausen Davie for her endless friendship and her boundless enthusiasm.

With reverence and deference, I offer my appreciation to all teachers who strive to both reach and teach, most notably to Gail Sider and Cathy Schaeffer who set the bar so tantalizingly high. I am grateful for and humbled by the stories of triumph and despair contributed by many dedicated teachers.

Thanks also to the creative team at Scholastic: phenomenal editor Kaaren Sorensen who both challenged and cheered me all the way through the second edition; editor-in-chief Tara Welty for ushering this book into the future; Virginia Dooley for first bringing this book to me and Joanna Davis-Swing for coaxing it out of me; designers Sarah Morrow, Michelle H. Kim, Jaime Lucero, and Jorge Namerow; managing editor Adrienne Downey; and creative director Tannaz Fassihi; and my prescient and persistent agent at Writer's House, Susan Cohen.

Finally, with all my love and gratitude, I thank my family:

Lou and Florence Boroson for their unconditional love and unwavering confidence. Always with me—even still;

Martin Boroson for his exhaustive edits, his exhausting ideas, and his inexhaustive support;

Andrew Dodd for entrusting and embracing me with his ring of truth;

Joseph Rutt for holding me up and backing me up, every single day;

Sam Boroson Rutt for inspiring me—literally;

and Leana Boroson Rutt, for inspiring me—literarily.

● ● ● ●

The art on pages 52, 58, 62, 64, 67, 118, and 175 was created with Boardmaker software, which was developed by DynaVox Mayer-Johnson, 2100 Wharton Street, Suite 400, Pittsburgh, PA 15203 Phone: (800) 588-4548 Fax: (866) 585-6260.

Cover Designer: Michelle H. Kim and Jorge J. Namerow
Editor: Kaaren Sorensen
Interior Designer: Sarah Morrow

ISBN: 978-1-338-03854-5
Copyright © 2016 by Barbara Boroson. All rights reserved.
Published by Scholastic Inc. Printed in the U.S.A.
First printing, June 2016.

6 7 8 9 10   40   23 22 21 20

Contents

Introduction

If you don't have a student on the autism spectrum in your class today, you will soon. The prevalence of Autism Spectrum Disorder (ASD) is at an all-time high, and more students on the spectrum are being placed in inclusive classrooms every year.

As of the publication of this second edition, one out of every 68 children is believed to be on the autism spectrum—and that number has been rising dramatically for decades (U.S. Centers for Disease Control and Prevention, 2014).

In combination with national shifts toward least restrictive programming and inclusion, these statistics mean that you'll see many students on the spectrum crossing the threshold of your suddenly inclusive classroom. In other words, students with Autism Spectrum Disorder are coming your way. You need to be ready.

And to be ready, you need to be up to date. An enormous amount has changed in the field of Autism Spectrum Disorder since the publication of the first edition of this book. That's why this book has been fully revised and updated to meet your needs now. In addition to all of the valuable, accessible ideas teachers loved in the first edition, you'll find tons of new information, concepts, strategies, and resources. Here's what's new:

- An expanded grade range (now K–8), in response to reader demand for middle-school support

- The latest developments on the autism landscape, including:
    - ✔ skyrocketing statistics reflecting the prevalence of Autism Spectrum Disorder
    - ✔ entirely new diagnostic criteria for ASD
    - ✔ dramatic innovations in classroom technology
    - ✔ the special challenges presented by the Common Core State Standards and other rigorous new state standards—and how to navigate them successfully

- Additional resources, including:
    - ✔ a brand-new chapter about collaborating with your colleagues to establish a truly inclusive school community

✔ reproducible fact sheets you can easily share with classroom paraprofessionals, building staff, and special area teachers

✔ a new feature called "There's an App for That," providing tips for using technology to support every area of challenge

And much, much more.

Within these pages you will discover what makes students on the spectrum tick (as well as what makes them *tic*). You will learn to identify Autism Spectrum Disorder, recognize what drives the responses and behaviors of students on the spectrum, and find out how you can help steer them toward success. You will learn how to hold it all together and how to keep your whole class running smoothly and your whole self feeling steady. And you will see that while this will be a year full of new challenges, it will also be a year full of powerful, emerging new perspectives, for you and for your entire class, about seeing and being in the world. Really.

The prospect of including these students in your classroom may fill you with anxiety: You may dread having to exert the extra effort and resent what feels like an intrusion on your comfort level and expertise. Or you may welcome the inclusion of these students as an exciting challenge and an opportunity to explore new territory and expand your professional horizons. Most likely, you find yourself vacillating somewhere in between. That's *your* spectrum, and wherever you find yourself on this autism-spectrum-support spectrum, help is in your hands.

Individuals Together

Every individual functions in and experiences the world differently on the basis of his or her own history, creativity, flexibility, adaptability, sensitivities, and sensibilities. There is no correct way to experience life. Some of us are excited by the taste of cayenne pepper; others find it overwhelming. Some of us meditate or read a book to relax; others relax by jogging or dancing. Some of us tend to get anxious; others get angry. Some of us feel and react passionately; others are stoic. None of these experiences or coping styles is right or wrong, just individual.

But we must all strive for the flexibility and adaptability to *feel when we need to feel, and deal when it's time to deal*. We must strike this delicate balance in order to be true to ourselves while functioning effectively within the context of the social world. Though many of the strategies in this book will help bring students on the spectrum closer to "mainstream" or typical functioning, all of your students will need to make the effort to embrace the diverse culture of your classroom.

Students on the autism spectrum share some common traits. But just like stars in the sky, each of these students possesses unique characteristics we can see only when we magnify the details. One of the fundamental goals of this book is to help you look closely enough to see and appreciate the stellar singularity of each student.

While this book seeks to highlight the brilliant and singular sparkle of each individual student, it also guides your efforts to create a *cohesive classroom community* that celebrates and draws together all kinds of learners and doers, thinkers and feelers, workers and players, walkers and talkers, actors and reactors, movers and shakers. With this book, you will learn how to help all students showcase their strengths and cope with their challenges within the context of the multifaceted classroom community. An inclusive classroom is a community built around mutual understanding, acceptance, and support. This is what inclusive education is all about, and when done well, every student grows and benefits from the experience.

The Spectrum of This Book

Every one of the unique students in your class possesses an assortment of strengths and challenges. Some of those strengths and challenges may be fairly typical and familiar to you; others may be quite remarkable and unfamiliar. The chapters in this book will familiarize you with the numerous idiosyncratic strengths, challenges, and factors that drive the functioning of students on the autism spectrum. Many examples and strategies are offered to help you prepare and respond effectively. In combination, the information in these chapters will help you lay the foundation to build a learning environment that is inclusive of and beneficial for every member of your class.

But no single chapter stands alone in guiding academic instruction. This is because academic instruction is possible only within the context of all of the issues in all of the chapters. You really cannot begin to teach curriculum to students on the autism spectrum if you haven't taken into consideration their challenges related to anxiety, regulation, sensation, engagement, socialization, communication, and organization, among others. When any of those systems is amiss, challenging behaviors may arise, so it is crucial to look *beyond* problematic behaviors to discover what is fueling them and what function they are serving. Each chapter of this book describes common behavioral triggers, guides you to decode the messages behaviors are communicating, and provides strategies for responding efficiently to effect lasting change. So please read the book all the way through at least one time, keeping your specific students in mind.

You'll see that most of the strategies in this book reflect *a way of thinking*, more than specific ways of doing. No one is asking you (or should be asking you) to upend your entire classroom or teaching style. As you read, you may want to focus less on implementing strategies and more on looking at your students through this investigative lens. Once you become familiar with the underlying sensitivities and challenges students on the spectrum face, differentiated problem solving should become second nature to you. And even if at first you make adaptations or modifications with only a few students in mind, once you start thinking along these lines, you'll see just how powerful creative thinking and differentiated styles of instruction can be for every learner.

In the meantime, this book provides lots of preventive and responsive strategies. Preventive strategies will be the most important tools in your box, both philosophically and practically. They will guide you toward thinking in a proactive, positive way. They will help you keep the heat down and prevent problematic situations from occurring and recurring. That's important because once a cycle of reaction has begun, it can be especially difficult or truly impossible to recover the day for your students on the spectrum.

So go ahead and implement whatever preventive strategies seem relevant and useful. But please don't try to use all of the strategies. You will be doing your students a disservice by not differentiating their needs, and, worse, you will use yourself up. Grab what makes sense today, and then put this book down. But don't put it far: The issues these students face and the ways they cope with them comprise an ever-changing landscape. So the parts of this book that feel irrelevant today may be lifesavers tomorrow.

Here's what you'll find in the pages ahead:

Ten Things You Can Do Before Day One, on page 10, is a quick checklist you can use to prepare yourself and your classroom before students on the spectrum join you. If you have limited time, try to implement the simple but critically important ideas on this list, even if you don't yet understand why they're so important. For now, just trust that these steps will pave the way for a smoother start. The rest of the book will put them into meaningful and compelling contexts for you.

Chapter 1, *Terms of Engagement,* defines and explains many of the terms, including the new diagnostic criteria, that you will encounter on your journey with students across the autism spectrum. This chapter also offers an overview of the special education referral and placement process.

Chapter 2, *The Power of Positivity,* offers suggestions to help you bring out the best in your students, in your colleagues, and in yourself. Progress for students on the spectrum can be almost imperceptible. You may feel frustration and discouragement rearing up against your every effort. And if you feel frustrated and discouraged, imagine how your students feel. This chapter will show you how to recognize and celebrate your students' strengths and how to keep yourself afloat even when you feel you're drowning.

Chapter 3, *The Simmering Pot,* describes why students on the spectrum cling to routine and consistency. Always guarded against unexpected input, these students live in a permanent state of anxiety. Learn how to structure a classroom to keep the weather calm and cool, enabling students to relax and rely on your structure to support their feelings of safety and fuel their independence.

Chapter 4, *Body and Soul,* illuminates the sensory systems of students on the spectrum. Discover why their systems may be on high alert in many ways you might not expect or even recognize. This chapter will describe the broad range of sensory experience, common sensory triggers and reactions, and other factors affecting self-regulation. Learn how to create an environment that nourishes each student with just enough—and not too much—sensory stimulation.

Chapter 5, *The Inner Sanctum,* uncovers why students on the autism spectrum, immersed in the comfort of reliable rules and static topics, may struggle to engage in the learning environment around them. Learn how to find the *hook* to capture their interest and keep them on board.

Chapter 6, *Meeting of the Minds, Part One,* introduces you to one of your most valuable resources: students' families. Find out where the families of students on the spectrum are coming from and how to walk in lockstep with them on the journey you are now on together. Combining your educational expertise with their whole-child, historical perspective, you will make a formidable team.

Chapter 7, *Meeting of the Minds, Part Two,* describes how to maximize collaboration with your colleagues regarding students on the spectrum. A truly inclusive program extends beyond the walls of the classroom. This brand-new chapter will help you work effectively with co-teachers, classroom paraprofessionals, therapists, special area teachers, and others in your school community to help create a seamless support system.

Chapter 8, *Something for Everyone,* unpacks the social struggles that students on the spectrum face when trying to read and interpret the perspective of others. Their need for sameness makes adapting to the unpredictable dynamics of interaction painfully elusive. Meanwhile, your other students may struggle to tolerate the quirks and behaviors of students on the spectrum. This chapter will help you make it work for everyone as you create a classroom community of support and acceptance.

Chapter 9, *Say What?,* explains the obstacles these students may face as they work to process and utilize language. This chapter articulates common areas of communicative challenge for students on the spectrum and offers strategies to support both receptive and expressive language, as well as nonverbal communication.

Chapter 10, *Boiling Up and Over,* details what happens when big behaviors erupt, despite all of the preventive measures you've implemented (as described in the previous chapters). When circumstances deviate too far out of the comfort zones of students on the spectrum, sensory systems overload and the anxiety that always simmers within overflows. Inside the student flares a sudden chaos of confusion, inadequacy, and panic. On the outside, we see a breakdown of coping skills and a loss of control. This chapter explores what is really being communicated by intense behavior. You will learn how to restore equilibrium with confidence and competence, how to find and address the true antecedents of behaviors, and how to help students develop more adaptive means of coping and communicating.

Chapter 11, *Info In, Info Out,* explains that conceptual processing and learning may happen in unusual ways for students on the spectrum. This chapter shows you how to break through, even in this challenging era of Common Core and other intense academic standards. Chapter 11 won't help you if you haven't read all of the chapters that come before. Only *after* you have attended to the full range of other issues—only once you have *reached* these students—can you begin to actually teach curriculum. That's why the chapter that pertains to curricular instruction comes last. Don't do it—don't jump ahead. You'll be fiddling with phonics while Rome is burning. It is only after the sparks have settled, the climate has cooled, and the forecast is stable that you can begin to teach academic curriculum to students on the spectrum.

Reproducible Fact and Tip Sheets—brand-new in this edition and found on pages 227–234 of the book—are provided to make it super-simple for you to share your wisdom. These double-sided information sheets are created to help others in the building who work with your students on the spectrum. Each contains basic facts about Autism Spectrum Disorder as well as tips to support interaction with kids on the spectrum, specifically geared to special area teachers, coaches and phys ed teachers, building and bus staff, and classroom paraprofessionals. Make a copy, add a few details about a specific student, and hand it off. They'll love you for it.

It's all here for the taking; once you've read it through, use it as you like. This book is not meant to be prescriptive. It's just full of ideas for you to think about and make your own. Pick and choose as you consider the ongoing and evolving needs of each member of your dynamic classroom community. Some strategies will resonate with you for some of your students; some may spark new and different ideas; others may sound ridiculous but might surprise you. Some may take a bit of work to create or implement, but trust that an initial investment of time and effort will pay off for months and years to come.

By taking the time to recognize, address, and support the strengths and challenges of students on the autism spectrum, you will discover ways to feature ability rather than disability. You will unearth innovative approaches that breathe fresh life into your curriculum and teaching methods to benefit all of your students. And as you develop your understanding of different ways of being in the world, you will open up new dimensions in your classroom constellation and inspire a panorama of remote stars to shine.

Ten Things You Can Do Before Day One

Every student on the autism spectrum will enter your classroom bearing a backpack full of worries. If those worries can't be put down on Day One, then toting that heavy load will become a way of life at school, a learned behavior. Each day these students will return burdened and compromised by the worries on their backs. Instead, seize this moment to help them offload their worries by preparing a classroom that exudes comfort, clarity, and consistency, even on Day One.

Here is a basic list of ten things you can do before Day One to lighten the load for students on the spectrum.

1. **Reach out to families.** Well in advance if possible, send home a copy of the questionnaire on page 49 (available to download at www.barbaraboroson.com), asking about strengths and challenges, what helps and what makes things worse. Encourage parents or caregivers to get in touch with you to discuss any specific concerns. Consider carefully whatever anecdotal information emerges from these contacts as you plan for Day One and beyond.

2. **Talk to colleagues** who have had experience with these specific students so that you can benefit from both their successes and failed efforts, and so that you can hit the ground running.

3. **Display basic classroom rules in clear, simple language.** Students on the spectrum may not intuit your rules, but once they learn them, these students may be your best rule followers. (Find out why rules rule in Chapter 3.)

4. **Prepare a visual schedule for the first day.** Always let these students know what to expect in advance. (See how and why to do this in Chapter 3.) Send a copy of the first day's schedule home *before* Day One; and better yet, do #5!

5. **Arrange a visit** before the hustle and bustle of Day One. For students on the spectrum, first impressions are *really* lasting impressions, so make it a good one. (Visit the section on visits in Chapter 3.)

6. **Set up the classroom** with sensible, plainly labeled spaces that have clear boundaries. (Find out why this matters in Chapter 10.)

7. **Avoid seating these students near expectable distractions or sensory provocateurs**, such as the gerbil cage, the bunsen burners, the windows, the microwave, and so on. It may all be perceived as much louder, brighter, and smellier by your students than it is by you. (Get a sense of sensory considerations in Chapter 4.)

8. **Keep classroom decorations to a minimum**, at least for a while. In the beginning, less is definitely more. (Learn why less is more in Chapter 4.)

9. **Designate a small corner of your classroom as a Cozy Corner or Sensory Space**, if possible. Soften it up with basic comforts: a small rug, a beanbag chair, a few stuffed animals, an assortment of friendly books and magazines, or whatever you've learned might comfort your specific students. This can become a comfy place for any student who needs to decompress a bit, but for your students on the spectrum it may be a sanctuary. (Get in touch with sensory corners and sensory tools in Chapter 4.)

10. **Brush away your doubts and polish up your confidence.** You can do this. (Find out why you should believe that in Chapter 2!)

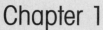

Chapter 1

Terms of Engagement

Spectrum and Special Education Terminology

Individuals with autistic traits have been perceived and identified in myriad ways over time. Despite evolving trends of ignorance, discrimination, questioning, research, clarity, and ambiguity (in that order!), a straightforward explanation of autistic-type challenges that really makes sense is hard to find.

For much of the 20th century, the term *autism* was used to describe only very remote individuals, people who were unable to communicate or engage with the world around them, who were inscrutable and unpredictable, lost in their own selves.

Beginning in 1994, several different subtypes of autism were identified and used for diagnosis, expanding the term *autism* to include many functional variations. Among them were Autistic Disorder, Asperger's Syndrome, and Pervasive Developmental Disorder, Not Otherwise Specified (PDD-NOS). While each of these subtypes fell under the broader diagnostic category of "autism spectrum disorders," they differed from each other in terms of significant variations in communication, socialization, and cognitive abilities.

But because every child on the spectrum is so different from every other, with unique combinations of strengths and challenges, distinguishing among the subtypes became an extremely complex and somewhat subjective business for diagnosticians.

That's why, in 2013, in the fifth edition of the Diagnostic and Statistical Manual (DSM-V, 2013), the American Psychiatric Association revamped the definition and criteria for autism spectrum diagnosis. Now the official diagnosis for all comers who meet the criteria is simply *Autism Spectrum Disorder*—an umbrella term beneath which all the varied and related symptoms huddle.

This cluster of symptoms is considered *neurodevelopmental* in etiology, which means that Autism Spectrum Disorder:

- involves the brain and nervous systems
- emerges during childhood and alters the course of a child's development

Across the spectrum one can find a rainbow collection of individuals who demonstrate similar autistic-type characteristics but who may function in very different ways and at very different levels. The image of a spectrum effectively evokes the *associated differentness* among the individuals covered by this colorful umbrella.

A Rose by Any Other Name

You may have students who, back in the old days (i.e., prior to 2013), were referred to with terms like Autistic Disorder, Asperger's Syndrome, High-Functioning Autism, Pervasive Developmental Disorder, and others. Some parents and older students—especially those previously diagnosed with Asperger's Syndrome—may still prefer to use these terms because they have become part of their identity, and meaningfully connect them to a specific peer group. Although those terms are no longer official diagnostic categories in the DSM-V, it is perfectly fine for students and their families to continue to use these descriptors if they choose to.

Autism Spectrum Disorder Today

Today, far more children are being diagnosed with Autism Spectrum Disorder than at any time in history. As recently as 2002, ASD was estimated to affect one out of every 150 children; however, according to the U.S. Centers for Disease Control (CDC), by 2010 that number had escalated to an astonishing one in 68. That means the prevalence of ASD diagnosis more than doubled in just eight years. (U.S. Centers for Disease Control, 2014).

Many possible explanations for this increase have been proposed over the years, and controversy swirls around them all.

Vaccines Redeemed

One theory about the increasing rates of ASD that gained disastrous momentum in the new millennium was based on the fraudulent claim that the MMR (measles, mumps, rubella) vaccine causes autism. This theory has been definitively disproven.

The baseless claim, originally made by British doctor Andrew Wakefield, was published in the highly respected scientific journal *The Lancet* in 1998. However, in 2010, upon finding that the study was undermined by falsified data, ethical violations, and financial conflicts of interest, *The Lancet* unequivocally renounced and retracted Wakefield's claims and he was stripped of his license to practice medicine.

But the damage was done. Immediately following publication of Wakefield's article, the rate of vaccination in many countries including the U.S. plummeted in response to a vigorous and tenacious anti-vaccine campaign, led by outraged parents and other activists. New and expectant parents, believing that they now had the power to fend off autism, refused vaccines in record numbers. Parents of already-vaccinated children on the autism spectrum, desperate to find an explanation for their children's challenges, now believed they had a place to lay blame. Lawsuits against the federal government and conspiracy theories attributed to vaccine manufacturers abounded.

And through it all, despite dramatically lower rates of vaccination across the U.S., the rate of autism diagnosis continued to soar. Bottom line? Study after study, conducted by unbiased researchers, has shown *absolutely no association between vaccines and autism, whatsoever.*

And yet, the vaccine myth has been extremely hard to shake in public perceptions about autism, with some parents remaining convinced that vaccines are to blame for their children's autism. Why is this? Probably because early symptoms of autism can appear as the loss of previously achieved developmental milestones. This developmental regression may occur at any time throughout a child's early years of near-constant cognitive, motor, and social development—including, *coincidentally*, following vaccination.

Still Searching

As researchers scramble to uncover a scientific cause for Autism Spectrum Disorder, numerous additional theories are being explored. Despite intense research and scientific advances, no single genetic or environmental cause of ASD has been identified. However, many studies are supporting a hypothesis that genetic markers may indicate a predisposition or susceptibility to autism when triggered by certain environmental factors. At this point, the kinds of environmental factors being considered are vast, including prenatal, perinatal, and postnatal experiences and exposures.

It is important to note that neither genetic markers nor environmental factors alone appear responsible for this complex disorder; and the combination of them does not result in autism in all individuals. Much more research is needed before we understand enough to solve the mystery of autism. Nevertheless, this promising line of investigation holds great potential for uncovering patterns regarding the interplay of genetics and environment and ultimately for developing ways to prevent or reduce and treat ASD.

Red in the Face

Although the CDC had triumphantly declared measles "eradicated" in the U.S. in 2000, unsurprisingly the occurrence of measles, which is potentially deadly in young children, soared during this frightening period of vaccine-refusal. In fact, more cases of measles were diagnosed in the U.S. in 2014 than in any other year since 1994 (U.S. Centers for Disease Control, 2014).

What's in a Number?

Another potential explanation for the soaring prevalence of ASD is that the numbers don't necessarily reflect more actual cases of ASD; instead the numbers may reflect a broadening of the definition and increased awareness of the disorder. For example, after Asperger's Syndrome emerged into public consciousness in the 1980s, the diagnosis of ASD eventually expanded to include many children—and adults—who might previously have not been diagnosed at all. And, as awareness and understanding of ASD has deepened, folks who had imprecisely received such diagnoses as Learning Disabled, Intellectually Disabled, or Other Health Impaired, for lack of a clearer diagnosis, might now be more accurately and meaningfully reclassified as being on the autism spectrum. In fact, some studies have shown that right alongside the dramatic increase in ASD diagnosis in recent decades, has been a decrease in related classifications (Polyak, Kubina, & Girirajan, 2015).

But unfortunately none of this speculation or information gives you the practical help you need today, as you stand before a classroom full of students, wondering what to expect from those who arrived with an array of evaluations, alerts, and acronyms accessorizing their school files. That's where this book comes in!

The rest of this chapter defines common terminology you will encounter in your work with students on the spectrum, so that you'll be able to talk the talk. After that, Chapters 2–11 will help you walk the walk.

> **Did You Know . . .**
>
> The CDC relies on three different data sources in order to obtain a comprehensive picture of ASD across the U.S. Their 1:68 statistic comes from the Autism and Developmental Disabilities Monitoring Network (ADDM), which culls data from medical and education records and boasts the largest sample size of the three sources.
>
> Another of the sources, the National Health Interview Survey (NHIS), reflects data collected only from parents. Although it represents a smaller sample size than the other sources, the NHIS study is considered to be the most longitudinal, the most up-to-date, the most in-depth, and potentially the most valid survey among the three. In 2015, the NHIS announced that its survey yielded a prevalence rate showing one in every 45 children to be on the autism spectrum—the highest national rate recorded to date (Zablotsky, Black, Maenner, Schieve, & Blumberg, 2015).

What Is Autism Spectrum Disorder?

Sounds like a simple enough question, right? And yet as researchers develop a better understanding of ASD and the many shades and colors that illuminate the spectrum, diagnostic descriptions seem to get increasingly hazy. What follows is a summary of the clinical description of autism spectrum disorder. Read it over. Get a sense of it. Then we'll start talking about real kids.

First, the Textbook Version

In order to qualify for the diagnosis of Autism Spectrum Disorder, individuals must meet, across multiple contexts, the DSM-V criteria A, B, C, and D as summarized below.

A. All individuals must have or have had *persistent deficits in social communication and social interaction* across contexts, not accounted for by general developmental delays, and manifested by all three of the following:

   1. **Deficits in social-emotional reciprocity**, ranging from atypical social approach and failure of normal back-and-forth conversation through reduced sharing of interests, emotions, affect, and response to a total lack of initiation of social interaction.

   2. **Deficits in nonverbal communicative behaviors used for social interaction**, ranging from poorly integrated verbal and nonverbal communication through atypical eye contact and body language or deficits in understanding and use of nonverbal communication to a total lack of facial expression or gestures.

   3. **Deficits in developing and maintaining relationships** appropriate to developmental level (beyond those with caregivers), ranging from difficulties adjusting behavior to suit different social contexts through difficulties in sharing imaginative play and in making friends to an apparent absence of interest in people.

B. All individuals must have or have had *restricted, repetitive patterns of behavior, interests, or activities* as manifested by at least two of the following:

   1. **Stereotyped or repetitive speech, motor movements, or use of objects** (such as repetitive mannerisms, echolalia, unusual use of objects, or idiosyncratic phrases).

   2. **Excessive adherence to routines, ritualized patterns of verbal or nonverbal behavior, or excessive resistance to change** (such as motoric rituals, insistence on same route or food, repetitive questioning, or extreme distress at small changes).

   3. **Highly restricted, fixated interests that are extreme in intensity or focus** (such as strong attachment to or preoccupation with unusual objects, excessively circumscribed or perseverative interests).

   4. **Hyper- or hypo-reactivity to sensory input or unusual interest in sensory aspects of environment** (such as apparent indifference to pain/heat/cold, adverse response to specific sounds or textures, excessive smelling or touching of objects, fascination with lights or spinning objects).

C. Symptoms must be present in early childhood (but may not become fully manifest until social demands exceed limited capacities).

D. Symptoms together limit and impair everyday functioning (American Psychiatric Association, 2013).

Because this broad diagnosis no longer uses subtypes to distinguish the many significant differences among folks on the spectrum, diagnosticians must now elaborate on the severity of the symptoms. Doctors must specify whether the condition occurs with or without:

✔ accompanying intellectual impairment

✔ language impairment

✔ a known medical or genetic condition or environmental factor

✔ another neurodevelopmental, mental, or behavioral disorder

✔ catatonia

Along the same lines, diagnosticians must also now rate the social and behavioral symptoms as specifically as possible, in order to characterize individuals and their level of need, as follows:

Level 1: Requiring support

Level 2: Requiring substantial support

Level 3: Requiring very substantial support

A key takeaway from the new diagnostic criteria is that Autistic Disorder, Asperger's Syndrome, and PDD-NOS no longer exist as official diagnoses. The good news here is that now diagnosticians don't need to differentiate among subtypes that allowed for subjectivity and variation in diagnosis. Also, diagnosticians must now indicate concurrent challenges; and they must specify levels of functioning, which is crucially important since the functional levels among folks with ASD are as varied as the functional levels of folks without!

Did You Know . . .

Another major change in the DSM-V is the creation of a brand-new diagnosis: Social Communication Disorder (SCD), which is not part of Autism Spectrum Disorder. This diagnosis was created to account for the many, many children who never quite met the criteria for ASD diagnosis in the past but were somewhat haphazardly lumped in there anyway. (They were often described as having Pervasive Developmental Disorder, Not Otherwise Specified.) A diagnosis of SCD describes an individual who exhibits social challenges similar to those on the autism spectrum but does *not* meet the criteria for restricted, repetitive patterns of behavior.

In Other Words . . .

Now let's look at all of that in classroom terms. What can you expect when a student arrives in your classroom with a diagnosis of ASD? Well, the fact is that even though students with ASD *must* meet the criteria above, they do so in an endless variety of ways. That means that every student with ASD will be dramatically different from every other—as different from each other as all of your typically developing students are from each other.

Still, there are several common characteristics—all falling within the two broad areas of social communication and behavior that drive the clinical definition—that you are very likely to see. Most students on the autism spectrum will demonstrate their own versions of the following characteristics. Please note that contained within these characteristics are some apparent contradictions. For example, both extreme and minimal reactions to sensory input are common on the autism spectrum—sometimes within one child. Yup, that's ASD.

Key Behavioral Issues

- preoccupation with certain activities and interests
- profound dependence on routines and sameness
- repetitive and stereotyped motor mannerisms
- extremely diminished or extremely intense responses to sensory input

Key Social Communication Issues

- delayed, limited, absent, or idiosyncratic expressive speech and language
- delayed, limited, or idiosyncratic receptive language
- repetitive and rigid use of language
- minimal eye contact
- limited development of peer relations and interactions
- rigid adherence to restricted topics
- lack of desire for socially or emotionally shared experience

Did You Know . . .

Frequently the diagnosis of Autism Spectrum Disorder is not made until later in childhood, in adolescence, or even in adulthood, even though symptoms may have been apparent since early childhood. In some cases, although the symptoms were noticed, they may not have interfered with functioning until social or other demands exceeded the individual's capacity. For some, demand exceeds capacity by age 2 or 3. For others, it's not until the curriculum and social expectations move from the concrete to the abstract (often around third grade) that demand exceeds capacity. For still others, this dichotomy doesn't become functionally problematic until adolescence or well into adulthood.

Never Judge These Books by Their Covers

Did you notice that the three descriptive functioning levels in the official diagnosis do not use the words *high-functioning* or *low-functioning?* Instead they describe *how much support* a student needs. This is an important distinction for you, as an educator, to understand.

Students with overt autism-related challenges have often been described as *low-functioning;* however, this label does them a serious disservice because quite frequently behind the flapping and beyond the lack of language is a brilliant intellect or gifted artist.

Meanwhile, students on the spectrum who present themselves as calm and articulate have often been tagged as *high-functioning.* This label does them an equally serious disservice because it neglects to look beyond the politely scripted greeting and robust vocabulary to find the intense cognitive, emotional, and social challenges inside.

Always keep in the front of your mind that some autism spectrum challenges manifest overtly, while others remain hidden from view. It is very important to be aware of both *external* and *internal* challenges and to address both in your work with and support of these students. Don't rely on first impressions; there is always a lot more to students with ASD than first meets the eye.

First Impressions

Some students in your class will have been identified as "a student in need of special education," "a student on the autism spectrum," or other similar designation prior to arriving on your doorstep. They may be first introduced to you via their Individualized Educational Programs (IEPs) and packets of evaluations, test scores, and recommendations. (See more on IEPs on pages 26–30.) Some will bear a painful personal history of failure, the cause of which has perhaps never been adequately identified or addressed. Still others will have issues that are first emerging as problems only now, as the academic and social demands at school intensify. Regardless of where they've been or what paperwork accompanies them, your journey together begins now. The weather forecast calls for variable sun and clouds.

Partly Sunny With Some Clouds

Since every student is so different from every other, you really can't know what to expect when you first meet a student on the autism spectrum. One student on the spectrum, for example, may present as surprisingly poised and socially related, greeting you with direct eye contact, a confident *Nice to meet you,* or an impressive exposition on the traffic conditions en route to school. You may find yourself wondering why he has been identified as he has—he seems "totally typical." But many of these factors may also be at play:

- The challenges for this student may be in such specific areas that they don't necessarily manifest in brief encounters.

- This student may have memorized the rote and predictable elements of a conventional greeting.

- This student may be very bright and highly articulate, but only on specific topics *of his choosing.* You may not realize at first that, despite the fact that he provided you with a highly specific report of the bus route and construction zones he encountered along his journey to school, he is unable to carry on a *two-way* conversation on this or any other subject.

- He may indeed seem absolutely typical as you get acquainted conversationally. But tomorrow he may try to engage you in the same conversation, verbatim, that he had with you today. It may be the only one he knows.

- While he performs scripted conversations and rote interactions with others, his inner world may be in disarray. He may be quietly consumed with anxiety and confusion.

- He may present superior speech or cognitive skills but be unable to make an inference, consider the needs or feelings of others, deviate from routine or expectations, use his language flexibly, or tolerate sensory input. Any or all of that may be simmering just below the sunny surface.

- He may be able to blend in seamlessly until something on his rigid roster of rules goes awry; then suddenly his "autism" shows in a big way (i.e., his symptoms become externalized).

My son, for example, presents as fairly typical in a brief first encounter. He looks put-together, and generally performs all of the expected rituals involved in a standard greeting. He is eager to please and always wants to do "the right thing." However, he has severe cognitive, processing, social, and sensory challenges. As eager as he is to do the right thing, he usually cannot understand or infer what the right thing is and is therefore often doing "the wrong thing." This dichotomy leads to misunderstanding and frustration for everyone. His polished external behaviors lead others to expect much, much more from him than he can deliver, causing him to feel like a failure at every turn.

Be aware that students who come with an Autism Spectrum Disorder diagnosis have been given that diagnosis for no small reason. If you can't see significant challenges, look harder.

Under the Radar

Some individuals on the spectrum have extremely strong cognitive abilities in select areas and impressive speech and language skills, and so can cope fairly well in certain contexts. It is not uncommon for them to pursue higher education in their specific areas of interest and expertise, and to meet with success in related careers. Often their chosen occupations are the sort that do not require the nuance and unpredictability of extensive social interaction. You might find these individuals doing coding behind a computer screen, calculating numerical figures in a CPA's office, or researching interactions between light and sound in a physics lab. You are less likely to find them working successfully in managerial positions or collaborative team environments that demand social versatility.

Many people who fit this description have grown into adulthood without ever being diagnosed. In 1994, Asperger's Syndrome became an official diagnostic category and many of those who had been previously undiagnosed found a home on the autism spectrum. Even though since 2013 the term Asperger's Syndrome has not been in use, the definition of "autism spectrum" still includes many individuals who fit this profile. They may not demonstrate many external challenges. But don't be fooled by a student who presents a shocking knowledge of technical detail, a staggering vocabulary, or expertly rendered manners. Internally, their struggles are often intense.

Partly Cloudy With Some Sun

On the other hand, some students on the spectrum wear their symptoms on their sleeves. A student like this manifests many external symptoms. Her behavior may be quirky or idiosyncratic. She may have an unusual rhythm or cadence to her speech, her language may be incomprehensible, she may make limited or no eye contact. She may flap her hands, rock in place, grimace, chirp, or exhibit other socially unexpected mannerisms.

Remember that a student like this may seem unavailable to you in conventional ways for any of the following reasons:

- She may be so deeply entrenched in sophisticated calculations or analytical processes that she cannot readily engage in social or other seemingly superficial expectations.

- She may actually be capable of engaging in advanced academic, esoteric, or other pursuits, but not in the context of overwhelming stimulation and not in a socially conventional way.

- She may be putting all of her energy into managing her anxiety, adapting to her sensory surroundings, curbing her impulses, or keeping her hands still, and has no capacity left to participate in a conversation.

- She may be very aware of and interested in the social world around her while profoundly unaware of how to enter it.

For example, one middle school girl I worked with was considered very intrusive by her peers. She would rush at them and poke them hard in the arm. Then, while rocking vigorously back and forth, she would call out, "Justin Bieber! Justin Bieber!" Not only was this a violation of her peers' personal space, but her behavior was physically unpleasant and socially "weird." Many kids moved away when they saw her coming. Others laughed and rolled their eyes or mimicked her. The peers who wanted to be nice would patiently explain, "No, Ashley, I'm not Justin Bieber."

As I got to know Ashley, I was able to recognize that she was desperate to socialize. She came right out and told me that the reason she pokes people is that she wants to be their friend. Although she was unable to explain why she kept yelling "Justin Bieber," I suspected that, like many kids on the spectrum, she had participated in a social skills group in which she had been taught to initiate conversation by talking about a topic that might be of interest to her peers, rather than only topics of interest to her. She had probably been given ideas for commonly popular conversation topics such as soccer, baseball, Star Wars, Taylor Swift, Justin Bieber, etc. Ashley had obligingly chosen one of those suggested topics and was determinedly trying to make conversation with it. She hadn't meant to be saying, *You're Justin Bieber!* Instead, she had been trying to say, *Let's talk about Justin Bieber!* Although Ashley clearly had a lot of fine-tuning to do, she was trying to connect.

Ashley needed to learn how to get someone's attention—without rushing at them and without poking. She needed to equip herself with a more complete and inviting opening sentence. We were able to teach Ashley to approach her peers with, "Hi Sonia. Do you want to talk about Justin Bieber with me?" and to keep her fingers to herself. Now her peers were willing and able to respond to her in more open ways. Now Ashley got responses along the lines of, *Okay, Ashley. Do you like his new CD?* and *Well, I'd rather talk about the social studies test. What did you get for Question 3?* and *I would, Ashley, but I'm busy now. How about later?* Even though Ashley was not yet capable of extending the conversations much beyond that, these exchanges left everyone feeling more positive about the interactions and about Ashley. And as she began to feel safer in the interactions, her anxiety went down so she had less need to rock back and forth, which helped even more. (See more about coaching conversation in Chapter 9.)

Climate Control

Regardless of how your students on the spectrum present themselves, the forecast for success in the classroom will depend largely on you. You are the weathermaker. You not only determine the seating arrangement and elements of the curriculum, but you also create predictable routines to keep the heat down. You are always on the lookout for ways to let the sun shine through. You set the barometer for social acceptance. You use sensory strategies to protect against sudden blustery squalls. And you keep your eye on the horizon, always watchful for the subtle signs of heavy storms brewing in the distance, and ever at the ready with the comfort of consistency, support, and acceptance when the rains come pouring down.

Astonishing Savants

Savant qualities are exceptional abilities or talents that stand dramatically apart from typical functional levels. In the movie *Rain Man*, Dustin Hoffman's character, Raymond, exhibited extraordinary calculation skills when he glanced quickly at a mess of hundreds of spilled toothpicks and instantly assessed exactly how many were scattered about the floor. Savant qualities are present among about 10% of people with Autism Spectrum Disorder (as opposed to among less than 1% of the general population), and when they appear they can be quite astonishing. Students on the spectrum who have savant qualities almost always demonstrate remarkable memory and often possess uncanny abilities in music, math, technology, calendar calculation, or other areas (Treffert, 2009).

Students as People

As we all know, the only thing consistent about weather is its variability. Every student you see on the spectrum may present and respond to you quite differently from day to day. It is possible that the intervention that left you feeling triumphant yesterday will get you nowhere today. But hang on to it. It may be the perfect answer tomorrow.

As the prevalence, research, definition, and awareness of Autism Spectrum Disorder have evolved over the years, I have encountered many children whose precise location under the umbrella of the autism spectrum remains unclear or inconsistent.

Did You Know . . .

Autism Spectrum Disorder is, on average, five times more likely to occur in boys than in girls (U.S. Centers for Disease Control, 2016).

And what I've discovered is that the details of their diagnosis alone do not dictate the details of their functioning, educability, or identity. The details are in the individuals. Every individual with Autism Spectrum Disorder is as unique as any other individual: She has her own strengths and challenges, her own likes and dislikes, her own patterns of action and reaction, her own past and future, her own personality, her own potential, and her own dreams. In other words, there is plenty of room under the umbrella; let it rain.

The Special Ed Process

Now that you understand some of the basic terminology of diagnosis and a bit of what to expect, let's look at the details of the process through which services and supports may be provided for students on the spectrum.

You may have students in your classroom who were diagnosed with ASD quite a while ago. These students may already have had many years of special education support and individualized services and arrive in your classroom with various supports and services already in place. (See the section on Intensive Therapeutic Programming later in this chapter.)

Other students, however, may not yet have been identified as having special needs when they come to you. These students may be so articulate and bright that they have been able to function adequately at school in the early years—presenting as a bit quirky, perhaps, but not raising any red flags. Yet as they move through the elementary years, the curriculum begins to require abstraction and higher-level thinking, and socialization begins to demand spontaneity and reciprocity. So, in the mid-to-late elementary years, "quirkiness" descends into "dysfunction," and the academic and social gaps become apparent and problematic.

Whether the students you work with are already known to be on the spectrum, or whether you only suspect that they are, you can be sure they will need more support than do typical students. They may need ongoing specialized instruction and individualized supports, both inside and outside the classroom, to enable them to function successfully in the mainstream.

Fortunately, there are many federal, state, and district guidelines and systems that exist to help. As you embark on this journey, know that having students with ASD in your class does not imply that you need to have all the answers or solutions. It does not mean that you should be staying up all night creating a parallel or modified curriculum for one or two students. It does not mean you need to upend your entire classroom or all of your best laid plans. And it does not suggest that you must single-handedly carry the burden of the diverse and intense needs of your whole class. Instead, make use of the services and supports that are out there. Rather than expecting or pressuring yourself to be a hero or a savior, try thinking of yourself as a champion, an advocate who can help students with ASD get what they need. Join the charge, along with the parents or caregivers and the multidisciplinary team at your school, to advocate for the programming and supports necessary to help these students find success.

Here is a description of some of the systems and supports that may be available and how to gain access to them. Going to bat for your students on the spectrum will rally a team of supporters around them and around you, and help make this placement work for everyone.

Response-to-Intervention (RtI)

Most likely, when you perceive skill or performance deficits in students, intuition guides you to modify your classroom or instruction to compensate for the deficits. Under the Individuals With Disabilities Education Improvement Act of 2004 (IDEIA), this previously intuitive approach went legislative. Response-to-Intervention (RtI) is an initiative that directs teachers to collect data over time, intervene and adjust instruction as needed, and monitor responses, all according to a tiered system.

While details can vary from district to district, a Tier 1 RtI plan usually indicates in-class supplemental instruction and group intervention to address minor skill and performance gaps among students considered to be at-risk based on standardized testing. Validated screening systems are utilized frequently to assess progress.

If skill and performance deficits are shown to persist in certain students after about eight weeks, RtI directs teachers to shift to a Tier 2 plan. In these instances, more targeted interventions are designed by the school's multidisciplinary, child-study, or RtI team and then implemented and measured. The interventions at this level can extend beyond the classroom to include instruction from reading or other academic specialists, or related services that can be offered in school by specially trained professionals, such as speech and language therapy, occupational therapy, physical therapy, and school counseling. Up to a full marking period can be devoted to Tier 2 interventions, and responses are closely monitored and adjusted as needed throughout.

Responding to Response-to-Intervention

By encouraging intervention before a student demonstrates failure, RtI effectively eliminates the long-standing "wait to fail" paradox (in which students could not obtain support until after they had accrued a proven record of failure).

However, RtI is controversial largely because its admirable emphasis on individualization limits its capacity for standardization. Though student responses to intervention must be quantified and documented in objective terms, the interventions themselves are created on an *ad hoc* basis, rendering this system subjective at its core.

If a student's skill and performance base is demonstrated as not responsive to Tier 2 interventions, a greater level of support is indicated. More intensive and individualized interventions are implemented, and in many cases, a comprehensive multidisciplinary evaluation process is initiated to determine the presence of a disability and the need for Tier 3 evaluation for special education intervention, which would provide a more intense level of support than can be provided at the Tier 1 and Tier 2 levels. Many districts require schools to provide documentation of their efforts at Tier 1 and Tier 2 RtI-based intervention before a referral for a Tier 3 special education evaluation will be accepted.

You will find that students who are or may be on the autism spectrum will likely need the more intensive supports that a Tier 3 special education qualification provides. When used in combination, differentiated strategies and special education provisions can make your classroom a fertile and responsive learning environment for all kinds of students. What follows is an overview of the steps necessary to obtain special education supports.

The Evaluation Process

A district-level Tier 3 multidisciplinary team will determine which of the following evaluations to conduct for any given student based on the challenges you have documented.

Psychological Evaluation: A psychologist assesses the student's intelligence (according to IQ testing) and emotional coping skills. The psychologist or other clinical professional may also meet with parents or guardians to assemble a social history, which would include developmental milestones, birth and family data, living circumstances, prior schooling, interventions, and therapies, and any other potentially relevant personal information.

Educational Evaluation: An educational evaluator assesses academic achievement in terms of broad and specific math and reading skills. These skills are scored according to age- and grade-equivalent norms.

Academic achievement findings can be especially informative when compared to IQ scores. A significant discrepancy between potential and achievement raises a red flag that there may be an important disconnect between the student's *capacity* to learn and his *actual* learning or his ability to demonstrate what he has learned. This could indicate the need for a different style of instruction or a different means of assessment.

Physical and/or Occupational Therapy Evaluation: A physical therapist assesses gross motor skills (such as climbing stairs, jumping, running, and so on). An occupational therapist assesses fine motor skills (such as gripping a pencil, cutting with scissors, manipulating small objects) and sensory integration (the way sensory input is received in the brain). In many cases a student's overall academic or behavioral functioning may be significantly compromised by matters of coordination or sensory integration. (See more on motor issues and sensory integration in Chapter 4.)

Bringing the Family on Board

Be sure to keep parents or guardians up to date throughout the entire evaluation process. Share with them, all along the way, the persistence of observed behaviors, the data you have collected, the interventions you have tried, the impressions of other professionals in the building, and the recommendations of the team. This way, they won't be caught off guard when suddenly a referral for evaluation is suggested. Encourage them to share their own interpretations of the issue. But be aware that this is usually very emotional territory for parents or guardians. Some will welcome your efforts, but others may reject your observations. Take a careful look at Chapter 6 before broaching new concerns with families.

Written consent from a parent or guardian is required to initiate a referral to the multidisciplinary team for Tier 3 evaluations. You or the school counselor should explain the evaluation process to parents or guardians, assuring them that a referral is a means of determining the best ways to support their child's success. Explain that students tend to enjoy the individual attention and the activities they do with trained evaluators. And assure parents or guardians that evaluations are conducted individually and confidentially and can be provided by the district at no cost to the family.

Speech and Language Evaluation: A speech and language therapist or pathologist evaluates the student's ability to receive and express information via the use of speech and language. Often even students who are quite articulate can have significant delays or distortions in their processing or use of language. Conversely, students who have very limited speech may in fact have strong language comprehension skills that might easily be overlooked. (See more on speech and language in Chapter 9.)

Results of Evaluation

When all evaluations have been completed, a meeting of the team is convened to synthesize all results and paint a complete picture of the student's functioning in terms of strengths, challenges, and needs. (Typically these meetings include the classroom teacher, the student's parents or guardians, all contributing evaluators, a special education teacher representative, a psychologist, the committee chair, and sometimes other professionals or family members as well.)

The goal of the evaluative process is to ensure that every student has access to a Free Appropriate Public Education (FAPE). If the process determines that the student's current educational program is not appropriate to meet her needs, program placement must be changed or modifications and accommodations must be enacted, in accordance with the IDEIA.

As a result of this process, an assortment of the following documentation, accommodations, and program options may be put into place.

Documentation of Student Needs

504 Plan: A student who is found to have a discrete physical or mental challenge that directly impedes her ability to function at school (for example, challenges related to walking, breathing, seeing, hearing, speaking, writing, reading, and so on) may qualify for a Section 504 Accommodation Plan under the Rehabilitation Act of the Americans with Disabilities Act (ADA).

This civil rights statute protects students from discrimination on the basis of impairment, and thereby grants certain accommodations to allow them equal access to education. A Section 504 Plan, which is individually crafted by the team according to ADA regulations, essentially levels the playing field, granting compensatory accommodations such as preferential seating, large-print texts, a ramp into the school building, assistive technology, and so on. Once provided with such tools, these students can reap the full benefit of their educational program. (See more on assistive technology in Chapter 11.)

IEP: An Individualized Education Plan (IEP) is a legal document under the auspices of the IDEIA. If it is determined that the student in question is in need of special education (also known as being *identified* or *classified*), the team creates an IEP according to IDEIA regulations.

IEPs are reserved for students who need more than a leveled playing field. Preferential seating or large-print texts would not be enough to give these students equal access to education. These students have conditions that require specialized instruction and support systems in order for them to learn and function in an educational setting. All provisions that might have been granted in a 504 Plan can be included under the broader reach of an IEP.

Based on the determinations of the evaluative team, an IEP does the following:

- classifies a student as being in need of special education

- mandates a type of classroom or school program and a student–teacher ratio

- mandates the types, frequencies, and student–teacher ratios of supplementary services

- grants specific program accommodations and modifications (see below)

- presents long-term goals and short-term benchmarks for every aspect of the student's program

The IEP is a blueprint for a student's learning environment and must be followed closely and updated every year. The student's progress toward meeting his or her IEP goals will depend on your efforts to do the following:

- actively pursue the acquisition of academic, social, and behavioral benchmarks with an eye toward long-term goal achievement

- oversee the implementation of accommodations and modifications

- keep data regarding progress and concerns

- stay alert to specific conditions or circumstances that affect the student's ability to function

- facilitate collaboration and continuity among all members of the team, including the family

- report on the student's progress at multidisciplinary team meetings

Accommodations and Modifications

Accommodations are changes made to a student's program to enable equal access to instruction or assessments. Accommodations do not alter the curriculum; they only seek to reduce the effect a disability has on the student's access to education. Accommodations can be granted according to the following four categories:

- *presentation of information*, which provides supports such as "talking textbooks" or "directions read and clarified"

- *response options*, which could allow students to fulfill assignments in alternative ways, such as by using spell check or other assistive technology (See more about assistive technology in Chapters 9 and 11.)

- *setting considerations*, such as "preferential seating" or "separate location for testing"

- *timing and scheduling adjustments*, such as extra time to complete work, or periodic breaks during work activities

Modifications, on the other hand, refer to changes made to the curriculum in order to meet the needs of the student. Some modifications are intended for use only during certain kinds of testing; others apply across the board. Common modifications include reducing the amount of class work and/or homework or simplifying the presentation of the curriculum to meet a student's level.

You will be expected to consider and recommend specific accommodations and/or modifications for your students who have 504 Plans and IEPs. Most districts use computer programs that generate 504 Plans and IEPs and offer menus from which to select appropriate accommodations, modifications, and relevant academic goals. All of these options are considered and discussed by the evaluative team before they are approved as a part of the official document.

Program Options

The evaluative team is obligated to pursue placement in the *least restrictive environment (LRE)* based on each student's specific needs. This means that every student must participate in mainstream programming and assessments, learning alongside typical students, to the greatest extent possible. For every student, the team is required to consider all placement options, beginning with least restrictive. Keep in mind that individual states or districts may have different options, or use different names and acronyms for the programs described here. When an appropriate placement recommendation is agreed upon, reasons for rejecting all less restrictive placements must be justified on the IEP.

Educational placement options for students on the autism spectrum range from least restrictive, such as a general education classroom setting, to most restrictive, such as homebound instruction or a residential facility. In between lies a wide variety of options mandated on the basis of a student's specific strengths and challenges. (Students in any placement may qualify for accommodations and modifications to their programs.)

Here is a list of class placement options, beginning with the least restrictive:

- **General Education Classroom:** A general education classroom is a full-size class run by one credentialed general education teacher.

- **Supplementary Services:** Regardless of educational placement, most students on the autism spectrum qualify for supplementary pull-out or push-in services in conjunction with their program. These individually mandated services may include occupational therapy, speech and language therapy, physical therapy, counseling, consultant teacher support, resource room instruction, reading support, and more. (Whether or not students qualify for in-school supplementary services, parents or guardians may opt to obtain these services privately outside of school, at their personal expense or with the help of medical insurance.)

- **Inclusion:** This model, which is the focus of this book, places students who have special needs together with typical students, all day, in a full-size class. Inclusion allows a student to remain in the general education classroom all day, incorporates a differentiated approach to mainstream curriculum, and provides additional classroom support, as needed.

Depending on the needs of each student and the constraints of the district, inclusion classroom support can range from the full-time collaboration of a credentialed special education teacher alongside the general education teacher, to occasional push-in support of various special ed staff, to a classroom paraprofessional or aide assigned specifically to a student who needs 1:1 support.

Inclusion settings offer the distinct advantage of providing students with full-time special education in the context of the general population. Many students on the spectrum benefit from this model in terms of academic, social, and emotional development. However, inclusion is not for everyone; some students simply cannot function in an environment as stimulating and relatively rigorous as a supported general education setting. (See more about the benefits and challenges of inclusion in Chapter 7.)

- **Special Class (also known as Self-Contained):** A special class is a small, self-contained special education class with a student–teacher–assistant ratio of 12:1:2 or even 6:1:2. These classes offer more specialized instruction and protection from the mainstream than inclusion classes do but less access to the social modeling of typical peers. In secondary grades, students often have the option of moving between special classes and inclusion classes on a per-subject basis.

- **One-to-One Support:** To support success in any of the above settings, some students are appointed a full- or part-time one-to-one paraprofessional, or aide. An aide's role is to provide individual academic, social, and behavioral support, while at the same time fading into the background whenever possible to facilitate independence. Aides may be appointed to support students on the spectrum in their efforts to engage, attend, communicate, transition, socialize, and modulate their reactions. (See more about classroom aides in Chapter 7.)

- **Out-of-District:** Often smaller public school districts, which have relatively small numbers of students needing special education, establish a system of reciprocity with neighboring districts. In these arrangements, special education services, resources, and funding are shared and available to students in both districts.

- **Non-Public Day Program:** If the district's evaluative team determines that the public school system does not have the ability or capacity to provide the kind of programming a student needs, they may suggest a non-public placement, which is a privately run, publicly funded, special education school. Since all of the students in this type of program have special needs, this is a more restrictive placement than any of the aforementioned. Non-public placements can be fully self-contained day schools or hospital- or clinic-based day-treatment centers.

- **Therapeutic Boarding School:** For students who need a more immersive environment, therapeutic boarding schools provide academic, emotional, social, and behavioral remediation in a fully self-contained setting.

- **Residential Treatment:** Students who are unable to be kept safe or to function successfully in their restrictive school setting or at home may qualify for a residential treatment center where they receive clinical supervision around the clock.

- **Homebound Instruction or In-Patient Hospitalization:** For crises or other extreme situations, some students may qualify for temporary homebound instruction or be referred for in-patient psychiatric hospitalization.

In addition to the program options listed above, some students may have received therapeutic programming from a very early age. The next section is a brief summary of several popular interventions.

Intensive Therapeutic Programming

Young children on the spectrum, through public early-intervention programs or private therapy, may receive intensive therapeutic treatments that seek to address global autism spectrum symptoms, such as responsivity, flexibility, regulation, socialization, and more. Students on the spectrum may have received many years of treatment or training prior to joining your class and may continue to receive intensive support outside of school. Providers of intensive treatment programs must be specifically trained and certified to practice each methodology. Although such programs are not designed to be implemented by general educators who are untrained in the techniques, it's helpful to have an awareness of the therapeutic approaches that may have loomed large in your students' backgrounds. You may also see trained special educators in your school, or even in your classroom, using some of these techniques.

Each of these programs features a different approach and all present demonstrated benefits that have inspired passionate supporters and advocates among therapists, teachers, and parents. Although the long-term benefits of some of the newer models have yet to be established, it is certain that they all seek the same goal: that of helping students achieve developmental milestones and pursue independence and engagement in the big wide world.

The most commonly used behavioral approach is Applied Behavior Analysis (ABA), which is the application of learning and behavioral principles based on the scientific study of behavior. Desirable behaviors are identified, taught, and encouraged through positive reinforcement, while undesirable behaviors are not reinforced or are gently discouraged. ABA therapists maintain careful, ongoing observation and measurement systems to assess progress.

Discrete-Trial Training (DTT), a teaching strategy integral to ABA, supports the acquisition of new skills by breaking down targeted skills and behaviors into achievable components. Many additional interventive models have spun off from the fundamental approaches first established by ABA.

The DIR (Developmental, Individual-differences, & Relationship-based)/Floortime model, developed by Stanley Greenspan, M.D., involves therapists joining in activities of the child's choosing, and influencing actions and reactions on the basis of the individual child's developmental levels. This approach generates rich opportunities for guiding and redirecting relationship development, potentially influencing a child's social and emotional functioning.

Other approaches, such as Pivotal Response Treatment (PRT) and Relationship Development Intervention (RDI), seek to integrate the best of both behavioral and developmental approaches. PRT is derived from ABA and focuses on behaviors that are considered "pivotal" to a child's development, such as motivation, self-regulation, and social interaction. The goal is that changes in these pivotal areas will yield generalized improvements in socialization, communication, behavior, and academic achievement.

RDI, developed by Steven Gutstein, Ph.D., is based on the belief that the brains of children on the spectrum are afflicted by "underconnectivity," which leads to rigid functioning. Interventions focus on supporting the development of "dynamic intelligence," including flexibility, coping with change, and understanding the perspective of others.

Social Communication/Emotional Regulation/Transactional Support (SCERTS) is also derived from ABA, and usually provided by special educators or speech therapists. This kind of support focuses on interventions in a variety of spontaneous situations and settings and with a variety of peers and adults, in what providers call an "authentic process" that promotes generalization.

Visual communication systems provide a means for non-verbal or minimally verbal students to communicate. Students use picture-based symbols to express their needs, thoughts, and feelings. A vast assortment of preprinted graphic icons can be purchased, and many picture-communication systems are available through apps and software programs. While most students on the autism spectrum who are placed in inclusive classrooms will have some verbal communication abilities, visual symbols can still be very helpful in supplementing the all-too-common gaps in both expressive and receptive language. (See more on picture-based communication in Chapters 3 and 8.)

TEACCH and Structured Teaching

TEACCH (formerly Treatment and Education of Autistic and Communication-related handicapped CHildren) is somewhat different from the programs listed above in that it is specifically school-based and is built on the belief that students on the spectrum have the capacity to function productively and independently if provided with a highly structured environment.

Though the TEACCH program can be implemented only by trained TEACCH instructors, many of the structured teaching elements of TEACCH are woven through the pages of this book, and can be implemented in any kind of classroom.

Some of the basic principles of structured teaching address the following:

- differentiating instruction and intervention (See more on differentiating instruction in Chapters 5 and 11.)

- organizing the physical classroom space in order to minimize distractions, maximize organization, and facilitate independence (See more on organizational and sensory strategies in Chapter 4.)

- adhering to visually presented schedules and routines to reduce anxiety, facilitate independence, and help students understand what is expected of them (See more on visual cues in Chapters 3 and 9.)

Complementary and Alternative Approaches

Some parents or guardians pursue medication or other complementary and alternative medical treatments outside the school environment. There is a dizzying array of options available and new approaches are being touted every day. Auditory Integration Training and listening therapy programs, for example, may help build new sensory connections and desensitize problematic reactions to auditory stimuli. Vision therapy, provided by a developmental optometrist, may improve visual processing and visual-motor coordination through the use of eye exercises. Additionally, acupuncture, biofeedback, chelation, chiropractic treatment, cranial osteopathy, gluten-free and casein-free diets, hippotherapy (therapeutic horseback riding), hyperbaric therapy, massage, meditation, multisensory environment therapy, neurofeedback, nutritional supplements (such as Omega-3 fatty acids, believed to improve brain function, and melatonin, believed to regulate the sleep/wake cycle), probiotics, and many other interventions have all been suggested to offer benefits. (Learn more about medication considerations in Chapter 6.)

These therapies may be time-consuming and/or very expensive, and in some cases the evidence of benefit is anecdotal rather than clinically proven. Some of these treatments, like chelation or hyperbaric therapy, may pose some risk. With others, like meditation and massage, there's nothing to lose and often much to be gained. These interventions may sound unlikely to you. But try to keep in mind that many professionals, parents, and caregivers believe strongly in their effectiveness, and parents have good reason to try just about anything that stands to help their children reach their greatest potential.

● ● ● ●

Now that you have a sense of who students on the autism spectrum are and where they may have been, it's time to prepare for what will be. Chapter 2 will help get you in the best frame of mind to approach the challenges ahead.

The Power of Positivity

You Can Do This!

As you begin this journey with students on the autism spectrum, you may be nearly as anxious as they are. Even though you likely have better-developed coping skills, greater flexibility, and savvier social instincts than they do, the prospect of attending to the needs of each individual student in your diverse class probably feels pretty overwhelming. Maybe you don't even feel up to the challenge. This chapter will explore ways to help you stay hopeful and to use your optimistic attitude to set an example for everyone around you, especially the students themselves. Your belief in their ability to grow and your efforts to make it happen will be the most powerful catalysts for success.

Keeping Yourself Going

If you had wanted to be a special ed teacher, you would have become a special ed teacher, right? Presumably, integrating students with significant special needs into your classroom is not what you bargained for when you signed up for general ed.

I would love to tell you that despite the challenges you and your students on the spectrum face together, the growth and development you see over the year will be breathtaking and rewarding; that by year's end you will be bursting with pride and basking in a bright spotlight, showcasing evidence of your stunning success, your miraculous ability to coax a butterfly from a seemingly empty cocoon.

I would love to tell you that. But I can't. It's just not going to be that flashy. Instead, progress is more likely to be resoundingly quiet, conspicuously subtle. If you don't look carefully, you might even miss it. But don't let yourself miss it because the progress you do make will be more powerful and more gratifying than anything you've ever done, as long as you tune in to a new set of personal goals and expectations. When your personal goal is to capture those brilliant moments that happen when you make a connection with a student on the spectrum—those fleeting moments when you reach *and* teach—you will catch a glimpse of that butterfly and you will be awed and renewed.

The Power of Progress

The ability to look for and recognize progress in unusual and unexpected places will go a long way toward helping you sustain yourself through your journey with students on the spectrum. Achievement and mastery of conventional goals may be elusive. So as you work to adapt your program to address the needs of these students, you will also need to adapt your idea of *progress*—expanding your own personal definition of what individual student progress looks like and what teacher progress feels like. Look carefully for huge victories in small places. For example, several months into kindergarten, Damien still drops his backpack on the floor in the middle of the classroom, where other students trip on it until he is prompted to put it in his cubby. When the day finally comes that Damien drops his backpack on the floor right in front of his cubby, unprompted, and *no one* trips on it, this *non*-event might go unnoticed. Even though Damien's backpack has still not quite made it into his cubby, for him this is terrific progress. Look closely or you might miss it.

Three Steps Forward, Two Steps Back

In some cases, progress will feel, at best, as though you're taking three steps forward and two steps back. You may need to walk certain students over the same two steps dozens of times, adjusting terms and expectations as you go, before you can move forward together. It takes patience. It takes hope. And it takes belief in your students and yourself.

It Takes a Village

There will be days when you just can't find anything to feel good about. Nothing seems to be getting through. Nothing. Remember that you are not alone. As you rally a team of support around your students on the spectrum, you are also rallying a team of support around yourself. No one person can adequately address the myriad needs of a student with "pervasive" challenges. Lean on those who have been there, who have had similar experiences, who have pushed through the frustrations, who may even be able to help you find something good to take from the day. Rely on colleagues who may be able to offer practical support: your co-teacher, the classroom paraprofessional, the occupational therapist, the speech and language specialist, the school counselor. Look through the pages of this book, especially Chapter 7. And visit www.barbaraboroson.com for more ideas, tools, strategies, and supportive words to help keep you going.

Learn the Language of Behavior

Most of the time, big struggles can be ameliorated by small fixes. When big struggles leave you feeling discouraged and depleted, try to hold on to the fact that very often the resolution is surprisingly simple once you determine the function of the challenging behavior. *All behavior serves a communicative function.* Behavior is a way all students signal that something is amiss. Many behavioral triggers that are common among students on the spectrum can be easily addressed and smoothed over, eliminating any need to act out behaviorally. Approaching behaviors according to this way of thinking will help you head off big struggles with competence and confidence.

First . . . Then

Each of the remaining chapters of this book (Chapters 3–11) describes an area of potential struggle— and they all come *after* this chapter, which is all about strengths and positivity.

By the time you finish reading this book, you'll be adept at figuring out what might have sparked a behavioral reaction or what is standing in the way of learning. You will be able to implement simple tweaks, quick adjustments that will make all the difference. Once you learn to recognize the antecedent of a challenging behavior, resolving the issue may be as simple as restating instructions in more concrete terms, changing some elements of the physical space in your classroom, or offering diverse tools or systems to your diverse collection of learners. Open your mind to creative ideas; your efforts have the potential to generate a lifetime of possibility for students on the spectrum and a world of difference for your entire classroom community.

If you keep watch for small signs of progress and trust in the ultimate potential for net growth among students on the spectrum, you will become a believer. And as long as you believe, anything is possible. Even if yesterday one of your students on the spectrum took ten steps back, even if his pot boiled over, and even if you got burned, begin today as a brand-new day, full of potential and promise. Thinking positive will keep you feeling positive, which will be the best predictor of success.

Spotlight on Strengths

Let's face it: the innumerable hardships of working with children on the autism spectrum flood into our minds unbidden, and spill readily out of our mouths. But if we focus only on the negative, then just like the students themselves, we run the risk of becoming pessimistic, getting lost in the struggles, and never finding our way out. What hope is there for struggling students when the people around them don't celebrate or even note their strengths?

This section will help you emphasize strengths so that you can maintain an optimistic outlook and model it for your students and for everybody else around them.

Putting Strengths on the Table

There are always strengths, even if they are only relative to areas of challenge. Look for competence in unexpected places, because otherwise, in the face of all the challenges, you might overlook them altogether.

For example, in Sasha's preschool class, the students were being taught to recognize their own names. The teachers had labeled each seat with the name of a student. Every morning, when students arrived for school, they were expected to find their names and sit in their designated chairs. However, later in the day, the chairs were redistributed around the rug for circle time and students were told to sit in any chair. Three-and-a-half-year-old Sasha routinely elbowed other students out of her way at circle time to get to the chair with her own name on it: She would not sit in any other chair, and no one could sit in *her* chair. Sasha would then direct Mira to the chair that said *Mira* on it, pointed Michael toward the chair that said *Michael*, Marcie to the *Marcie* chair, and so on.

Sasha's teachers were frustrated with her "inflexibility" and "aggression" and "inability to follow classroom rules," and they asked me to come in for a consult. Indeed, Sasha had been showing some rigidity and impulsivity in other areas that warranted further investigation. But in this particular circumstance, I first pointed out that the on-again, off-again assigned seating system was, in fact, confusing and inconsistent. We resolved that problem easily by putting the students' names in fixed positions *on the tables* instead of on the chairs. Now the labels had consistent value, and the chairs were freed up for more flexible use.

But another issue had become apparent as well. While focused on maintaining order in the classroom, all three teachers had completely overlooked the fact that Sasha was demonstrating, at three years old, that she had learned a dozen sight words: not just her own name, but the names of every student in her class. That fact, no one had noticed.

Why Accentuate the Positive?

The struggles of students on the autism spectrum pervade most areas of their functioning. There is little that they do that is not made more difficult by their wide array of challenges. This compilation of overwhelming experiences and failures is relentlessly stressful and anxiety-provoking for them. It is also a tried-and-true recipe for low self-esteem, depression, and self-destructive behavior. Those debilitating secondary conditions are frequently seen in adolescents and adults with Autism Spectrum Disorder.

Paradoxically, individuals on the spectrum who seem more socially related are at even greater risk for depression than their less-related peers on the spectrum. This is, in part, because students on the spectrum who are more socially adept are both blessed and cursed with awareness of their condition and their differences. My own son, who is on the spectrum, cried many nights in bed as he reflected on the hurts of the day, coming to terms in painful increments with the facts of his disability and his deepening feelings of differentness.

All students arrive in your classroom already in possession of specific strengths. Among students on the spectrum, these strengths, remarkable as they may be, are often heavily overshadowed by concomitant challenges. As a teacher, you know to look for strengths; but others in their lives may not look past their obvious quirks and inadequacies. The world around these students will offer a steady stream of negative feedback, failure, and rejection.

While the special strengths or interests of students on the spectrum may not be in conventional academic areas, they are still worthy of admiration and recognition. Find them and *use them*—even if they don't specifically fit into your curriculum—as a way to blaze a trail of respect all around those students, weaving it among their families, among their peers, among your peers, and within themselves.

Special Interests and Abilities

Here are some common strengths students on the spectrum often possess. Find out whether students in your class have any of these or other exceptional strengths. Then read on to see how to *use* those strengths to promote an atmosphere of positivity, acceptance, and respect.

Strength: The Expert

Many students on the spectrum become experts in areas of special interest to them. They may excel in assembling jigsaw puzzles or solving mazes, or demonstrate a remarkable sense of direction. Others may have exceptional talents in the arts, such as painting, sculpture, musical performance, or acting. Some have in-depth understandings of the intricate inner workings of cars, planes, computers, or any other type of technology.

> **Yeah, But . . .**
>
> See Chapter 5 to learn about the social challenges that result from preoccupations with special interest areas and what you can do to help.

They may be internal schedule keepers, keeping track of anything from your classroom schedule, to classmates' birthdays, school holidays, city bus schedules, or lunar phases. They may know the date of every Thanksgiving going back to the Kennedy assassination, or keep track of what television shows aired on each network during prime time hours dating back twenty years. You will find that some have an astonishing capacity for memorizing information such as mathematical facts, movie trivia, classroom rules, historical dates, state capitals, maps, species of dinosaurs, baseball statistics, train routes, international flags, and more.

Strength: The Cooperator

Chances are, no one will be more invested in your classroom rules and schedule than students on the autism spectrum. These students will cling to your classroom structure as a lifeline for guidance and reassurance. By providing a clear structure of expectations, you enable them to anticipate and mentally prepare for whatever comes next. It is truly their pleasure to adhere to—and enforce—your rules and schedule. When they know exactly what's expected of them, students on the spectrum recognize a rare opportunity to strive confidently for success.

> **Yeah, But . . .**
>
> See Chapter 3 to learn about the challenges related to rigid rule-following and what you can do to help.

So you may find students on the spectrum to be extremely eager to please and cooperative. *As long as your schedule is clear*, these students will likely be first in line—always aware, for example, of when it's time to move on to the next lab station. *As long as your expectations and organizational systems are clear*, they'll be reliably prepared, always wearing their sneakers on phys ed day, always armed with three sharpened Number 2 pencils on testing days. *As long as your rules are clear and routines are consistent*, they may well be Jiminy Crickets on your shoulder—reminding you that you had said there would be a quiz today, or that Czechoslovakia is not called Czechoslovakia anymore.

Strength: The Truth-Teller

Lying is a tool that some people use purposefully to evoke specific reactions in other people. To lie, we need to first anticipate how another person will react to our words, and manipulate those reactions to our own benefit. We have to consider: *If I tell the truth, I might hurt her feelings.* Or *If I tell the truth, I might get in trouble.* Or *If I tell the truth, everyone might laugh at me, but if I make up something cool, everyone will like me.*

> **Yeah, But . . .**
>
> See Chapter 8 to learn about the social challenges related to honesty and what you can do to help.

So, believe it or not, being *dis*honest requires the ability to understand and predict the feelings, thoughts, and reactions of others—a skill that is often quite limited in individuals with Autism Spectrum Disorder.

Without the capacity to *put themselves* inside other people's minds and anticipate reactions, many students on the autism spectrum have no concept of dishonesty or manipulation. Recognizing no reason to lie, perhaps even unaware of the concept of lying, they may be naturally, spontaneously, and often refreshingly honest. (Learn about *mindblindness* in Chapter 8.)

Honesty is a great strength to celebrate with students on the spectrum. Enjoy your faithful truth tellers. Though unmitigated honesty may not be socially savvy, let us remember that honesty is still, generally speaking, the best policy.

Using Strengths to Blaze a Trail of Respect

Since students on the autism spectrum are not always able to put their best foot forward, here are some ways you can showcase their strengths to help them step out in style.

Promoting Positivity Among Classmates

Your attitude toward your students on the spectrum will shape how they are viewed and treated by peers. If you allow yourself to focus on challenging behaviors, other students certainly won't be able to see beyond them. Classmates have the capacity to see their peers on the spectrum from many perspectives: They may see them as weird or annoying, as scapegoats or victims, or even as geniuses—depending in large part on how you set the tone. If you demonstrate how much you value and appreciate the strengths of your students on the spectrum, and represent them as people who are more than their challenges, your words will grant them overt status as contributing members of your classroom community, and you will be modeling an atmosphere of true acceptance. (See more on building classroom communities in Chapter 7.)

Take a moment to consider what strengths your students on the spectrum can contribute, and actively look for ways to utilize those strengths publicly, by assimilating them into your classroom language. Here are some examples:

- If a student's strength is schedule-keeping, demonstrate your confidence in his skill: *Ravi, please tell everyone what time our midterm exam will begin.*

- If a student's strength is memory, show the class that you trust her: *Jessica, what was the name of that man who showed us around the museum last month?*

- If a student's strength is knowing the state capitals, consult him as an authority: *Antoine, help me out here: What's the capital of Wisconsin?*

Creative thinking and conscious effort on your part will open and establish new channels of association between your students on the spectrum and their classmates.

Promoting Positivity for Parents and Caregivers

Ravi cannot stop wiggling his fingers in front of his eyes. Jessica's handwriting is illegible. Antoine can't find his way around the school building. But when you're talking to parents and caregivers, try opening with remarks like these:

- *Ravi is right on top of the schedule. He is always where he's supposed to be.*
- *Jessica has an amazing memory. I count on her to remind me where we left off every day.*
- *Antoine is our best geography player.*

These kinds of comments are important in several ways. Your acknowledgment of students' strengths gives their parents and caregivers something to feel proud of. They will be pleased to hear how their children can incorporate atypical skills into useful classroom tools. Remember, these parents and caregivers probably have not had many gratifying moments when discussing their children with teachers. Your positive presentation will not only warm their hearts; it will also foster a positive relationship between you and them, which will facilitate the parents' or caregivers' ability to hear, accept, and collaborate when you go on to present your concerns.

Promoting Positivity for Your Team

Team meetings and impromptu collegial conversations are valuable opportunities to vent negative feelings and bounce ideas off each other—and that's important. Whatever frustrations you're feeling, chances are other professionals who work with students on the spectrum feel them, too. But interspersing anecdotes of positive experiences helps uphold the perspective that these students are more than their challenges. Your effort to look for and talk about strengths will reflect your optimism and ability to see the whole child. As the primary teacher, you are in the best position to model positivity for the team, just as you do for your class. (Share your wisdom by giving out copies of the fact sheets on pages 227–234 in this book.)

Promoting Positivity for Students on the Spectrum

The greatest benefit of being positive in the classroom is the message you're sending Ravi and Jessica and Antoine. Imagine how good students on the spectrum will feel when they are given the opportunity to offer their skills to the class; when they get singled out for what they *can* do, and not only for what they can't.

Laura, a third-grade teacher, knew that computation was an area of strength for one of her students. Juan had memorized the times table before the school year began and knew multiplication facts instantly. Even though he was struggling socially and was way behind on reading comprehension, Laura saw an opportunity to let him shine. One day, when Juan had completed his multiplication worksheet before anyone else had, she asked him to have a seat at her desk. She told the other students to hand in their worksheets to Juan, gave him her red correcting pen, and invited him to help her out by correcting the worksheets. Juan was thrilled not only to be singled out to correct the worksheets, but to be given a seat of honor and the authoritative red pen with which to do it. Years later, Juan still remembers that moment as his favorite experience of elementary school.

Praise the Process

There are many opportunities to criticize and correct students on the spectrum. Even when we look closely at their strengths, we notice that frequently the work they produce is not reflective of their potential because they get derailed along the way. They may lose focus or misunderstand instructions. They may be hindered in their efforts by sensory, social, language, organizational, motor, or other challenges. Don't wait until the worksheet or the project or the interaction is completed to comment on it, because the final outcome may not seem praiseworthy. Once you correct the completed math test, you may find that many of the problems were done incorrectly. At that point, the student's good effort will have been overshadowed by a poor outcome, and an opportunity for praise and encouragement will have been missed. You and they will get discouraged.

✱ **Catch the Moment:** Whenever you see a student on the spectrum working diligently, sitting quietly, listening attentively, interacting positively, reacting calmly—whenever you catch them *in the moment* of doing the right thing—that's the moment to comment. Praise the *process*. For example, *Ravi, you are really trying to keep your hands still. Jessica, I see you being careful with your handwriting.* This will inspire students to keep on doing their best and will signal to them that their excellent effort is noteworthy and valuable in and of itself, and cannot be negated by a less-than-excellent product.

The Diversity of Diversity

In the mid-1990s, the spectrum community has itself developed a term to describe folks who are not on the spectrum. The term is *neurotypical*, or *NT* for short. This term quickly gained popularity both in and outside of the spectrum community. It is now used to describe anyone who has no neurological challenges or developmental disabilities like ASD, ADHD, dyslexia, intellectual disability, Tourette's syndrome, and the like.

More recently, a related, broader term has emerged: *neurodiversity*. This term inclusively portrays natural variations in neurological functioning as benign, implying that all neurological functioning lies on a spectrum. In this sense, every one of us has a place on that universal neurodiverse spectrum.

Many proponents of the neurodiversity movement believe that Autism Spectrum Disorder and other neurological and neurodevelopmental differences should no longer be considered deficits, and therefore do not need to be "cured." Instead, they promote the celebration of autism spectrum behaviors and communication styles; they seek to raise awareness among neurotypical society that all kinds of neuro-functioning are valid. They encourage the neurotypical community to meet folks on the autism spectrum *where they are* and to stop trying to *normalize* them. And they work to develop lifelong programs that allow all folks with autism to be themselves.

Peter Smagorinsky, a professor of English who was diagnosed with ASD as an adult, speaks for others on the spectrum when he offers this perspective:

> *Neurotypicals—people within the normal range—are incomprehensibly obsessed with conforming to social rules, adherence to which wastes time and energy that could better be put toward singular, more useful, and often relatively asocial ends: mastering the details of the vast Pokémon universe, building monumental and complex structures with Legos, repeatedly watching every episode of* The X-Files, *and otherwise achieving total immersion in a narrow, esoteric area of interest. With such a necessary and compelling project demanding my urgent and unabated attention, who cares if I am still in my unmatched pajamas or haven't brushed my hair in three days?*

Ultimately he asks the provocative questions: "Whose rules provide the center of gravity for considering what counts as appropriate behavior? Why are those who don't understand or follow those rules viewed as being in deficit, of having a *disorder*?" Do folks on the spectrum have a disorder? Or do they simply follow their *own* order? (2011, pp. 1713–1717)

Simon Baron-Cohen, professor of developmental psychopathology and Director of the Autism Research Centre in Cambridge, England, tries to resolve this confounding question. As cited in *Far From the Tree* by Andrew Solomon, Baron-Cohen suggests: "Autism is both a disability and a difference. We need to find ways of alleviating the disability while respecting and valuing the difference" (2013, p. 367).

In your classroom, appreciating neurodiversity does not mean that you can or should alter your goals of helping students on the autism spectrum comply with class rules and expectations. Indeed, those are the goals supported throughout this book! But the concept of neurodiversity may help you to appreciate some of the behaviors and communication styles you see as valid differences—valuable variations of natural expression.

The Language of Positivity

As we look for and emphasize strengths, we need to be mindful of the language we use regarding students on the spectrum. These are not just semantic nuances to help you be diplomatic or politically correct. Instead these distinctions represent key ways of thinking that will inform the relationships between you and your students and between your students and everyone else. By being mindful of how you think and what you say, the degree of acceptance your students on the spectrum achieve is in your hands . . . or really, in your mouth.

What follows are some simple ways to use positive language that will inspire and reflect your positive attitude and inclusive approach.

✳ **Speaking of Strengths:** Consider that the inverse of *strength* is not necessarily *weakness.* The inverse of *strength*, in my book, is *challenge.* Again, this is a semantic difference that packs a big punch. The word *weakness* has a negative connotation and implies permanency. The word *challenge,* on the other hand, reflects a belief that a struggle is fluid and surmountable. A *challenge* is an invitation to work harder and an opportunity to grow.

✳ **That's Just So Typical:** Consider the commonly used word *normal* and its inverse, *abnormal.* Anything that is not *normal* must be *abnormal,* which means *defective.* Though students on the spectrum may be different from your other students in many ways, it serves no one to think of them as abnormal or defective.

Typical and its inverse *atypical,* however, are kinder and more accurate descriptors of students or behaviors that are different. *Atypical* is much more neutral and accepting than *abnormal,* implying difference rather than defect. Surely you already use the word *unusual* instead of *weird* for the same reasons.

✳ **What We've Got Here Is Failure to Communicate:** Students on the spectrum often speak or act in ways that are incomprehensible to others. Sometimes we cannot understand the verbalizations of these students because of their profound articulation challenges, or because their linguistic constructions are inscrutable, as in, *Who put the bus?* **Who put the bus?**

Other times students on the spectrum use their bodies in ways we don't understand—flapping their hands, spinning, and so on.

In many cases these expressive efforts seem to be non-communicative, disconnected from the topic at hand or disconnected from our reality. And so, because they are not *apparently meaningful,* professionals tend to dismiss them as *meaningless.*

While indeed these seemingly non-communicative words and behaviors do not conform to conventional definitions of meaning, they do hold meaning for the students who use them. So just because *you* don't know why a student is doing what he's doing, that doesn't mean his words or actions are without meaning. The problem is not an absence of meaning; it is a *failure to communicate meaning.*

We, ourselves, need to rely on context clues, background information, and gentle questioning to extract meaning. Based on context, is it more likely that the question *Who put the bus?* is about an actual school bus that might be late or idling in a different location than usual? Or is this more likely about a misplaced toy bus? Or a bus on a TV show? Are there words missing? Words misused? Or something else?

✱ **Moving Beyond Tolerance:** Consider the difference between *tolerance* and *acceptance*. A fifth-grade teacher with the best of intentions eagerly told one parent that her son's classmates were "really learning to tolerate him!" Why did this not make the parent feel good? Because the word *tolerate* does not mean *accept. Tolerate* means "to endure without repugnance; put up with." Is that our goal? Is that the best we can do? No. We must strive for *acceptance,* which is a full-on welcoming as an equal member of society—or in this case, the classroom.

● ● ● ●

Creating a positive atmosphere around all of your students and within yourself will keep everybody optimistic. And staying optimistic will optimize progress, thereby fueling the positive atmosphere. It's an upward spiral. As you read each of the remaining chapters, hold on to your strengths-first outlook as we examine how the many challenges of students on the spectrum will manifest in your classroom. Learn what they are trying to communicate and how you can address their needs calmly, confidently, competently, and . . . positively.

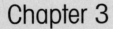

Chapter 3

The Simmering Pot
Keeping the Heat Down on Anxiety

S tarting with this one, each of the remaining chapters in this book addresses a specific
area of challenge and offers strategies to help you prepare for, prevent, and respond to it.
We begin here, with anxiety, because students on the spectrum carry it with them to every
situation, every minute of every day. Continually braced against unfamiliar situations, ill-
equipped to handle whatever might come next, anxiety almost always simmers just below the
surface, and boils over in a flash.

   This chapter will help you recognize what students' anxiety may be communicating and
guide you to prepare yourself and your classroom to keep things cool, even before Day One.

Why So Anxious?
The challenges that result from having Autism Spectrum Disorder pervade nearly every aspect
of students' lives as they try to function in the social world. The term *social world* here is
not meant to imply a world full of birthday parties and play dates. Instead, it refers to the
communal context in which we each live an individual life while necessarily participating in the
lives of others.

   In the context of this social world, we are all confronted by innumerable influences that
are beyond our control. These unpredictable elements range from the words, actions, and
reactions of other people to the whims of technology, culture, health, weather, transportation,
and many others. Really, we never know what's coming next. Yet generally we are able to adjust
our functioning automatically from moment to moment to cope with new situations or changes
to our expectations.

Neuro-Connections: A Snake in the Grass

Recent research in neuroscience has demonstrated different trajectories in the brain development of some children on the spectrum. Instances of accelerated growth have been noted in the fear-recognition centers of the brain (i.e., the amygdala and the insula). Additionally, weak connections have been detected between the fear centers and the frontal cortex, which is responsible for controlling emotions and making decisions.

Mikle South, Tiffani Newton, and Paul D. Chamberlain, neuroscientists at Brigham-Young University, explain, "It's the job of the frontal cortex to put the brakes on anxiety. It tells us, 'Hey, that's just a garden hose and not a snake coiled in the grass.' What we're seeing suggests that many people with autism can't easily discriminate when to feel safe. In that situation—when we don't know if a situation is safe or not—our natural default is for fear. That's just instinct to help keep us alive" (2012).

As you'll see throughout this book, the assortment of challenges students on the spectrum bring to the social world leaves them seriously compromised as they approach nearly any novel situation. Significant obstacles often stand in the way of socialization, engagement, communication, sensation, organization, abstract thinking, learning, self-regulation, and many other areas. Moreover, since their coping skills are inadequate to compensate for their challenges, these students learn from experience to doubt their abilities. So anxiety is always on the burner.

The next section will explore common triggers that spark anxiety for students on the spectrum and will describe how and why these students may cling tightly to certain anchors for comfort and safety.

Anxiety Triggers

Consider your own sources of anxiety. Maybe you bristle at the sound of interference on the radio or the feel of wool on your skin. Perhaps you can't stand being late or you feel uneasy leaving home without double-checking the door locks. Individual flexibility and tolerance levels vary across the many experiences we encounter in a day, but any situation can cause anxiety for someone who is sensitive to it. Generally, most of us are able to manage our reactions to our anxieties. We cover our ears, scratch our itches, take a different route, and reassure ourselves about nagging doubts.

But for students on the spectrum, when all is not in order, senses are heightened, flexibility and rationality fly out the window, and reactions can be intense, boundless, and uncontrollable. The triggers for unexpected behaviors are as variable as the potential reactions to them. Every day, the senses of these students are relentlessly assaulted, every deviation from expectation threatens equanimity, and social demands force students out of their comfort zone into perilous territory. Conventional means of verbal and nonverbal communication are out of reach, and self-regulation relinquishes control over impulses. Most likely, students on the spectrum are unable to alert you to their mounting distress along the way. Sometimes their only form of communication is behavior.

For example, in his memoir *Look Me in the Eye* (2007), John Elder Robison, an adult with ASD, recalls playing with blocks as a young child: "I never mixed my food, and I never mixed my blocks. Blue blocks went with blue blocks, and red blocks with red ones. But Doug would lean over and put a red block on top of the blue ones. Couldn't he see how wrong that was?! After I had whacked him, I sat back down and played. Correctly. Sometimes when I got frustrated with Doug, my mother would walk over and yell at me. I don't think she ever saw the terrible things *he* did. She just saw me whack him" (p. 7).

In the situation Robison describes, his behavior does not effectively communicate his anxiety to his mother. She makes no connection between the anxiety trigger and the behavior. And why would she? Who would have guessed that mixing the colors of blocks would trigger such a reaction? But it did. As mentioned in Chapter 2, one of the most valuable strategies to use when working with students on the spectrum is to *look past a behavior to its function. In other words, find what's behind it, what's fueling it, what the behavior is communicating.* Many sources of distress can account for difficult behaviors, such as sensory challenges, social challenges, and more. These are discussed in each of the following chapters of this book. But right alongside most of those sources of distress, anxiety is churning.

Comfort Anchors

To cope with their ever-simmering anxiety, many students on the spectrum rely heavily on certain elements of their lives to provide the consistency and predictability they crave. These are anchors that can help them feel more sturdy and in control. For example, one student may need to wear the same pants every single day. Another may need to be greeted in the same way every morning. Another may feel that all is right in the world as long as she has a baseball card in her pocket—but only if it's David Ortiz on Mondays, Wednesdays, and Fridays, and Mike Trout on Tuesdays and Thursdays. Equilibrium may depend on those specific anchors.

Local Coherence

Kamran Nazeer, the author of *Send in the Idiots: Stories From the Other Side of Autism* (2006), calls the act of finding comfort in the familiar "local coherence." In his book, Nazeer describes walking into a party with his friend Craig. Both men are highly educated adults, both of them articulate and worldly, and both on the autism spectrum. Despite their achievements, being at this large, posh party is very stressful for them. They don't know exactly what to expect. They move among clusters of conversation, but find none to be on topics about which they are well versed (or really, well rehearsed). Their anxiety builds.

But Nazeer has been in this type of situation enough times that he has a plan—an ace in the hole, or more specifically, a clip in his pocket. Nazeer goes everywhere with an "alligator clip" in his pocket. Like a binder clip, this is a small clip that can be squeezed on one end and opens and closes on the other. When Nazeer feels overwhelmed, he invisibly shifts his mental focus to the clip in his pocket.

He recalls, "I opened this clip and I closed it. I opened it and held it open. I put a finger between its jaws and let go its sides. . . . The alligator clip provided . . . local coherence. I could focus on what I was doing with the clip and other matters could become just a backdrop. I didn't have to worry about what I was achieving at the party. I could take a break and worry about the clip instead, which was a simpler thing to worry about, a simpler thing to understand and manipulate" (pp. 121–122). (Make *local coherence* more coherent for yourself by reading more about it in Chapter 11.)

Boiling Points

In the classroom, keeping the temperature low means recognizing and respecting not only the sources of anxiety for your students on the spectrum, but also the comfort anchors they cling to and rely on. You really can't afford to wait until simmering anxiety boils over. Equilibrium in these students is precarious—easily upset and very difficult to restore. Worse yet, often a loss of control sometimes sets off a chain reaction of disruptive events: Because he is upset, a student on the spectrum may unwittingly violate his own precious external or internal rules; the class schedule may get delayed; and other things he relies on for consistency may suddenly go awry. The disorganization of the situation snowballs. That's why you're going to want to find out about your students' specific anxiety triggers and comfort anchors before Day One.

For each student the triggers are different, but consider the possibilities. When Tomás arrives at school, he spends the morning yelling out "Remember the Alamo!" over and over

Alert! Alert!

Danny Reade and Hayden Mears are two young entrepreneurs with ASD who have created an online service called Asperger Experts. Their goal is to help folks with ASD—and those who love them—to understand the spectrum "from the inside." They describe living with ASD as being constantly in "defense mode," a hypervigilant state of defense against potential threats, resulting in a full retreat from everyone and everything. Everything feels threatening. "Basically, Defense Mode forces you to forfeit all higher human functioning in a desperate, last-ditch effort to numb yourself and preserve your well-being. Additionally, your mind and body remain on high alert and are constantly busying themselves with ensuring your safety instead of enjoying and engaging in life . . . . What does this mean? Well, it means complete cognitive shutdown" (2015).

and over. You have absolutely no idea why. Your challenge (in addition to the mighty task of maintaining focus and patience among all of your other students) is to recognize that Tomás's disruptive behavior is his signal to you that something is wrong, and that it most likely has nothing to do with the Alamo. It's time to for you to go exploring—but not necessarily in Texas.

What you may not know when he walks in yelling, is that when Tomás woke up this morning, he found that the shirt he had expected to wear was dirty, and this new shirt he ended up with has a scratchy label. His sister urgently needed to use the toilet so he had to wait to brush his teeth. There were no more waffles. It's snowing, so he had to wear boots when he expected to wear shoes. The bus was late. The driver was different. The number on the bus was changed. His usual seat was unavailable. The driver took an alternate route to school. Anxiety crept up and up and up.

Tomás's reliance on routine situations proceeding as expected may be critical anchors to his functioning, so all of these sensory challenges and deviations from routine raised his anxiety and may have already sparked a meltdown, before he even got to school.

Plus, there's no telling how the responsible adults in Tomás's life responded to his anxiety around these changes. How much do they understand about his needs? What skills and strategies do they have in place to help mitigate his reactions? How much time and patience do they have? How much patience do they have left after last night's three-hour meltdown when his favorite television show got preempted? For better or worse, the reactions of parents and other adults can also contribute to the degree of anxiety that spills into your classroom as your students on the spectrum cross the threshold each morning.

The goal of this chapter is to help you tamp down problematic situations before anxiety ever flares up. More than in any other area, when it comes to anxiety, prevention is overwhelmingly your best strategy. (In Chapter 6, pick up strategies for arming yourself with crucial information from the family. And in Chapter 10, find out how to respond when, despite your best preventive efforts, the pot boils over.)

Common Anxiety Triggers and How to Avoid Them

Clearly, getting through the day—getting through even a moment—can be painfully challenging and anxiety provoking to students on the spectrum. Chances are, as you read this, your anxiety is bubbling up, too. Life at the helm of a roomful of students is demanding enough without always having to be braced against students' seemingly unpredictable eruptions.

Unfortunately, the fact is that many circumstances can set off anxiety reactions in students on the spectrum. This section will introduce you to common anxiety triggers for these students and will help you prepare your classroom to include steady anchors for support. Even if these strategies seem time-consuming now, your investment of time in advance will save you and your students hours of anguish throughout the year by keeping anxiety on a low burner, and may very well make the difference between success and failure.

Since anxiety triggers are unlikely to be mentioned on students' IEPs, this information will need to be collected anecdotally. Here are two general suggestions to ease your way.

✱ Ask the Families: Send home a form *before* students on the spectrum join your class, if possible, inquiring about areas of strength, sensitivity, and challenge. (See example, below.) Parents and caregivers will likely welcome your proactive, individualized approach and be more than happy to warn you about what they've learned the hard way. Request that completed forms be returned to you quickly so you'll have a chance to plan accordingly.

This questionnaire may be the most important tool you have to get the year started on the right foot. This form will clue you in to each student's unique strengths, challenges, hot spots, and anchors, allowing you to plan and prepare for them before any triggers get pressed. You'll see that your efforts to implement many of the strategies in this book will be based on information you obtain from this form.

✱ Ask the Team: If possible, even before you meet your students on the spectrum, consult with their school support team (school counselor, occupational therapist, speech and language therapist, and so on), and previous teachers. Ask about the students' anxiety triggers. What has helped? What hasn't? Prepare yourself to approach each student using tried-and-true productive tools to establish continuity and, of course, try to avoid known provocations and pitfalls.

Once you have familiarized yourself with what to expect from these new relationships, give your students on the spectrum that same opportunity by easing their transition into their new classroom, as described in the next section.

Parent/Guardian Questionnaire

Dear Families,

Please fill out the following questionnaire and return it to me by _____ . Thank you for your support.

Child's Name: _____ Nickname?_____

Parent(s)/Guardian(s)

_____   _____

Phone numbers: Best times for me to reach you:

#1. _____   _____

#2. _____   _____

#3. _____   _____

#4. _____   _____

Siblings (names and ages)

_____   _____

_____   _____

Please tell me some of your child's specific strengths and/or special interests (e.g., technology, arts & crafts, history, pets, sports, books, etc.)

_____

_____

_____

What does your child find most challenging? (e.g., math, reading, taking turns, listening, etc.) _____

_____

_____

What kinds of situations make your child anxious or upset? (e.g., loud noises, transitions, large crowds, etc.) How does he/she tend to react? (e.g., crying, yelling, running, hiding, striking out, etc.) _____

_____

_____

_____

What comforts your child when he/she is anxious or upset? (e.g., quiet time, a favorite toy, etc.) What makes it worse? (e.g., being asked questions, a touch on the shoulder, etc.) Please be specific: _____

_____

_____

_____

Please share any specific goals, hopes, or dreams you have for your child this year (e.g., social, emotional, academic, etc.): _____

_____

_____

_____

Are there any other concerns or issues you would like me to know about or to watch out for? (Feel free to continue writing on back.)

_____

_____

_____

The best way for you to reach me is via _____
at: _____

Thank you. I look forward to working with you and your child.

Barbara Boroson © 2011. For a reproducible version of this form, please visit www.barbaraboroson.com.

Facing Something New

One of the most overwhelming new situations students on the spectrum can face is a new school year. Everything they grew comfortable with last year is now upended. New room, new faces, new routines, new rules, new expectations—all at once.

But a little preparation can minimize the unexpectedness of it all. When you take care to address specific anxiety triggers ahead of time, students on the spectrum will recognize that they are starting off on solid ground. This is particularly valuable because students on the spectrum tend to associate certain environments with certain feelings. Those associations can become imprinted. If the first day of school feels overwhelming, then a high level of anxiety may become associated with school. This association is a learned behavior and it can be unlearned over time, but that's a much, much bumpier road. A better bet is to make the first impression as positive as you can.

✱ Arrange a Visit: All students on the spectrum need to be given practical information in advance. Reach out to your elementary students on the spectrum before the first day of school.

Secondary students on the spectrum should be given their schedules before the school year begins. Hopefully a school counselor will invite them to visit their classrooms and walk through their schedule a few days before school starts. Try to make yourself available to chat for a few minutes.

Students at any age will be very reassured by familiarizing themselves with practical information such as what you look like, what your classroom looks like, where they will be sitting, and how to find the bathroom. Students with specific sensory needs may be comforted by exploring what the classroom smells like, what they can see from their desk, what the chairs feel like, what kind of clock is on the wall. Plus, any of these elements can serve as comfort anchors, reliably awaiting the student's arrival on the first day. Take a little time to get acquainted, answer their questions, show them around the room and school, and learn about their interests and anxieties.

What's Next: Life on Schedule

Even once students have seen your face, heard your voice, and explored the classroom, the actual events of a day in your class are still unknowns. Most students on the spectrum function best when they know exactly what is coming next. That's where visual schedules come in, especially for elementary students on the spectrum. While most secondary students on the spectrum who are in inclusion classes can probably manage a written schedule, some will need words paired with visuals. Regardless, the key is specificity. Read on about visual and written schedules, how to create them, and why you'll want to have some version of a schedule in place before Day One, so students can familiarize themselves with it during their visit.

An ideal day for students on the spectrum might be like the movie *Groundhog Day*—every day the same as the day before. So the best way to start out is to try to create an environment that is as predictable as possible (given the circumstances), to minimize the likelihood of surprises and unexpected turns of events. The more preparation students have for any new experience, the less anxiety they will bring to the table.

Since most students on the spectrum are primarily visual learners, visual daily schedules are essential tools to add predictability to the day. Visual schedules can be used to help students *see* what's coming next. When the environment remains predictable, students know what to expect and can learn when and how to respond to it. Each time a familiar stimulus arises, they know they can be successful by using a previously learned response.

> *"If I can't picture it, I can't understand it."*
>
> —Albert Einstein

The schedule is a comfort you can provide to enable students to function easily and effectively throughout the day. Fortunately, in most cases students on the spectrum have both the capacity to learn a classroom schedule and the motivation to adhere to it, though some modifications may be required. This section will address how to help students calmly navigate the many unpredicted twists, turns, and transitions they face in a school day.

Types of Modified Visual Schedules

The presentation of your ordinary schedule may need to be modified and expanded for specificity and clarity in order for it to be useful to students on the spectrum. The goal is to make the schedule concrete and straightforward. Specific modifications will depend on each student's style of functioning. You may choose to integrate elements of several styles. You may choose to adapt your whole-class schedule, if you have one, or you may prefer to create individual schedules for students who need the extra support.

Guess What?

Dr. Pawan Sinha, a professor of brain and cognitive science at the Massachusetts Institute of Technology (MIT), recently identified what he feels is a key factor in much autistic behavior. According to a summary of his findings in *MIT News*, "autism may be rooted in an impaired ability to predict events and other people's actions. From the perspective of the autistic child, the world appears to be a 'magical' rather than an orderly place, because events seem to occur randomly and unpredictably. In this view, autism symptoms such as repetitive behavior, and an insistence on a highly structured environment, are coping strategies to help deal with this unpredictable world" (Trafton, 2014).

Poor prediction, in combination with limited reading or interpreting of context clues, can also account for other challenges. Without the ability to anticipate the words and actions of others, social skills are compromised. Without prediction, motor planning becomes a shot in the dark and sensory assaults seem to erupt from nowhere. (Find out more about prediction challenges as part of Executive Dysfunction in Chapter 4.)

Regardless of the approach you choose, the day's schedule should be in place before the students arrive in your classroom every morning. Individualized schedules can be posted alongside the whole-class schedule, or you might place them on desks, in manila folders, in three-ring binders, on clipboards, or in relevant locations around the room.

Schedules that use removable and reusable icons allow you the most flexibility as you try to manage multiple schedules. They also allow students to interact with their schedules in a tactile way, posting the icons themselves, or perhaps removing icons after an activity is complete. Invest in strips of Velcro and be prepared to use them. Once you have a stash of icons outfitted with Velcro, you can simply reuse and rearrange them as schedules dictate.

Which kind of schedule would suit your students on the spectrum best?

✶ Concrete: For some young students who cannot read and are extremely concrete, you might need to post actual objects on the schedule. Using Velcro, mount a pencil on the schedule to denote journal-writing time; a tiny ball to represent phys ed, a plastic fork to indicate lunchtime, a linking cube for math, and so on. This format provides a concrete and realistic representation of each activity, and offers visual and tactile options to pre-readers or multisensory learners.

✶ Photographic: If you think a student does not require actual concrete representation on the schedule, post photographs of the student himself doing the expected task. Photos offer a student very specific visual representations, by enabling him to see himself doing the expected activities. But this format also offers greater challenge because he will have to infer that the photographic objects represent real objects before he translates that information into real action.

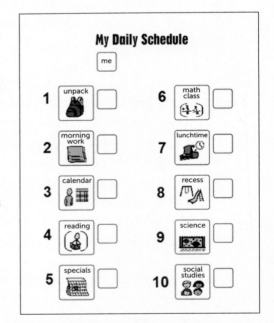

The Picture Communication Symbols ©1981–2010 by Mayer-Johnson LLC. All Rights Reserved Worldwide. Used with permission. Boardmaker™ is a trademark of Mayer-Johnson LLC.

✶ Representative: Most students on the spectrum who are in inclusive elementary classes will be able to utilize a schedule comprised of representative drawings accompanied by words. These stick figure–like pictures are less concrete than photographs—they only vaguely look like real people with real objects. Many icons of this kind already exist. You can purchase premade icons, print them from downloadable programs, or draw them yourself. (For links to resources for supplies like these, visit www.barbaraboroson.com.)

✶ Written: For upper-elementary or secondary-level students, a schedule of words alone may suffice. Following a written schedule may be a long-term goal for students on the spectrum. But if your students don't achieve that this year, that's fine. The first goal is to find a schedule format that provides comfort for each student right away. Some may use the same schedule all year. Others may be able to progress from pictures to words as the year progresses.

Success With Schedules

Even having made significant modifications, do not take for granted that the meaning of a schedule is self-evident. Be sure to incorporate these characteristics:

✻ **Clarity:** Explain exactly what each icon on the schedule represents and implies, and then check for understanding. For example, clarify that a pencil on the schedule means that it is time to use a pencil only for writing, and not for sharpening, drawing pictures, or poking peers. Verify that a student understands the icon by asking her to restate the meaning in her own words or demonstrate to you what she will do when she sees it on her schedule.

✻ **Specificity:** If your students on the spectrum seem lost and confused, despite the schedules you have made, don't give up on schedules. Instead, streamline them, concretize them, make them even clearer to ensure that they are understood.

✻ **Consistency:** Try keeping a *Check Schedule* icon in your pocket. When a student comes to you for guidance, refer her to the *Check Schedule* icon. This will remind and empower her to find the answer to her question on her schedule—and on her own.

Visual Schedules: There's an App for That!

While physical schedules can be manipulated, providing a concrete, tactile benefit, other benefits can be gleaned from digital schedules. In addition to the instant and motivating engagement many children on the spectrum experience with technology (more on this in Chapter 11), older or more socially aware students on the spectrum won't feel singled out by a personal digital schedule as they might by a physical schedule. Free or inexpensive schedule-making apps offer a vast array of images and sounds, customizable video and audio upload options, interactive calendars and checklists, visual planning tools and prompting, multiple viewing formats, and file sharing. Some go on to include support for waiting (such as taking turns and not interrupting) and for emotional regulation. Others take children on visual journeys to help them know what to expect in different situations.

As of this writing, popular schedule-making apps, adaptable for all ages, include *First-Then* by Good Karma Apps, *Functional Planning System* by The Conover Company, *Choiceworks* by BeeVisual, and *Model Me Going Places* by Model Me Kids. New and improved apps are being created all the time. Search under "visual schedules" in your app store. You're sure to find an app for that.

Off-Roading: Planned Deviations From the Schedule

Though many students on the spectrum may wish real life were like a movie, the fact is we cannot rewind and replay the same day over and over. Nor should we, because again, our ultimate goal is to help students on the spectrum adapt to the ever-changing social world. So there will be change and there should be change, but it needs to be supported. If your students struggle with change, here are some ways to support their efforts.

Change in the Classroom

Routine in your classroom is not limited to the realm of schedule and activities. As discussed earlier, the need for predictability also prevails when it comes to students' physical space.

Walking into the classroom to find that the desks have been unexpectedly rearranged or work centers have been relocated can be disorienting and distressing to students on the spectrum. Seemingly small changes that you think won't matter may matter deeply.

For example, a fourth grader named Nikola refused to enter his classroom one morning. Despite the teacher's efforts to coax and cajole, Nikola's behavior escalated: He threw himself to the floor, kicking and flailing. With no other recourse, his teacher called the principal who was able to bring Nikola to her office where he calmed down quickly. Nikola spent the entire day working quietly in the principal's office, still unwilling to enter the classroom.

It wasn't until he got home that afternoon that Nikola was able to express what had triggered this outburst: Cut tennis balls had unexpectedly been placed over the bottoms of all of the classroom chair legs (to prevent the chairs from scratching the floors). This turn of events was unacceptable to Nikola. Not only was it an unexpected deviation from the classroom environment of the day before, but it violated a rule that was fixed and, to him, inviolable—that tennis balls are for playing tennis; they are *not* floor protectors and they do not belong on chair legs. Having been given no advance notice, no opportunity for discussion, adaptation, or participation, Nikola was unable to reconcile this new use of a familiar object with the rigidly preconceived notions he had in his head.

You can avoid rocking the boat in your classroom with a little planning and participation, as follows:

✱ **Heads Up:** Take the extra minute on Friday afternoon, for example, to notify students if, when they arrive on Monday morning, the desk groupings will be different or the computer will be against the opposite wall.

✱ **Participation Perks:** Recruit students to help you do the rearranging. Having a hand in making changes allows students to feel they have some control over the situation, and seeing the change unfold gradually before their eyes may make it less of a blow.

Change in the Schedule

Try to be as specific as you can when creating the schedule and update it daily to reflect any changes that you can anticipate. An assembly, a birthday celebration, or a guest in your classroom can represent a jarring interruption to the rhythm of a day. Put these special events on the schedule. And for major deviations, such as field trips, your students will benefit from some advance planning and preparation as well.

Feeling Grounded

Some students on the spectrum are partial to wearing baseball-style hats with brims. Brimmed hats often help students on the spectrum feel protected from overwhelming visual input, as the brims reduce their field of vision. Also, by eliminating skyward views, brimmed hats help students on the spectrum feel more connected to the ground—literally *more grounded*. Consider allowing hats for outdoor activities and field trips.

Field Trips

Field trips are especially difficult for students on the spectrum as all bets are off in terms of familiarity and routine. Try these strategies to ease anxiety before the big excursion:

✱ **Show:** Show photographs of your destination. Or, take the class on virtual field trips in advance of actual field trips. You may find a video tour on the location's website. If not, check YouTube for footage that other visitors have posted of their own visits there. Show it to the whole class or share the links with certain students. This is a great way to prepare your students for exactly what to expect, easing anxiety and, therefore, maximizing engagement.

✱ **Tell:** Talk through the details of an upcoming field trip with the class. (Remember to clarify whether or not you will be going to an actual *field*!) Describe as best you can what will happen on the trip: how long you will all be there, what time you plan to return. You might even want to create and bring along a basic schedule for the trip.

✱ **Think:** Take a minute to think about each trip in terms of your students' specific anxiety triggers. Will there be loud noises? Will it be crowded? Will there be strong smells? Will it be muddy? Will there be academic or physical challenges? Students on the spectrum may be better able to manage a field trip if they can prepare for such sensory and other challenges. Giving students the opportunity to bring ear plugs, wear boots, and so on, is an easy way to ease their adaptation to challenging environments.

✱ **Script:** Remind all of your students that they are representing your school in the community and so you expect them all to be their *very best selves*. But spell out for your students on the spectrum what their *best selves* look like. Discuss very specifically what actions and behaviors you expect from your students throughout the trip. Let them know if you want them to maintain school rules—i.e., raising their hands to speak and using inside voices, or if school rules will not apply. If they will be assigned to a group, review turn-taking, collaboration, and partnering skills. Let them know whose instructions they must follow, since you may not be the trip leader. Specify that they must afford tour guides and hosts and parent chaperones the same respect and courtesy they (ideally) give to you and other authority figures. (If *respect* and *courtesy* are not words you would use to describe the way your students on the spectrum relate to you, find out why—and what you can do about it—in Chapters 5 and 10.)

✱ **Plan:** Consider asking your school administrator to boost your student–teacher ratio for field trips if you anticipate that any of your students may become overwhelmed by the deviation from their usual day.

At Exactly What Time Will We Be Spontaneous?

Even an activity you think will be a treat for your students, such as an extra outdoor recess on a beautiful day, might be received as an unwelcome violation by students on the spectrum. Any deviations from the norm may cause them confusion, worry, and fixation: *What else is suddenly going to change? And when are we going to get back to what we are supposed to be doing?* Without warning, your "treat" could become another anxiety trigger.

✱ **Put Spontaneity on the Schedule:** Post planned surprises on the visual schedule in the form of a question mark or smiley face icon. Giving students the opportunity to *expect the unexpected* reduces some of the jolt caused by unscheduled events. Be sure, especially at first, that the "surprise" activity is an adequate payoff for the extra effort the student had to expend to withstand not knowing. Make it surefire fun for your most vulnerable students. This is a great exercise in slowly introducing students on the spectrum to being flexible and beginning to allow deviations from their schedules.

Power to the People

Empower students who rely on the schedule by encouraging them to help you post the next day's schedule every day. Their participation in this activity will allow them to feel more in control and less reliant on your presence to maintain order.

Off-Roading: *Unplanned* Deviations to the Schedule

Sometimes changes in the classroom or routine happen quite unexpectedly, offering no opportunity for you to forewarn your students. The sink floods, the gerbil dies, the pencil sharpener breaks. These unscripted situations, which violate expectations and trusted systems, can prove very distressing to students on the spectrum. Respect that there is big meaning in a big reaction. If students become extremely upset over the sudden breakdown of something in the classroom, that item was likely a comfort anchor for them and had a vital role in their routine.

While you cannot prepare your students on the spectrum for truly unexpected events, you can prepare them for the *possibility* of unexpected surprises by mapping out plans for those random moments. What follows are some common surprises that may arise, as well as strategies to help you prepare your students for them.

Anchor's Away

An absent teacher is one of the most threatening disruptions for students on the spectrum. The implication of having a substitute teacher is that everything will be new, different, and not okay. And many times, that is indeed the case. Sometimes you have the chance to prepare the class for this event, and sometimes not. When you do know ahead of time that you are going to be absent, alert students (in as much detail as possible) about *what* and *whom* they might expect the next day.

But because you often won't know ahead of time when you're going to be absent, try to put these preventive strategies in place:

* **Dibs on Subs:** Discuss early in the year with your principal why it might be important for your class to have the same substitute teacher whenever possible. This is particularly important if you do not have the continuity of a co-teacher or paraprofessional in your classroom.

* **Share What Works:** Try to alert the substitute to your students' special needs or anxiety triggers, to whatever extent you feel necessary. Emphasize the importance of following the schedule and any other specific strategies you have found to be effective, such as using a quiet voice, allowing extra time, and so on.

* **Best Laid Plans:** Get in the habit of always posting the next day's schedule *before you leave each afternoon*. This way, the schedule will be there in the morning, even if you are— unexpectedly—not.

* **Just in Case:** Periodically review a "just in case I am absent" protocol with the class. Reassure students about those elements of the day that will proceed in ways that are comforting and familiar, while giving them a heads-up about what could be different.

* **Step Right Up:** Draw on the strengths of students on the spectrum by soliciting their help. Share with them that substitutes will try to follow the schedule, but may need help. Encourage your most vulnerable students to be special helpers.

Fire!

Fire alarms can be overwhelmingly stressful to students on the spectrum for many reasons:

- Fire alarms require an instantaneous, pressured response with no advance notice.
- Many of students' rigid internal rules must be broken, such as going outside without a coat and hat or without a backpack, or going out a different door.
- The sound of the alarm may be truly painful to your students who have sensory issues. It is very common to see students on the spectrum during a fire drill with hands over their ears and tears in their eyes, or even screaming, just to drown out the shrill noise of the alarm.

Overscheduled?

The schedule itself is a comfort anchor. Students on the spectrum are sustained just knowing it's there, and so they tend to review it many times per day. Some teachers worry that students' adherence to the schedule restricts the development of independence. But consider the alternative: Without the schedule, these students might be done in by anxiety or consult you constantly for information and reassurance. Instead, using schedules, students can calmly access information on their own and enter into activities without your direct facilitation. That's independence.

✻ **Tip Them Off:** Usually the administrators in your school will know ahead of time when there is going to be a planned fire drill. Find out and tip off your most vulnerable students beforehand.

✻ **Know the Drill:** Use a Social Story (which is a prewritten guide for challenging situations) about fire drills to help acclimate students on the spectrum as to what to expect. (See more on Social Stories in Chapter 8.)

✻ **Schedules-to-Go:** For those times when the fire alarm surprises everyone, have a fire-alarm schedule in the attendance book that you take with you when the class has to evacuate the building. Hand copies of it to specific students as they walk out the door. This provides a script for this unexpected event as well as a transitional object onto which your students on the spectrum can redirect their focus, away from the chaos.

The Picture Communication Symbols ©1981–2010 by Mayer-Johnson LLC. All Rights Reserved Worldwide. Used with permission. Boardmaker™ is a trademark of Mayer-Johnson LLC.

Transitional Moments

Now you have provided students with a layout of the day so that they can predict what activity will be coming next, and what will happen after that. This will take you a long, long way toward smoothing out the bumps and keeping the heat down. But now let's look even more closely at another trouble spot: transitional moments. These are the moments that sneak in *between* structured activities. These moments are loose, undefined, disorganized, even chaotic, and are frequent triggers to students on the spectrum. Transitions require students not only to complete what they were doing before, but also to shift, physically and mentally, to whatever comes next. Even though transitions are often brief, they can be packed with provocation for students on the spectrum. If you have students who need support shifting from one activity to the next, here are some common transitional challenges and strategies to help.

Shifting Gears

During a transition, what may have been a quiet, organized activity abruptly explodes into action. Suddenly everyone is talking loudly. Chairs scrape against the floor as classmates get up to put away their materials or prepare for the next activity. Bodies are moving in every direction.

Even more challenging for students on the spectrum—who may have trouble regulating their moods—may be those moments when a transition requires a shift from loud, lively, and energetic, to quiet, organized, and still. Either way, suddenly nothing is as it was the moment before.

Transitional moments demand regulation, spontaneity, flexibility, organization, focus, sensory adaptation, language processing, motor planning, and much more—all at once. As you'll see in forthcoming chapters, none of these skills comes easily or automatically to students on the spectrum.

For example, your simple words, *Okay everybody, wrap it up*, at the end of a math project demand immediate response, yet are heavily loaded with implied meaning. On hearing those words, students are expected to perform several actions:

1. Heed your call to attention.

2. Decode your idiomatic language.

3. Adjust to the fact that what had become familiar and comfortable is now over; it's time again for something new.

4. Adapt to the sudden surge of noise and energy in the room.

5. Stop working immediately, regardless of whether their work is complete, even if their expectation had been to finish.

6. Clean up their work stations, sorting which materials should be put away and where (e.g., the calculators go back on the third shelf, the worksheet goes in the classwork bin, and the pencils remain at their desks).

7. Determine the multiple steps necessary to prepare for the next activity.

It's pretty amazing that for most typically functioning students all of this happens automatically and almost instantaneously. But for students on the spectrum, just as they process all of those elements and begin to get in gear for this change of course—just as they begin to get a handle on all that was implied in your words—the moment has passed and it's on to the next activity. Now the class is already gathering on the rug or sitting back down with new materials or heading out the door for next period. And chances are your students on the spectrum are still sitting, math worksheets and calculator aglow, pencils in hand, brows furrowed, hands flapping, anxiety building.

But transitions don't have to go this way. By unpacking the challenges presented, we can help smooth out those in-between times, too, as described in the following strategies:

✱ **Warning, Warning:** Time prompts can be effective for the whole class. Alert students five minutes before an activity is going to end. This will give them time to finish up their work and prepare for the upcoming change.

An additional two-minute warning along the way will help students gauge their progress toward the transition. At the two-minute warning, have them stop working briefly to give you their attention. Explain specifically what you expect to happen during the transition: *When I say it's time to stop working, please turn off your calculators and put them on the third shelf of the bookcase by the window. Put your papers in the classwork bin. Then you may start reviewing for the quiz.*

Keep in mind that for some students on the spectrum that would be too many steps and too many words to process at once. If so, separate the instructions, and then reiterate them as needed, or list them in writing.

✴ **Follow Protocol:** Break down the expectations for a transition and put them on the schedule or on the board. Jed Baker (2001), a psychologist and expert on social-skills training, suggests setting up two- or three-step mini-protocols for various transitions. For example, if you expect students to begin independent reading, have a rubric like this one at the ready to display:

> *Getting Ready for Independent Reading*
>
> > *Quiet hands and feet*
> >
> > *Eyes on book*
> >
> > *Ready to work*
> >
> > *Quiet mouth—read in your head*

✴ **Carrying Comfort:** Let students keep a small transitional object with them as a thread of continuity and comfort as they move from one activity to the next. Sometimes transitional objects can be small enough to be discretely tucked into a pocket, available as a comforting touchpoint as needed.

✴ **Straight Talk:** Be careful to avoid using idioms or slang when giving instructions. Students on the spectrum are very literal, so your instruction *Okay everybody, wrap it up* might ultimately get you a calculator carefully wrapped in a math worksheet.

Separation

One especially challenging transitional moment for young students on the spectrum can be separation. Given their multifaceted anxiety and difficulty coping with change, many students will struggle with saying goodbye to everything that is home and family, as they move into a different environment. If this is an issue for your students, consider incorporating bits of home into their day.

✴ **My Life in Pictures:** Invite students to bring in photographs of their families. These can be posted on desks, used to decorate notebooks or folders, or posted on a classroom wall in a family collage.

✴ **Home Aroma:** Suggest that students wear something that belongs to a parent or other family member, such as a T-shirt or sweatshirt, which might be soothing to touch and might carry just enough scent of home to be a comfort. Or suggest a dab of mom's perfume or dad's cologne inside their shirt collar in the morning to provide reassurance through the day.

✻ **Getting in the Groove:** Allow students to ease into the new day by creating a routine warm-up activity to serve as a comforting transition and help them to shake off lingering longings. (See Chapter 4 for specific ideas.)

Behavioral Expectations

Maintaining routine refers to more than the organization of time and space. In your classroom, you create a set of routine rules for all students to know and respect. As discussed previously, students on the spectrum rigidly depend on rules not just to guide their actions but to manage their anxiety.

Unruly Rules

Consider just how challenging it is for students on the spectrum to follow rules with rigid precision. Temple Grandin, a world-renowned professor of animal science who is on the spectrum, still struggles to generalize rules and sort out their gradations. She works hard to make sense of the confusing (and un-rule-like) fact that rules themselves do not follow predictable rules. Some rules are inviolable, some can be manipulated within reason, and some rules are meaningless. Other rules seem to exist even though they were never stated as rules.

Grandin has created for herself some *rules for rules* by categorizing rules into four types along these lines:

1. **Rules for Illegal and Unacceptable Actions:** These are rules that can't ever be broken. Killing and stealing are against the law and are never okay to do.

2. **Rules for Illegal but "Acceptable" Actions:** These are rules that people often break even though doing so is against the law. Speeding and littering are, in fact, against the law. Nevertheless, many people do them and rarely get in trouble.

3. **Rules of Courtesy:** These rules are not laws and they are okay to break, but only sometimes. For example, in certain circumstances it's okay to say *Yeah* instead of *Yes, please.* (Grandin has also struggled to recognize that courtesy violators do not necessarily need to be corrected by her!)

4. **Unspoken Rules:** These hidden rules address actions that should not be done, even though there are no stated rules against them. These refer to behaviors that are considered "common sense," such as not pulling the arm of someone who is holding hot coffee, not banging a rock against a flagpole, not licking magic markers, and countless others. Have you actually ever stated rules prohibiting these kinds of actions? Did you ever think you'd need to? Probably not . . . until you needed to.

Rules Rule

When rules are well understood, students on the spectrum will likely be the first to remind you if you are not upholding them exactly as you have presented them. So when you find these students breaking the rules, there's probably a compelling reason. Here are some of those reasons.

Rule Rigidity

Like all other aspects of the social world, rule compliance requires nuanced abilities such as inference and generalization. Even rules you think are crystal clear may not be clear at all when interpreted by literal and inflexible thinkers.

Okay, Now What?

Sometimes students on the spectrum will follow a rule only to the extent that you have stated it and will not infer beyond that. When you see that students have stalled, consider that they might be awaiting further instructions. A classic example is when a teacher hands out a test and tells the students, *Do not begin the test until I tell you to . . . Okay, you may now pick up your pencils.* All the students begin working on the test, except for the student on the spectrum who is sitting still, holding her pencil. Why? Because the instruction was for the students to pick up their pencils; no one said to *begin testing.* A more specific and productive instruction might have been: *Okay, now you may pick up your pencils and begin working on the test.*

Ready to Work

Sit on chair

Feet on floor

Fold hands

Take 3 deep breaths

Count to 10

Ready to work

The Picture Communication Symbols ©1981–2010 by Mayer-Johnson LLC. All Rights Reserved Worldwide. Used with permission. Boardmaker™ is a trademark of Mayer-Johnson LLC.

Caught in a Bind

Other times, students on the spectrum will stick to rules too rigidly, not understanding the nuance and inference often required of living in the social world. For example, when he was in middle school, my son's peers thought it was funny to turn off the lights in the boy's bathroom while he was in a stall. Because there were no windows in the bathroom, my son was plunged into total and complete darkness. When he shared this terrifying experience with me later, I told him: "If that ever happens to you again, I want you to take your cell phone out of your pocket, turn it on, and use the light from the phone to guide your way out of the bathroom."

He looked at me and gasped, absolutely horrified at the idea. "I could *never*!"

"Why not?" I asked.

"We're not allowed to turn our phones on at school!"

In that moment my son's rigidity left him in a desperately frightening situation with no perceived solutions.

(By the way, even though rigidity prevented my son from breaking the rules just enough to solve his immediate problem, it did not prevent him from finding a way to solve the larger problem once he had some distance from it. A few days later, my son wrote a persuasive letter to the assistant principal which resulted in all of the bathroom light switches in the school being changed to sensors. Now no one at that school will ever be left in the dark in the bathroom again!)

Rule Continuity

Various adults in your students' lives are likely to have different sets of rules and expectations. Art, music, and phys ed teachers, as well as occupational therapists, school psychologists, cafeteria workers, recess aides, and bus drivers all have their own styles and expectations. This inconsistency can be confusing for students on the spectrum. Collaborate to develop continuity across the school day to whatever extent is possible. Share experiences about approaches that seem effective. Share copies of the fact sheets provided on pages 227–234. (And gather more information about collaborating in Chapter 7.)

Three Rules for Setting Rules

1. Be sure your rules are incontrovertibly clear to every student.
2. Be sure your rules are reasonable and enforceable.
3. Differentiate rules flexibly for specific students as needed, but then uphold them with consistency.

Like the schedule, behavioral expectations should be posted in comprehensible terms, explained, clarified, and checked for understanding. To further your efforts for clarity, consider using a behavioral system, as described below, to support students who need concrete feedback on their behavioral progress.

Hey! That's Not Fair!

Learning disabilities specialist Rick Lavoie suggests that when other students balk at individualized adaptations, explain to them that fair does not mean everyone gets the same. *Fair means giving each student what he or she needs.*

Token Economy Systems

The behavior of your typically functioning students may be reinforced simply by your smile or even by the self-satisfaction of doing something well. Such students may not need to participate in a token economy system to produce positive behavior. In fact, when we find students who are self-motivated, it's better not to diminish their positive predisposition by imposing unnecessary, external token rewards.

However, students on the spectrum are usually unmoved by (or unaware of) unspoken reinforcements. They need concrete reinforcements to support their effort and progress.

Less tangible incentives, such as extra reading time or extra screen time, may work for older students, and may eventually motivate even some of your younger students on the spectrum— but most will benefit from starting with the concrete incentives of a token economy system.

If you have students who need concrete incentives, set up a system whereby each student who needs the system has the opportunity and motivation to earn tokens by demonstrating differentiated target behaviors. When a student earns the necessary number of tokens (incentives), he may exchange them for a valued "treasure" (reinforcement). But remember that in most cases, when students on the spectrum are off-task or misbehaving, the reason goes much deeper than motivators and prompts. Again, every behavior is a form of communication. Please take the time to read through this book to understand the many, many triggers that can upset the equilibrium of students on the spectrum, and can spark a behavioral response. You will learn simple strategies for adapting the environment to reduce anxiety, support sensory needs, enhance engagement, and bolster communication. Then you may find you'll have no need for behavioral systems at all!

Tokens can take the form of tickets, points, coins, stars, checkmarks, stickers, or whatever motivates specific students. (For more inventive incentives, visit www.barbaraboroson.com.) Here are some tips for enhancing the value of your token system:

✱ **Set Up Success:** Be sure the goal you set for each student is achievable. (Make it *easily* achievable at the beginning.) You can be sure that your system will backfire if you set up a highly motivating incentive that a student is incapable of achieving. Try to differentiate expectations for each student.

✱ **So Far, So Good:** Let students see how many *more* tokens they need in order to earn the treasure. Create or download free printable templates with delineated spaces into which students attach tokens as they earn them. This allows them to see clearly how many spaces they have yet to fill. (See sample template below.)

✱ **Follow Through:** Treat this system like a contract. If students uphold their end and earn the designated number of tokens, be sure to uphold your end and provide the contracted reinforcement. Be consistent; don't change the rules along the way or you will lose credibility and your system will lose its effectiveness.

✱ **Emphasize Effort:** Students on the spectrum get more than their share of negative reinforcement every day. Avoid giving consequences if good effort has been applied. Practice noticing and acknowledging effort and progress: *André, since you raised your hand a few times today, you've earned a star.*

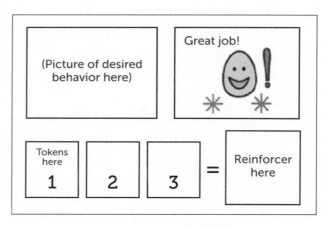

The Picture Communication Symbols ©1981–2010 by Mayer-Johnson LLC. All Rights Reserved Worldwide. Used with permission. Boardmaker™ is a trademark of Mayer-Johnson LLC.

Tomorrow, let's see if you can raise your hand and wait quietly. Remember, there will be no straight lines here; what was achieved yesterday may fall by the wayside tomorrow when André's shirt feels scratchy, or his bus arrives late, or he gets a paper cut on his finger. Your short-term goal is to encourage positive effort. True mastery may be a long time coming.

✱ **Pair It With Praise:** Always tell students precisely what they are doing that earns them a token. This clarity serves two purposes: First, it reinforces the likelihood of students repeating desirable behaviors. And second, it helps teach them to connect the good feeling of getting a token with the more abstract reinforcement of praise. Someday, maybe, praise or pride alone—with no concrete token—will be enough.

✱ **You'll Get It Next Time:** When you feel that students on the spectrum have not put forth their best effort—*all* things considered—clarify for them exactly what action failed to meet your expectations. Explain that because of that action, they did not earn a token this time. If you don't tell them what they did wrong, they will not recognize the relationship between their action and your reaction.

Behavioral Systems: There's an App for That!

For older students, or those who are more socially aware, behavioral systems can be strictly digital, rather than displayed on the bulletin board for all to see. Many apps now allow teachers to easily create behavioral systems for individual students, which enhances your ability to maximize interest and motivation. These apps make it easy for you to set goals, reinforce positive behaviors, track rewards, and demonstrate progress to students. Many icons for commonly sought skills are provided, but additional, customized tasks and rewards can be added as needed.

As of this writing, popular apps for behavioral charting include *iPrompts Pro* by Handheld Adaptive, *iReward* by Grembe Inc., *Smart Charts* by Happy Face Kidz, and *Working4* by Pyramid Educational Consultants. New and improved apps are being created all the time. Search under "behavior trackers" in your app store. You're sure to find an app for that.

✱ **The Meta-Token:** The loss of a possible token may be perceived as a very negative consequence by some of your system-dependent, rule-following, rigid students. So be gentle with your explanation, keep it positive, and check for understanding: *Now that you understand why you aren't getting a star today, I know you can do better tomorrow. What will you do differently tomorrow to get a star?*

A parent recently shared with me that one day in 2016 her well-behaved son expressed that he was feeling extremely anxious about ever breaking a rule at school because he might not earn the coveted end-of-the-day reward. His mom tried to reassure him: "Oh, I really don't think you need to worry about that! After all, when was the last time you didn't get your reward?"

The boy replied, without hesitation, "January 10, 2014."

So be aware that your behavioral systems may hang heavily over the heads of your students. Apply them gently.

If you have a student who can't tolerate the loss of a potential token, then that behavioral response itself may be one to be remediated. Offer strategies for staying calm. (Learn more about coaxing calm later in this chapter and in Chapter 4.) And then offer her a token when she is able to calmly tolerate not earning any other tokens!

Rousing Reinforcements

Reinforcements can be of high value to students of any age while still being of low cost to you. (See www.barbaraboroson.com for links to online stores that offer dozens of inexpensive products.) Here are some simple ideas to maximize the value of reinforcements available to students:

✳ **Make It Meaningful:** Individualize your choice of reinforcements based on both age and interest. Since students on the spectrum may have a very narrow range of interests, reinforcements must be meaningful to each targeted student or they will not be effective. When selecting reinforcements, whether physical or digital, make personal motivation the priority, even if the treasure seems thematically disconnected from the activity.

✳ **Think Outside the (Treasure) Box:** Reinforcements can include a pizza party; an indoor-recess-board-games tournament; the chance to sit in the teacher's chair; the opportunity to tell a joke over the loudspeaker during morning announcements; earned access to a coveted app or computer game; a VIP lunch with the principal; or a few minutes of hat-wearing or another usually restricted activity.

✳ **Aim for "Age Appropriateness":** By consulting with students and with parents or caregivers, try to choose a variety of reinforcements that are meaningful but also "age appropriate." Even if your seventh grader on the spectrum would be motivated by Nemo and Dory stickers, the spectacle of his shirt covered in these too-childish stickers would sabotage his efforts to socialize with peers. But if Nemo and Dory are where he's at, maybe he could earn "cooler" sea-themed items, such as fish-themed playing cards, hand-held water ring games, Yu-Gi-Oh sea serpent trading cards, fish fortune-teller magic tricks, plastic water snakes, or extra screen time on apps like Ninja Fishing, iQuarium, or Splashy Fish.

✳ **Offer Shoppertunity:** Let students who earn enough tokens shop for their treasure. Offer a wide variety of options from which they can choose. This also encourages students to set goals for what they would like to earn next week including "big-ticket" items that might require longer-term budgeting.

Optimizing Optimism

In many cases, you will find that your behavioral aspirations for students tend to be about correcting negative actions, such as *Stop kicking the chair legs* or *No grabbing scissors*. Challenge yourself to reframe these into positively worded, outcome-oriented goals that convey what you want students *to do*, rather than what you want them not to do. Tell them: *Keep your feet still* or *Wait your turn for scissors.*

By framing goals in the positive, you also cultivate a culture of optimism and are more likely to notice when students apply positive coping skills where they had previously struggled: *I like the way you wait your turn for the scissors now.* This kind of quiet progress may be easily overlooked, but is not easily achieved. Look for quiet improvements such as handling disappointment, good waiting, accepting *no*, stopping on time, and coping well with making mistakes (Baker, 2009).

Expressing rules in the form of positive goals instead of *Don'ts* will also enhance clarity and boost students' motivation and ability to comply: *The rule in our class is: We wait our turn* or *The rule is: We keep our feet still.*

Coaching Coping

Unfortunately, the incentives and reinforcements described in the section above will have little effect on students who have no internal control over their impulses. Not only are specific tasks difficult for students on the spectrum, but the skills required to cope and persevere with those difficulties may be inaccessible, due to regulatory challenges. When sensory overload kicks in or anxiety bubbles up, waving tickets or stickers before these students is only setting them up for frustration and disappointment, exacerbating an already overwhelming experience.

Rather than letting disquieting situations escalate into crises, you can offer your students tools to support self-regulation. Here are some tools and strategies that may help students recognize their feelings and try to modulate their own responses:

✱ **Pack a Coolbox:** Don't just expect the unexpected— *prepare* for it. Create a relaxation folder or a small *coolbox* that a student who struggles with anxiety can use when she needs to calm down. Use the information you collected from parents, caregivers, and colleagues to fill the box with individualized affirmations, calming cues, and comfort objects.

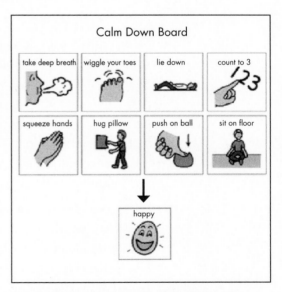

Affirmations might include statements like these:

> *I am a great swimmer!*
>
> *I can name every movie Matt Damon has ever been in!*
>
> *I can recite pi to 27 digits!*

Calming strategies can include:

> *Drawing a picture helps me relax.*
>
> *Taking deep breaths helps me feel better.*
>
> *Counting to ten helps me calm down.*

The Picture Communication Symbols ©1981–2010 by Mayer-Johnson LLC. All Rights Reserved Worldwide. Used with permission. Boardmaker™ is a trademark of Mayer-Johnson LLC.

Reinforcing the Negatives
of Negative Reinforcement

In most classrooms these days, the behavioral atmosphere is upbeat and optimistic, emphasizing incentives and positive reinforcements. Here are a few reminders about why negative reinforcements are negative, especially when working with students on the spectrum.

- Most negative reinforcements are more suppressive than instructive. Students on the spectrum cannot intuit why their behavior caused a consequence and then change their behavior spontaneously. These students require specific, proactive re-education in order to learn replacement behaviors, and in some cases environmental modification may be necessary as well.

- Negative reinforcements tend to be set as class-wide or school-wide policy, with consistency of enforcement as a primary goal (as is the case with a zero tolerance policy). But students on the spectrum have IEPs because they cannot be held, across the board, to the same standards as typically functioning students. Class-wide and school-wide systems fail to differentiate the special modifications or accommodations students on the spectrum need and deserve. When necessary, try to use natural consequences that emerge—by definition—*naturally*, in response to individual situations.

- Many negative reinforcements restrict learning opportunities. For example, suppose a student routinely tosses the game board when he realizes that he lost the game. If the response to this behavior is that he can no longer play games, he has lost all opportunity to learn game-playing skills. He needs to be re-educated about game playing and may need the game to be modified. If a negative reinforcement seems necessary, a better choice might be requiring the student to clean up all the spilled pieces—a natural consequence, but not a restricting one.

- Often negative reinforcements are issued in the heat of an exasperated moment and without careful consideration. With students on the spectrum, this could mean inadvertently removing comfort anchors. Impulsively confiscating a beloved squeeze ball or an element of the regular schedule would only make an anxious student more anxious and thus more likely to erupt again.

Add comforting objects, specific to each student, to the coolbox. These might include items such as:

- representations of familiar topics or special interests, such as family photographs, a small stuffed animal, a tiny globe, a motorcycle magazine

- a Social Story about staying calm (See more on Social Stories in Chapter 8.)

- sensorily supportive objects such as a squeeze ball, a massage ball, an iPod with earbuds, resistance bands, or noise-canceling headphones, carefully differentiated according to each student's sensory needs

- an index card that lists affirmations (as described on page 67) and other ideas for calming down. (You might want to work with the student, in a calm moment, to create it. Keep the card in the box.)

> *"The more you know about your emotions, the more you can control them instead of letting them control you."*
>
> —Tony Attwood, Ph.D. (2009)

✱ **Headed Toward Red:** Teach students to take their own emotional temperature, using a graphic of a thermometer with color-coded emotional gradations. Moods range from cool, calm blue to hot, raging red. Students can learn that when they recognize that their emotional temperature is headed toward red, it's time to take a break, take out the coolbox, or use whatever soothing strategy has been prearranged. (See a full-color, reproducible version of the Emotions Thermometer at www.barbaraboroson.com.)

Encourage students to browse through their coolboxes periodically, even during calm moments, in order to practice and reinforce these self-regulatory skills and help prolong the current state of calm.

(Read about more ways to modify the sensory environment, including creating a sensory corner, in Chapter 4.)

Barbara Boroson © 2011

✱ **Coded Communication:** Coordinate a signal that individual students can use to alert you when they feel they are beginning to heat up or lose control. Have a plan in place so that both you and the students know what will happen as a result of that signal, depending on the comfort needs of each student. A peek through the coolbox, a trip to the water fountain, a moment with you in the hall, or some other regulatory activity may be just enough to help students get back on track.

✳ **Model Coping Strategies:** When you find yourself struggling with something, vocalize your own process and coping strategies aloud. *I know that when I'm calm, I'll be able to figure this out. I'm going to take a deep breath to calm down so that I can solve this problem.* Show students how you persevere and don't give up, explaining, *Wow, this is hard, but I believe in myself. I'll persist. I know I can get it.*

Emotional Regulation: There's an App for That!

Very often for students on the autism spectrum, digital devices are calming comfort anchors in and of themselves. Why not maximize their effect by offering some apps that help students monitor and regulate their own emotional states? Some apps allow students to curate a library of images, sounds, and words that calm them, resulting in a virtual happy place. Others provide guided steps and prompts and simple exercises for calming down.

As of this writing, *Tap Me Happy* by Smart Apps for Kids and *Calm Counter* by Touch Autism are popular for these purposes. New and improved apps are being created all the time. Search under "emotional regulation" in your app store. You're sure to find an app for that.

Fading Structure

Put preventive strategies in place and keep them there. In time, you will likely see problematic behaviors abate significantly. That's a wonderful thing; that's success. Chances are, your students on the spectrum are doing well in large part *because* of your consistent strategies. If so, you are off to a great start together. Keep it up.

But watch yourself for signs of complacency. With successful preventive strategies in place, we can be easily lulled into believing that problem areas are no longer problem areas, and we can grow lax about maintaining these strategies.

For example, suppose you make a point of always notifying students ahead of time when you know you will be absent from school. So far, that system works well; your students on the spectrum seem to do fine with a substitute teacher. You might begin to think, *They do fine every time I have a substitute, so I don't need to prepare them anymore.*

Hold on. Give yourself some credit. Trust that your students on the spectrum are doing fine *because* of your careful preparation, and then stick with it. One brief hiatus can allow an otherwise avoidable problem to develop and set off the downward spiral you've worked so hard to avoid.

Instead, let nature take its course. There will be plenty of times when circumstances will result in an unavoidable deviation from the schedule (such as when you are *unexpectedly* absent from school, when there is an *unplanned* fire alarm, and so on). If, on the basis of reactions to such unavoidable events, you believe you can scale back some modifications, do so very slowly—one element at a time—per individual student. Do not risk triggering more anxiety. Make a small change only when you are sure your student is ready for it, and then watch carefully for any ramifications.

● ● ● ●

Here's what *you* can expect: No matter how much you work to prevent them, there will be occasional situations that get red hot. And there may be times when someone gets burned. In Chapter 10 strategies are offered to help guide you through the moments when the pot really gets boiling. But please read through the chapters between here and there first, because they will give you loads of insights and strategies to help you keep the heat down. By the time you get to Chapter 10, you will be a master chef, expert at maintaining just the right temperature under your busily simmering pots so that they very rarely boil over.

Chapter 4

Body and Soul
Regulation and Sensation

Imagine walking into the school cafeteria at lunchtime. Imagine that your hearing is so sensitive that common sounds are truly painful to you. The clatter of every fork stabs into your ears, the scratchy screech of every Styrofoam tray makes you shudder, and the cacophony of voices roars like a lawn mower in your ears. Your ears and eyes are sensitive to fluorescent light, so the glaring overhead bulbs buzz relentlessly, while their incessant flickering makes the room spin. Your senses of smell and taste are so acute that the combined aroma of turkey tetrazzini, boiled hot dogs, reheated green beans, and commercial coleslaw, overlaid with the caustic odor of cleansers and ammonia, makes you gag. Your body awareness is so precarious that the chaos of people moving in all directions makes you dizzy and disoriented, and now you can't find where you are supposed to sit.

You close your eyes and cover your ears to shut it all out, but you can still feel the press of the crowds while the smells linger in your nose and throat. Someone taps your shoulder to ask if you're okay, and your sensitivity to touch perceives it as a slap. Your fleeting impulse control has now vanished completely, and you whirl around and strike the offending arm away.

Now you hear voices yelling at you, your coping and problem-solving skills are maxed out, and all you know is that you can't be here. You begin to rock back and forth in a soothing rhythm but cannot block out the pressure pulsing in your temples. You spot the door and bolt out onto the empty playground. You sink to the ground under a tree, gulping in the fresh air, soaking in the silence around you and the stability of the tree behind you and the ground beneath you, and now the lunch monitor is hollering for you to get back inside.

Enjoy your lunch!

Overwhelming situations like these are common for students on the spectrum because their sensory and regulatory systems do not function in typical or self-protective ways. Often, their behaviors are interpreted as aggressive, oppositional, or antisocial. But in fact, these students may be at the mercy of intense sensory input and may possess limited ability to regulate their responses. This means they may seem to overreact, underreact, or react impulsively, indiscriminately, and inexplicably. Difficulties with regulation manifest in areas of behavior, organization, socialization, focus, and more, and can forcefully derail students' physical and emotional well-being. This chapter will explain two major factors that affect self-regulation—executive function and sensory processing—and will show you how to recognize and address these challenges.

Executive Function

Executive function is the ability of the brain to think through situations and, when necessary, override impulsive or automatic responses. For example, executive function enables some of us to eat only one piece of birthday cake after lunch, even as the whole cake beckons. We have the capacity to think it through by examining various options and outcomes: We reflect on whether or not we are still hungry. We recall that the last time we binged on cake, we felt sick for hours. We recognize the possibility that others at the table might want some cake, too. We remember that we decided to cut back on sweets for health reasons. We speculate that too much cake now will ruin our appetite for the dinner celebration that is planned for later in the day. We use self-talk to mull over the decision: *I really shouldn't. It's so good, though! Maybe I should leave it for everyone else. But it's my birthday! No—I'll be glad later if I don't have any more now.*

For those of us with adequate executive functioning, the frontal and prefrontal lobes in our brains operate as Chief Executive Officer, micromanaging every choice we make and everything we do. Executive function effectively orchestrates or regulates our actions and reactions in the context of conscious consideration and learned experience. When this system operates properly, we have access to useful planning skills such as objective thinking, prediction, reflection, flexibility, impulse control, and empathy, as well as critical coping skills such as waiting, tolerating frustration, staying calm, and shifting gears.

Students with executive function challenges struggle with many skills:

- considering the perspective of others
- interpreting and understanding the motivation of others
- modulating their own demeanor to fit a certain context
- generating ideas or initiating topics
- planning ahead (foresight)

- learning from their mistakes (hindsight)
- focusing
- coping with frustration
- putting a thought or action "on hold"
- thinking objectively (reframing)
- thinking flexibly
- staying calm
- managing time and pace
- shifting gears or attention
- navigating transitions
- maintaining organization
- following instructions or directions
- adding new information to existing knowledge (working memory)

The absence of these skills can cause students to appear inconsiderate, rude, impulsive, rigid, manic, careless, stubborn, inattentive, highly reactive, thoughtless, impatient, disorganized, or disoriented. But, in fact, they are at the mercy of intense executive dysfunction.

Acting and Reacting

When the executive function system is impaired, nothing inhibits impulsive, distracted, or otherwise dysfunctional behavior. In other words, students with executive dysfunction simply act and react. That cake is a goner. Students may give no thought to how an action will affect them or others in the future or to what the consequences of that same action were in the past.

Brakeless Behavior

Martin Kutscher, a pediatric neurologist, explains that students with executive dysfunction live in the moment. For them, there is only this moment. And this moment. And this moment. The future and the past don't exist. These students get swept away by whatever is happening to them in any instant, uninhibited by any kind of self-regulatory controls. Kutscher calls this disinhibition "brakeless behavior," a term which vividly conveys not only the impulsivity of some behaviors, but also their unstoppableness (2004, p. 7). This may contribute to the tendency of students on the spectrum to repeat the same words or behaviors and may explain why those behaviors can be so intractable: There is no effective intrinsic system in place that signals *enough* and then shuts the behavior off. (See more on the repetition of words and behaviors, also known as *perseveration*, in Chapter 5.)

Why Are You Laughing?

Limited self-regulation may also cause students to respond to emotional or other situations in ways that are socially unexpected. They may laugh at or underreact to serious situations, and they frequently overreact to seemingly minor situations. They tend to go too far in any one direction, getting too wild or too silly, struggling to shift their moods efficiently from one register to another.

Executive Function Strategies

Since the minds of students with executive dysfunction dart so quickly from one moment to the next, it is very difficult to insert a lesson on self-regulation *between* those impulsive moments. So a better approach is to weave the use of general skills that support regulation across the curriculum. If you have students who struggle with executive function issues, here are some strategies to help them practice skills that encourage reflection, prediction, impulse control, and other components of regulation. Not all of these strategies will apply to every student. Use those that resonate with your students and feel doable to you. Pick and choose; you can always come back for more if you need them. (Find additional information on this topic and more strategies at www.barbaraboroson.com.)

Teaching Reflection and Prediction

Students on the spectrum benefit greatly from learning to reflect and predict, because those skills introduce the new *idea* of thinking before acting. Once this concept becomes familiar, you can begin prompting students to apply reflection and prediction skills *between* impulsive moments. And here are some prompts to help you make that happen:

✱ **Cause and Effect:** To support foresight and hindsight, practice connecting cause and effect by using concrete examples in natural contexts: *Uh oh. We left the papers near the open window and the breeze caused something to happen. What was the effect of the breeze on the papers?*

✱ **Looking Forward:** Have students make predictions about stories or classroom events: *The iPads are stacked very high. Does the pile of iPads look stable? Why not? What do you predict will happen if we leave them stacked so high? Why?* Support students' efforts as they try to apply these skills to social and other more abstract situations.

✱ **Looking Back:** Debrief both successful and unsuccessful situations with students on the spectrum. If a situation was stressful, you may need to provide time for students to calm down and regroup before you debrief. But as soon as possible, and without criticism, make conscious for your students whatever positive efforts and missteps they made. Remember that these are difficult new ways of thinking for students on the spectrum, so ask your questions slowly and allow plenty of time for language and thought processing. If you do not overtly connect the cause to the effect, these students will not learn from their mistakes (or from their successes); they will not spontaneously make the connection between their actions and the outcome of the situation.

For example, since Kenji does not think through what will happen if he keeps poking Anya's shoulder, talk him through the learning process:

- reflection: *What happened last time you poked someone?*
- empathy: *How would you feel if someone were poking your shoulder?*
- prediction: *So, then, how do you think Anya feels when you poke her shoulder?*

You may be surprised to note that this very basic line of reasoning seems to yield a new epiphany every time. Keep at it because these kinds of connections are not happening automatically. Your words are sinking in, albeit slowly. Encourage students to plan how they might handle the same situation even better the next time. And always clarify that by "next time," you don't mean only next time, but every time!

Teaching Impulse Control

Impulsive students are unable to make conscious choices about their behaviors because they are unable to stop and think before doing. But *some* students on the spectrum may be able to understand that choices can be made about handling situations. Try to explain, to those you think might understand, that they can *learn to choose* whether to raise their hands or call out. They can *learn to choose* whether to get in the back of the line or cut in front. They can *learn to choose* whether to kick an adversary or walk away. This section will guide you to help students locate that elusive moment of choice and use it to apply their new reflection and prediction skills. Again, these strategies will not work for everyone.

✳ **Look Behind the Scenes:** Students' impulse control can be affected by an overwhelming sensory environment (as shown in the lunchroom example on pages 72–73). Modifying the sensory environment to meet the needs of sensitive students can go a long way toward facilitating impulse control. (See "Sensational Strategies" on page 92.)

✳ **Stop and Think:** Bolster students' efforts to control impulses by providing clear, natural incentives and positive reinforcements: *Since you're interrupting, I cannot listen to you. If you stay quiet and raise your hand, I will listen to you.* The goal is to help students capture that instant, just before impulses take over, in which they can independently remember that prompt and make a conscious choice: *Oh! If I raise my hand instead of calling out, I will get a turn to answer. So I will stay quiet and raise my hand.* Be patient; this is a lofty goal.

✳ **Don't Miss a Beat:** Be sure to notice the amazing progress evident when students verbalize their efforts to stop, such as when a student interrupts by calling out, *I'm not going to call out! I'm going to raise my hand and wait to be called on!* This kind of statement indicates that this student has been able to wedge a beat into that instant; she is thinking before doing. Of course the intention was instantly overtaken by impulse, but still, there is great progress there. Acknowledge this powerful intermediate step that is well on the way to impulse control: *Good job remembering to not call out! Next time, do that great remembering in your head and don't let it out of your mouth!*

Along these lines, I worked with a kindergartner who would get very angry with me whenever our time together came to an end. Every time I got ready to leave, Julian would glower and yell at me and accuse me of being a "bad person" for leaving. To ease the transition,

I showed him a schedule of what he would be doing right after I left. To acknowledge his feelings, I told him I understood that he was sad to see me go and I showed him our next meeting on a calendar. I reflected to him that when he called me a bad person, it hurt my feelings. And I suggested that, if he feels sad at the end of our visits, he might use his words to say, *I'm sad that you have to go.*

Julian and I replayed this entire scenario regularly for weeks with no change in his behavior. Finally one day, as I was getting ready to leave, he muttered glumly, *I'm going to call you a bad person . . . tomorrow.* There it was; there was the beat. There was the moment in which he stopped and thought, in which he made a choice to not call me a bad person. He couldn't entirely not-say-it yet, but he had caught himself before the words burst forth. We were on our way.

Teaching Advance Planning

Students with executive function challenges may struggle to plan ahead. This may cause them to be chronically unprepared for certain tasks or activities, always showing up without the necessary tools or gear. Others may struggle with planning in terms of pacing themselves. Impulsivity may drive them to finish their work as quickly as possible just to get it done. Others meander dreamily through their work with no awareness of expiring time. You can support planning and pacing by implementing some of the following strategies:

✱ **Count It Down:** Try using countdowns for time remaining in an activity. But be aware that while countdowns can help some students pace themselves, your frequent interruptions (*five minutes left . . . four minutes left . . .* and so on) may be distracting and disorienting to others.

✱ **Time Time:** For students who are easily derailed or are visual learners, use visual timers, which are clock-face timers that graphically represent elapsed and remaining time. These timers, available in both hands-on and digital forms, show students exactly how much longer they will need to wait, comply, or attend to the task at hand, so they can pace themselves accordingly. (The original physical visual timer is the Time Timer®. Many digital versions of visual timers are now available.)

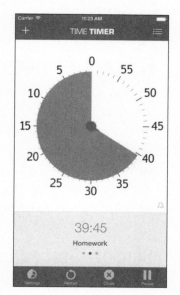

✱ **Chunk It:** Break assignments into small chunks, so that students can feel gratified and energized by mini-accomplishments, rather than having to sustain their attention and effort along the way toward a larger goal. For example, if you expect students to research the founding dates of each of the 50 states and put them on a timeline, try assigning the activities as separate tasks. You might try listing them on the schedule using separate icons: one for research, another for sequencing, and a third for plotting on the timeline. This way, students can more easily achieve success and move on confidently to the next challenge.

✻ **Finish Later:** Students on the spectrum often have an urgent need for closure, a rigid, intrinsic pressure to complete whatever they've started. No matter how appealing the next activity may be, they may be unable to stop whatever they're doing until it's finished. The suggestion that they might "go back to it later" is too amorphous to offer any comfort. Try overtly scheduling an opportunity to tie up loose ends by putting a *Finish Work* icon on their schedule for later in the day. Or give students a folder called "Work to Finish Later." These strategies offer a kind of semi-closure, providing visual substance to your words and a tangible means of "putting a project where it belongs," even if just temporarily.

Teaching Waiting

Waiting means deferring want, which is especially difficult for impulsive students with limited executive function. Worse, when students on the spectrum are told to wait, they often do nothing but that. There is no notion of finding something else to amuse themselves *in the meantime* or occupying themselves *while* they wait. They just wait, and focus single-mindedly on what they are not getting. And that makes waiting interminable.

Offer alternatives to just waiting: *While you are waiting, please pick up five scraps of paper from the floor and put them in the recycling bin,* or *While you are waiting, go through your coolbox. I'll come get you when I'm ready.* Give students opportunities to practice deferring want for increasing increments of time and offer incentives for good waiting.

Even though drawing on these strategies helps students on the spectrum develop regulatory skills, powerful sensory triggers may severely undermine their efforts to stay calm and consider or modulate their reactions to stimuli. The next section describes the overwhelming obstacles that can be presented by sensory challenges and offers many simple but critical ways to adapt the environment so that these sensitive students can cope.

Sensory Integration

Sensory information is processed in the brain through a system called *sensory integration*. When the sensory integration system works well, sensory input is efficiently and productively received by the brain, where it is organized and responded to in predictable ways. However, when the system is not adequately integrated, sensory input is processed in a way that does not yield an organized or predictable response. Disruptions to sensory integration can affect any or all types of sensation and can sabotage students' efforts to learn, socialize, and stay calm. The sensory system can be so brittle that even one sensory offense can derail a whole day.

Sensory Processing Disorder

Significant disruption to the sensory integration process is called Sensory Processing Disorder. Though Sensory Processing Disorder (formerly known as Sensory Integration Disorder) is not an official diagnosis in DSM-V, it is a discretely defined condition, and sensory challenges are among the criteria considered when making an autism spectrum diagnosis.

Sensory challenges can be difficult for teachers to get a handle on because responses vary from student to student. Even more challenging is that responses can vary widely within the same student depending on the type of sensory input she faces. And more confusing still, responses to particular input can even vary within the same student from day to day.

If you can't keep track of the many ins and outs and ups and down of your students' sensory challenges—or even of an individual student's sensory challenges—it may be helpful to simply hold on to the concept that these students' sensory systems are most often *calibrated differently* than others'. It's as if, sometimes, the dial is set too tightly closed, not allowing enough sensation in. When this happens, students seek sensory input. Other times, the dial is set too far open, allowing way too much sensation in. When this is the case, students do whatever they must to avoid the overwhelming input.

Sensory processing issues can cause a classroom decorated with brightly colored posters or artwork to be visually overstimulating to students on the spectrum: They don't know where to look; colors swim before their eyes or give them headaches. The cluster-seating arrangement, which places your socially inept and distractible students in the midst of the other students, may be disorienting. The social environment feels incomprehensibly disorganized; faces are everywhere. The flashing lights you use to indicate the end of an activity can be blinding and frightening. The sound of the rhythmic clapping you use to bring the students to attention may actually be painful to their ears.

Indeed, at school the sensory assault of noise, movement, transitions, personalities, and more constantly swirls around, whipping up a menacingly stormy sea for these students. They may have an entirely different experience of your classroom than you might guess.

Since sensory assaults often spring up without warning, students are often on guard against them. Living with that relentless tension contributes significantly to the anxiety that is so common among students on the spectrum. But many aspects of the sensory environment can be mitigated and student responses can be modified. The next section describes what kinds of sensory triggers students face, followed by a long list of simple strategies to help settle those senses.

> "Be aware that even though [you] may have created a uniform experience for [your] class, this child's understanding of the experience, his interpretation of it, may be different than what we assume it would be."
>
> —S. Jay Kuder (2003)

Did You Know . . .

Sensory Processing Disorder often occurs in the absence of Autism Spectrum Disorder. However, it is uncommon to find ASD without sensory processing challenges. Ninety percent of individuals on the autism spectrum manifest sensory processing challenges (Schoen, Miller, Brett-Green, & Nielsen, 2009). And more than 75% of individuals on the autism spectrum are found to meet the full criteria for Sensory Processing Disorder (Sensory Processing Foundation, 2016).

The Process of Sensory Processing

Effective sensory processing is a multistep system that depends on three separate areas of sensory function: *sensory modulation, sensory discrimination,* and *sensory-motor integration*. Challenges can occur in any or all of these areas.

Sensory Modulation

Sensory modulation is the ability to regulate responses to sensory input. Students with modulation challenges commonly respond in any or all of these three ways:

1. **Sensory Avoidance:** When students are highly responsive to sensory stimuli, they may try to avoid sensory input. Seemingly innocuous or mild sensory input can be so painful to them that they hide from it or seek to defend themselves against it. These sensorially defensive efforts lead them to be fearful and cautious, or defiant—braced against sensory input and ready to react with a fight-or-flight response. Sometimes the use of more than one sense at a time can be entirely overwhelming.

2. **Sensory Indifference:** When students are minimally responsive to sensory stimuli, they may be oblivious to sensory input. They may seem sluggish, experiencing limited perception of pain and requiring intense sensory input to get in gear. Students whose senses are minimally responsive can appear inattentive, self-absorbed, and disengaged.

3. **Sensory Pursuit:** Students who are in need of intense sensory stimulation may hungrily seek input. These students are on a constant quest for more, more, more. They are hyper-alert, always into everything. These are your bumpers and crashers, your risk takers. They hum, bite, sniff, touch, climb, jump, and spin, craving sensory input all the time (Kranowitz, 2016).

True to Their Experience

When students exhibit large and loud reactions, they are perceived as being *overly* responsive, as if they are making a big deal out of nothing. They tend to be dismissed as melodramatic. Instead, respect that these students react on the basis of what they feel. What they feel, they feel big. Sure, they seem extremely reactive, but if so, their intense response is perfectly suited to the degree of sensation they are receiving. Try to think of them as *highly* responsive, not *overly* responsive.

Similarly, when students seem oblivious to what's going on around them, they tend to be viewed as under-responsive, dull, or out of it. Sure, they seem tuned out; but if so, respect that their low-key response is perfectly suited to the degree of sensation they are receiving. What's happening around them or within them, they scarcely notice. Try to think of these students as exhibiting *low* responsivity, rather than as being *under*-responsive.

Topsy Turvy: Sensory Imbalances

Just to confuse the picture, be aware that one student can have elements of all three challenges to modulation: highly responsive to some kinds of stimuli, minimally responsive to others, and oblivious to still others. One student may find the fire alarm so loud that it makes her cry, but she doesn't notice when you call the class to attention. Another student may crave the deep pressure of a tight hug, but can't tolerate a light tap on the shoulder. And another student may respond entirely differently to a specific sensation today than she did yesterday!

Sensory Discrimination

Sensory discrimination is the ability to perceive differences among various sensations. Some students may have such keen discrimination abilities that they can detect or focus on input so subtle that others may overlook it completely. I call this *sensory detection*. When a student has keen sensory detection, she may be the first to notice the smell of smoke, or the only one who can tell that the cafeteria changed its chicken nugget supplier.

But more often students with sensory discrimination issues experience *sensory jumbling*. They may struggle to differentiate sounds (such as musical tones or rhyming words), pictures (such as same versus different or foreground versus background), or smells and tastes. They may not recognize the difference between a gentle tap on the shoulder and a sharp poke in the arm—a confusion that has important social implications.

Others who struggle with sensory discrimination may not realize when they are dizzy, hungry, or nauseous. They may have trouble determining the distance and speed of a moving vehicle when crossing the street, or may have figure-ground recognition challenges that make it difficult for them to interpret or sequence pictures.

For example, while consulting in a first-grade class, I worked on jigsaw puzzles with a student named Mateo. I noticed quickly that Mateo was unable to sort straight-edge pieces from middle pieces. Though I showed him the difference again and again and taught him how to run his finger across the straight edge, he did not seem to get it.

Finally I asked him to show me the straight edges on his incorrectly chosen pieces. To my surprise, he pointed out not the edges, but the straight lines drawn *on the pieces* as part of the picture. Even after I explained to him the difference between straight lines and straight edges, Mateo still could not differentiate the shape of a piece from the picture on it. He could not shift from looking at the image to looking at the shape.

It was only when I turned every single piece face-down to conceal the images—making all of the pieces uniformly gray—that Mateo was able to notice the shapes of the pieces and solve the puzzle quite efficiently—without the so-called "benefit" of the pictures.

Sensory-Motor Integration

Sensory-motor integration is the ability to plan and execute physical responses to various situations or stimuli (also known as *praxis* and discussed on page 91). Students who struggle with sensory-motor integration have difficulty with coordination and movement. They may exhibit weak muscle tone and body control, slumping in their chairs, sprawling out on the rug, appearing generally floppy and clumsy.

Can You Hear Me Now?

When students seem to exhibit inadequate seeing or hearing abilities, parents or caregivers may wisely seek an evaluation with an ophthalmologist or audiologist to rule out a physiological problem. But if the root of the issue is, in fact, sensory processing, students may score just fine on seeing and hearing tests. In these cases, the disconnect is happening in the way visual and auditory input are being *processed* by the sensory system.

Coping With Sensory Processing Challenges: Stims

When sensory input is troubling to those of us with *typical* sensory processing, we can often regulate the intensity of the input by altering our relationship with the external environment. When necessary, we cover our ears, close our eyes, hold our noses, and so on. But for students with sensory processing challenges, that same input may be overwhelming, causing them to seek comfort any which way they can. And that's when we get disruptive, socially unexpected, and other difficult behaviors. That's when we get a student holding her ears, moaning, and rocking back and forth to block out the noise of the scraping chairs, or a student repeatedly shaking his hands in front of his face to block out the fluorescent lights. And sometimes those behaviors bear no apparent resemblance to whatever's triggering them. So it's hard to know *why* our students are behaving as they are, unless we understand the core challenges and then look closely at the environment to see what could be triggering the behavior.

Many of these self-regulatory kinds of behaviors are called *stims*, which is short for *self-stimulatory behaviors*—behaviors that serve to stimulate or regulate the sensory system. Stims help students in one or more of the following ways:

- stimulating their sensory input
- blocking out overwhelming sensory input
- releasing excess energy or excitement

Common Stims

You may notice students on the spectrum exhibiting any of the following stimming behaviors:

- grunting, chirping, or snapping fingers, which may help remind them to tune in and listen up

- humming or repeating words or sounds, which may help them tune out the overwhelming noise of the classroom

- blinking at lights or wiggling fingers in front of eyes, which may help stimulate the eyes to focus

- lining up objects or looking out of the corners of the eyes, which may help structure or limit an otherwise chaotic visual field

- scratching, hair twirling, or tapping, which may provide necessary tactile input

- sniffing objects or other people, which may provide olfactory input

- licking or tasting inedible objects, which may provide necessary oral input

- spinning, rocking, hand flapping, toe walking, jumping, or bouncing, which may help reestablish body position relative to the earth

- crashing, stomping, leaning, head banging, biting, chewing, or teeth grinding, which may stimulate muscles and joints

Flapping, On the One Hand

Stims may help jumpstart the senses of students who are minimally responsive to sensory stimuli, like flipping the *on* switch in an otherwise sluggish sensory system. For these students, stimming can be pleasurable and helpful in activating their focus and engagement.

Flapping, On the Other Hand

Paradoxically, students who are highly responsive to sensory stimuli seem to stim more often when overstimulated by the external world. They lose themselves in the comfort of these repetitive behaviors in order to block out overwhelming input or release excess stimulation. For these students, stimming tends to increase when they are under stress or overexcited, and can serve a soothing function.

Stemming Stimming

Granted, those are behaviors we might very much wish would go away. But know this: Simply extinguishing stims cannot be our goal because stims and other behaviors are *symptoms*— reactions to a deeper problem. Stims are necessary for self-regulation and may be vital to a student's ability to function. That's why students use them! Instead, use the following section to help you understand the wide range of sensory processing challenges that can affect the equilibrium of students on the spectrum. Then, at the end of this chapter, you'll find strategies to help you adapt the sensory environment to mitigate the impact these sensitivities have on your students and reduce the need for stims.

Types of Sensory Processing Challenges

Sensory processing challenges can affect any area of sensation, including not only the senses we are cognitively aware of, but also other body-centered senses we may not consciously perceive. If you work with students who seem to fit the descriptions above, the following section will describe how their challenges may manifest in your classroom, sense by sense.

The Basic Five

The senses that we are most readily in touch with, so to speak, are these basic five: hearing, seeing, touching, smelling, and tasting. Here is an overview of how students with sensory challenges may respond to each of the five basic senses.

Sound

1. *Sound Avoidance:* Students who struggle with high auditory responsivity often hear sounds others cannot hear at all or may be affected by sounds in intense ways. A variety of basic classroom sounds can be irritating or downright painful. Common auditory triggers include the constant buzzing of fluorescent lights, the scraping of chair legs against the floor, the blare of the lunch and dismissal bell, the squeaking of dry-erase markers on the whiteboard, the creaking of Styrofoam, as well as tapping feet, crinkling paper, and so on.

> **Did You Know...**
>
> Auditory sensitivity is very common among students on the spectrum. Students with high auditory sensitivity can often be found trying to avoid input by covering their ears, tuning out, or acting out. Some resort to flapping or other self-stimulating behavior in an effort to refocus their energy away from the unbearable input. Paradoxically, some students actually scream when they hear an overwhelmingly loud sound. This enables them to drown out the offending noise with a sound of their own making.

2. *Sound Indifference:* Students with low auditory responsivity, like those with auditory processing challenges, may seem oblivious to ordinary sounds, and respond very slowly or only to exaggerated or very loud sounds. When the classroom marble jar crashes to the floor, shattering into pieces and sending marbles spinning about the room, sensory disregarders

> **Did You Know...**
>
> Many students on the spectrum hear music more accurately and intuitively than they do spoken words. Only one-tenth of one percent (.001) of people in the general population have perfect pitch. However, a full five percent (.05) of people with Autism Spectrum Disorder exhibit perfect pitch (Heaton, Williams, Cummins, & Happé, 2008).

don't even look up from their books. (See more about central auditory processing in Chapter 9.)

3. *Sound Pursuit:* Students who crave auditory input seek or create loud noise, prefer the volume on the radio or television to be turned way up, enjoy crowds and noisy places, and tend to speak very loudly.

Layout Logic

Despite the many proven benefits of seating students in clusters, old-school classrooms with desks organized in neat rows were actually easier for students on the spectrum to manage. Freestanding desks in straight lines created a less distracting, less interactive environment and a clearer, more structured space. If you have students who are overstimulated or distracted by sitting face-to-face with other students, consider this alternative: Intersperse some two-person, side-by-side clusters among the others. This handily cuts social challenges and distractions in half.

Sight

1. *Sight Avoidance:* Students with high visual responsivity may be overwhelmed by bright colors, busy visual fields, and certain kinds of lights. (See Lights Out box on p. 86.) They may cover their eyes or make poor eye contact and appear inattentive or hypervigilant.

2. *Sight Indifference:* Students with low visual responsivity may react slowly to approaching objects or people, fail to notice obstacles in their path, have limited visual-spatial recognition, and may seem to look right through you.

3. *Sight Pursuit:* Students who crave visual input may seek lots of screen time, gravitate toward shiny or spinning objects, or flick their fingers in front of their eyes.

Walking and Chewing Gum at the Same Time

For many students on the spectrum, using two senses at once is overwhelming. For example the instruction *Look at me when I'm talking to you* may serve only to ensure that you get no response at all. Asking students to take notes while watching a movie or to hang posters while socializing could cause a shutdown or a meltdown. You may need to accept one or the other, looking or listening, walking or talking. Try to limit expectations to one sense at a time.

Lights Out

Fluorescent lights are ever-present in schools and have posed a distinct problem for students on the spectrum. Many fluorescent lights buzz and flicker incessantly and emit a harsh glare. Just being in a room lit by these lights may be unbearable.

Manufacturers of newer fluorescent lights, such as compact fluorescent lights (CFLs), claim that the flicker is now imperceptible to the human eye. Even so, the cool, blue-ish light of CFLs can have debilitating non-visual effects on the nervous system. Studies have shown that exposure to CFLs raises physiological stress reactions in the body, such as raising blood pressure and heightening the startle response.

Additionally, scientists are pursuing the possibility that the visual processing of fluorescent light is draining, especially to individuals with ASD, depleting their mental resources and making them more vulnerable to anxiety, agitation, self-stimulatory behaviors, and disruptive behaviors (Dunkley, 2014).

The best way to support a student who struggles with this is to keep those overhead lights off. Often natural sunlight will be enough to light the classroom. If you are unable to function without the overhead lights, try using only some of them. Consider replacing bulbs with colored or softer diffused-light bulbs. Consider purchasing translucent, fabric light filters that diminish the glare and muffle the sound. If necessary, be open to allowing some students to wear light-colored sunglasses or a baseball-type cap with a brim to shade their eyes from the glare.

If light poses an ongoing problem, suggest to parents or caregivers that they consult with a developmental optometrist, who may be able to provide custom glasses using Irlen lenses that are specially developed to filter out offensive elements of light.

Touch

1. *Touch Avoidance:* Students with high tactile responsivity may flinch when others approach, find a light touch to be painful and therefore may react angrily to innocuous physical contact. These students tend to avoid messy activities such as those involving paint or glue and be intolerant of getting wet. They are likely to find certain fabrics, seams, or clothing labels to be painful or unbearably irritating. Or they may prefer to wear long sleeves and long pants even in summer to protect themselves from bruises and scratches.

2. *Touch Indifference:* Students with low tactile responsivity have poor body awareness. These students are not likely to notice that their shoes are on the wrong feet, that their face is dirty, or that their nose is running. They may not notice that they have bumped into someone or not realize when they are being too physical with others.

3. *Touch Pursuit:* Students who crave tactile input seek or create messy activities and tend to touch everything and everyone, often at unexpected times or in socially unacceptable ways. They may also rub or bite their own skin, twirl their hair, chew on their fingernails, collars, or pencils, and prefer being barefoot.

Don't Be Indifferent to Indifference

Some students on the spectrum may seem unaware of touch unless it is intense, and therefore they may have a diminished perception of pain. They may not realize it when they are significantly hurt, so watch them carefully, especially after a fall or collision.

By the same token, these students may not be affected by extremes of temperature, feeling perfectly comfortable in situations that are extremely hot or cold to others. They must be monitored in this regard as well, as they can fall victim to heat exhaustion or hypothermia.

Smell

1. *Smell Avoidance:* Students with high olfactory responsivity can be powerfully affected by smells that may be undetectable to others. They may get physically overwhelmed by individual smells or by combinations of smells. The lunchroom, the bathroom, the gym, magic markers, pencil shavings, fresh photocopies, hand lotion, and more are all potential offenders at school.

2. *Smell Indifference:* Students with low olfactory responsivity seem oblivious to smells. They may not be affected by the various body emissions that their peers react to with loud objection and, more important, may not detect the smell of smoke or leaking gas.

3. *Smell Pursuit:* Students who crave olfactory input may seek to learn about their environment by smelling it. They may sniff at new objects to differentiate them from others, or may find certain smells soothing or exciting.

Taste

1. *Taste Avoidance:* Students who have a high responsivity to taste are often very picky eaters, avoiding certain flavors and certain textures of food.

2. *Taste Indifference:* Students who have a low responsivity to taste tend to be indifferent to the flavor of food or types of cuisine.

3. *Taste Pursuit:* Student who crave taste stimulation may seek out spicy foods, crunchy foods, or seek to learn about their environment through taste, which may lead them to bite or lick inedible items.

Let It Be

You may find a certain behavior to be unusual, even unwelcome. But if it is not dangerous, destructive, or disruptive, and if it's quietly under the social radar, simply let it be. When Sheila is able to stay calm in class by stroking a scrap of corduroy fabric under her desk, great. If Marcel wears eye glasses with non-prescription lenses in them, just because the weight of the frames on his face helps him stay focused, good for him. Kudos to your students for being open to adaptive ways of obtaining comfort, and kudos to you for knowing a good thing when you see one.

Plus Two: The Interoceptive Senses

The interoceptive senses relate to our awareness of our own internal states, including balance and position, as well as hunger, thirst, fatigue, illness, and other types of physical discomfort. Generally speaking, students who have a high responsivity to internal input may seem hypochondriacal. But in fact they are feeling every internal irregularity quite acutely.

Students who have a low responsivity to internal input, on the other hand, may not know when they are sick, feverish, or off-balance, and may miss the signal when it is time to use the bathroom. (Be careful not to blame students for persistent toileting problems. Offer support to the parents or caregivers, who are surely exasperated, by explaining that this stubborn situation could have a sensory explanation. Consult with the occupational therapist for strategies.)

Two specific areas of interoception are *proprioception* and *vestibulation*.

Proprioception

The proprioceptive sense relates to perceiving where our bodies are in space, based on input or pressure received by muscles and joints. Proprioception tells us what our body parts are doing or should be doing in any situation. When working effectively, this sense would, for example, guide our muscles to clench when someone puts a heavy book in our hands. Students who struggle with proprioception may not be able to regulate the force of their high-five or the pressure of their pencil.

1. *Pressure Avoidance:* Students who have a high responsivity to joint and muscle input tend to be physically rigid, avoid hugs, and steer clear of activities like jumping, running, or rolling.

> **Did You Know . . .**
>
> The words *kinesthesia* and *proprioception* are often used interchangeably. In fact, *kinesthesia* refers more to the sense of the body's movement, whereas *proprioception* refers to the sense of the body's position in space.

Chapter 4: Body and Soul: Regulation and Sensation

2. *Pressure Indifference:* Students with a low responsivity to joint and muscle input may trip and fall frequently and be unaware of their position.

3. *Pressure Pursuit:* Students who seek joint and muscle input are bumpers and crashers: running full tilt into walls, tipping their chairs back, pratfalling over obstacles. They tend to run their hand along the wall in the hallway, may lean or press against objects, stomp their feet when walking, crack their knuckles, or use proprioceptively stimulating behaviors such as head banging, toe walking, or hand flapping.

Four Is Shy and Quiet: Synesthesia

Heightened responsivity to sound allows some individuals with auditory sensitivity to make extraordinary connections to music because they can perceive elements others do not hear. Similarly, individuals with heightened sensitivities to any kind of sensory input can demonstrate remarkable multisensory relationships with activities such as painting, sculpting, cooking, dancing, and more.

On rare occasions, individuals with unusual sensory perception experience synesthesia. *Synesthesia* is the perceptual joining together of sensations that are usually perceived separately. People who experience synesthesia may see sounds, hear colors, taste shapes, smell textures, feel music, and more. Thought to be caused by an over-connectivity of certain neurons, synesthesia occurs in 7.2% of the general population, but can be found in 18.9% of individuals on the autism spectrum (Baron-Cohen, Johnson, Asher, Wheelwright, Fisher, Gregersen, & Allison, 2013).

In his memoir, *Born on a Blue Day* (2007), Daniel Tammet, an adult on the autism spectrum, describes his extraordinary capacity with numbers. Tammet associates every number with a specific shape, color, texture, and personality. By intuitively visualizing numbers in a vivid pictorial landscape, Tammet has memorized and can recite the value of pi up to 22,500 digits.

Vestibulation

The vestibular sense tells us which end is up, based on the position of our heads in relation to the earth. Movement and balance activities such as spinning, turning upside down, and jumping are regulated by the vestibular system. Depending on the functioning of the vestibular sense in each student, these kinds of activities may be either unbearable or unstoppable.

1. *Movement Avoidance:* Students who have a high responsivity to movement struggle to maintain their sense of balance and physical equilibrium. They may have low muscle tone, slumping in their chairs or resting their heads on the table. These students are commonly disoriented by movement activities such as biking, running, sledding, swinging, sliding, or spinning. They tend to be cautious and afraid of falling; they clutch your arm as they walk

in the hall or cling tightly to banisters when on stairs. They may appear uncooperative—for example, refusing to get up on the chorus risers—but in fact, they are afraid.

2. *Movement Indifference:* Students with a low responsivity to movement can spin for a long time without feeling dizzy. They may be unaware when they are off-balance or unstable, and fail to protect or remove themselves from precarious situations.

3. *Movement Pursuit:* Students who seek movement are constantly in motion. They are thrill-seekers and daredevils. In school, they tend to fidget and wiggle, swivel in chairs, leap down multiple steps, and hang upside down.

Wiggle Room

Be open to the idea that some students learn better in unconventional ways. For example, ten-year-old Kaneesha does her nightly reading by putting her book on the floor and doing handstands over it—reading while she is upside down. Her ability to focus is greatly enhanced by the added proprioceptive and vestibular input.

In some schools, students have access to adjustable-height desks that allow them to stand as they work. These desks come with swinging footrests which allow for fidgeting, as well as adjustable-height stools to give students the option of standing or sitting as their mood dictates. Teachers who have been using these desks in their classrooms find that stand-up desks give students the flexibility to expend energy, enabling them to focus more on learning than on having to sit still.

Occupational Therapy

Occupational therapy (OT) is the go-to place for students who have sensory processing or motor issues. Most students on the autism spectrum need occupational therapy and have it mandated on their IEPs. Occupational therapists are qualified to use specific sensory integration therapy techniques during sessions with students. These techniques can be highly successful in helping to integrate the mind-body connection needed to regulate sensory input.

Sensory interventions may include joint compression and deep pressure (which help to regulate proprioceptive input), therapeutic swinging (which helps to regulate vestibular input), and therapeutic brushing (which helps to desensitize nerve endings by stimulating them with a special brush). These kinds of activities can support the organization of the sensory systems to calm students down and set them up for learning.

Occupational therapists are an integral part of the multidisciplinary team that supports students on the spectrum. Pick their brains for creative ideas for classroom modifications and specific adaptations for certain students. Occupational therapists can suggest or provide tools for the classroom and can teach parents and caregivers how to carry through some of these therapeutic techniques outside of school as well. If you are working with a student who does not receive OT but you think would benefit from it, speak to the special ed director or your principal about getting an OT evaluation. With the parents' consent, this evaluation can be performed in the school district and can yield quite far-reaching benefits.

In addition to improving self-regulation, sensory processing, and adaptive responses, occupational therapy can also address the following related motor challenges that students on the spectrum may face:

- *Praxis (motor planning)* is our ability to plan a motor activity and then actually execute it. Students with dyspraxia struggle with crossing midline (i.e., performing visual or motor tasks that involve crossing over to the opposite side of the body, such as tying shoes, reading across a page, or drawing a circle with a compass), bilateral coordination (i.e., using both hands together), and organizing body movements. Tasks that can be made more difficult by dyspraxia are activities that require use of both hands at once or multistep motor activities like getting dressed, typing and mousing, taking notes, throwing a ball, playing piano, riding a bike, swimming, and many others.

- *Fine motor coordination* is our ability to use small muscles with strength, dexterity, and control. Students with fine motor challenges struggle with handwriting, cutting with scissors, and more.

- *Hand-eye coordination* is our ability to synchronize the use of our hands with visual input. Students with hand-eye coordination challenges struggle with skills such as fastening buttons, stringing beads, and keeping their place while counting objects.

- *Oral-motor coordination* is our ability to use the muscles in and around our mouths with strength and control. Oral motor challenges can include chewing, drinking, and blowing bubbles.

- *Visual-motor coordination* is our ability to use the muscles in our eyes with strength and control. Students with visual-motor challenges struggle to track left to right while reading, use both eyes together, and more.

- *Activities of daily living (ADLs)* are the necessary basic tasks of everyday life. Success with ADLs depends upon capacity with many of the fundamental skills listed above. Challenging ADLs may include personal hygiene, getting dressed, and eating with utensils.

Physical Therapy

Gross motor challenges, which do not tend to have a sensory basis, fall into the realm of physical therapy. Physical therapy works to improve muscle control and motor coordination related to the larger muscles used in walking, climbing, throwing, and so on.

Sensational Strategies

In the context of the sensory environment, intense reactions may be involuntary and stimming behaviors become vital comfort anchors. If we simply try to extinguish behaviors, they will be replaced by others that serve the same sensory function. But by addressing the underlying function of the behavior, we can actually eliminate the need for it. Read on to collect strategies for meeting sensory needs in ways that will allow your students have a calmer, steadier experience in the classroom.

Modify This: Creating a Sensory Friendly Classroom

Knowing your students' sensory triggers will guide you to modify the classroom's sensory environment so students won't need to rely on stims or other behaviors to regulate their sensory systems.

Many of these classroom modification strategies are easily implemented using supplies you already have in your classroom. Others require specialized sensory tools that can be provided by occupational therapists or ordered online. (You can find links to sites that sell these kinds of tools as well as many additional sensory strategies at www.barbaraboroson.com.)

✳ **Keep It Clean:** Try to keep physical spaces well organized, free of clutter, and clearly delineated.

✳ **Go Soft:** Print worksheets on gray, tan, or other pastel-colored paper. These soft colors do not reflect as much light as brighter colors and white paper do.

✳ **Turn Down the Sun:** Face students away from the glare of sunlight (which can change over the course of the day) and turn off some of the overhead lights.

✳ **Noises Off:** Seat students away from open windows and the hallway and away from the dripping faucet, dehumidifier, and any other source of auditory distraction.

✳ **Make It Snug:** No need to cover the whole floor; scattered rugs will help absorb sound and keep the room quieter. (Small area rugs also serve the important function of helping to visually define the boundaries of work and play areas.)

✳ **Pursue Minimalism:** Limit decorations on your walls, at least at the beginning of the year. Add elements gradually, watching for signs of distraction or disorganization.

✳ **Less Is More:** Minimize the amount of work on any one page. Use reading guide strips that highlight only one line of text at a time. Or create a cardboard cut-out template students can use to frame small amounts of work, effectively hiding everything else on the page.

✳ **Try Not to Make Scents:** Minimize unnecessary odors in the classroom. Purchase only unscented markers, use unscented hand lotion, avoid eating hot food in the classroom, and encourage your school to use eco-friendly unscented cleaning solutions. (Everyone will benefit from not inhaling those unnecessary chemical additives.) Seat students away from the gerbil cage, the bathroom, painting supplies, Bunsen burners, open windows, and any other source of potential odors.

* **Stand Firm:** Alert phys ed teachers and recess monitors of balance and equilibrium issues so that these students are closely monitored for risk-taking behaviors.

* **Chew on This:** Offer an extra snack break during the day or allow gum chewing to stimulate the senses when focus is flagging.

* **Heads Up:** Offer plenty of movement breaks during which all students have the opportunity to get physical input. Try whole-class jumping jacks or yoga moments. Just one minute spent in the "downward-facing dog" position can reboot engagement and focus for students who need the vestibular input. For students who cannot tolerate turning upside down, try still, upright poses such as the "mountain pose." (Display photographs of these yoga positions on the interactive whiteboard.)

* **There's No Place Like Om:** Try doing a moment of whole-class meditation. The expenditure of a few meditative minutes across the day could pay off with hours of calmer, more focused learners.

* **The Pressure Is On:** Offer natural opportunities for weight-bearing or input-stimulating activities, such as stacking chairs, distributing text books, rubber-stamping papers, using a hole-punch, and so on.

Sensory Spaces

All students welcome opportunities to retreat and regroup. For everyone's benefit, consider setting up a sensory corner in your classroom. Find an available corner of your room and partially wall it off (using shelves, bookcases, or bulletin boards) to minimize visual and auditory stimulation and to allow some privacy. Make it cozy with a soft rug, cushions, pillows, or beanbag chairs.

Stock the space with a collection of sensory tools that students can choose among whenever they need to calm down or rev up. Tools can include squeeze balls, textured or weighted balls, stress balls, bubble wrap, kinetic sand, therapeutic putty, linking cubes, pull tubes, Slinkys, scraps of textured fabrics, beads, picture books, music with earphones, and noise-canceling headphones. Some students will busily push, pull, touch, and so on, while others may crawl under the beanbag chair and close their eyes.

Students who struggle to keep their composure in the classroom may fare even better when they have access to a soothing space outside of the classroom. Your school might be lucky enough to have a separate sensory room, outfitted with many of the tools and comforts used in a sensory corner, along with thick mats, weighted blankets, a swing, a mini-trampoline, and a soothing sound machine. But if not, and if you have students who might benefit from this kind of special space, see if the occupational therapist can help you justify the need for a sensory room and present the idea to school administrators. The one-time set-up costs will be more than compensated by the high-intensity crises it will help avert for many years to come.

Modify That: Offering Sensory Options

When students are crashing into walls or biting and poking other students, for example, they are usually seeking tactile or proprioceptive input. Instead of issuing consequences for "bad behavior," try to offer alternatives that serve the same sensory function in a more socially acceptable way. A weighted vest provides continual input to the muscles and joints, and naturally reduces a student's need to crash into walls or poke other students. Chewelry® offers an array of FDA-approved silicone necklaces and bracelets designed to stimulate joints and muscles around the mouth, jaw, and neck in a way that is safer than chewing on pencils, crayons, fingernails, or classmates. Bouncy Bands are thick bands of sturdy rubber that stretch across the legs of a desk to provide movement opportunities for feet while allowing students to stay seated.

The key to creating a sensory environment that supports all kinds of sensory processors is offering options. Since some students in your class may represent unpredictable combinations of sensory avoidance, indifference, and pursuit—while the majority of your typically functioning students are probably healthy sensory thrivers—there is no one-size-fits-all solution. Instead, provide opportunities for students to regulate their own degree of exposure to sensory stimulation. This means offering flexible options and expectations. Since your students' needs are highly variable, the options you make available should be as well. Consider these varied strategies:

✱ **Comfort on Demand:** Allow students to keep a small soothing sensory object—whether it's a scrap of soft fabric, a ridged pebble, a stress ball, a fidget toy, a tiny stuffed animal, or whatever works—with them throughout the day. This can serve as a touchstone in their pocket for whenever they need it.

✱ **Sound Judgment:** Some students need noise-canceling headphones to block out all background sound while doing quiet work. Others focus better with rhythmic music pulsing through those same headphones. And others won't be able to tolerate even the feeling of headphones against their ears.

✱ **Glop On, Glop Off:** Even though many young students love the feeling of immersing their hands in paint, others cannot tolerate the damp texture of fingerpaint on their hands. Offer access to latex gloves, or paintbrushes, paint markers, sponges, cottonballs, and toothpicks.

✱ **Don't Push It:** Some students don't exert enough pressure to write or draw with pencils or ball-point pens; they need access to felt-tip pens or markers. Others press so hard they poke through the paper; they may need to do their work in crayon.

✱ **Get It Together:** If glue produces anxiety, offer glue sticks, paste, rubber cement, tape, paper clips, or staples.

✱ **Fear Not:** Allow the use of worry beads, squeeze balls, or other fidget toys.

✱ **Hold On:** Provide pencil grippers for poor pencil grasp or vibrating pens to increase grip awareness.

✱ **Please Be Seated:** Check that chair height is appropriate so that students' feet rest squarely on the floor, to support balance and security. Seat cushions and footrests can be used to make minor adjustments. Wiggle or "bumpy" cushions can offer vestibular input to reduce disruptive fidgeting.

Sensible Screen Time: There's an App for That!

Many sensory and motor needs can be supported through the use of apps. Visual, tactile, and auditory stimulation are part of the appeal of most apps, in general, and many also happen to require tracking, hand-eye coordination, and motor planning. Some apps are specifically designed to stimulate sensation, while others are actually designed to soothe the senses. Popular sense-stimulating apps, as of this writing, include *Cause and Effect Sensory Light Box* and *Cause and Effect Sensory Sound Box*, both by Cognoble, and *Gloop* by Run, Swim, Fly. Others, like *Fluidity* by Nebulous Design and *Laser Lights* by PDJ Apps, are soothing. *Brain Works* by Sensational Brain prompts kids and teens to take customized sensory breaks on a schedule they can plan themselves, supporting not only their sensory needs but also their self-monitoring and regulation skills. New and improved apps are being created all the time. Search under "sensory processing" in your app store. You're sure to find an app for that.

• • • •

As you have seen in this chapter, most students on the spectrum face an unrelenting onslaught of sensory challenges from all directions and lack the skills to regulate their responses. As long as they are out and about amid the social world, unpredictable input swirls around menacingly. Really, the safest place is *in*. The next chapter will lead you on a tour of that remote inner sanctum and show you how to bridge the gap.

Chapter 5

The Inner Sanctum

Crossing the Bridge to a Remote Student

Challenges in the areas of socialization, communication, regulation, and sensation comprise a heavy burden that students on the spectrum bring to every encounter. If that's not enough to carry, pile on the anxiety that results from facing the world with so many challenges, and we can understand why every encounter feels overwhelming.

Does anxiety force these students to retreat into their predictable inner worlds as protection from the assault of external stimuli? Or is their remoteness the *cause* of their difficulties with the external world? There may be no simple answer, but there is no doubt that the *interplay* of remoteness and anxiety is powerful and self-sustaining. It produces fearful, socially separate students who are frequently lost in their own heads, not tuned in to what is happening around them, and seemingly unavailable to others.

Some students seem content to stay inwardly focused and do not welcome interlopers into their private inner world. They may not have the natural motivation to make contact with you, to establish a relationship, to keep open the lines of communication. Others clearly want to engage but don't know how to do so in pro-social ways. They may have the motivation but be unable to demonstrate it in a way that is meaningful to you. Still others may come and go—one moment, totally engaged, and the next, nobody's home.

While remoteness may serve as a protective barrier for students, it also insulates them from important stimuli that actually must break through—like education and socialization. Surely you have many tricks up your sleeve to engage students; your lively demeanor and creative curriculum are designed to excite and draw students toward you and toward the learning opportunities you offer. But unfortunately, students on the spectrum will not simply come to you. So even while you're busy tending to the needs of the rest of your class, you'll have to take the time to go and get them. This chapter describes why students on the spectrum seem so far away and offers strategies you can use to reach them.

Life on the Island

It is almost as though each student on the autism spectrum is on a remote island— alone. The waves wash in and out, the sun rises and sets, and there is a soothing, predictable rhythm to the day. The island may be beautiful and peaceful, but it is also solitary and stagnant. There is no learning, no growth on the island; just more of the same, day after day. If that is all your students on the spectrum know, they are missing out on the richness that life on the mainland has to offer.

This will be quite a journey—one students cannot make by themselves. They need the psychic push to step up onto the bridge, the skills and stamina to make the journey across, and the ongoing support to manage the chaos, demands, and stimulation of life off the island. And even if you have numerous students on the spectrum in your class, you can be sure that they do not all inhabit the same island. Each dwells on a solitary island with its own culture and values. Each student will need to cross his own bridge, at his own pace, and only to the extent that he is able.

Early in your relationship, you may need to travel almost the entire way across the bridge to reach a student. Take some time there to get to know the island, look around, listen to the sounds, check out the sights, get a feel for the culture there. What's it all about? What's the buzz on the island?

Then slowly begin to use what you know to draw the student toward you, coaxing a few steps at a time, helping draw him across the bridge toward the social world.

The View From the Bridge: Looking at Eye Contact

Eye contact is one of the most obvious challenges for students on the spectrum. The absence of eye contact contributes to your perception that students are disengaged. Students who do not make eye contact are also deprived of the benefits of *joint attention*, which is the sharing of experience with others (more on this on pages 101–102) and *social referencing*, which is the use of our eyes to confirm what we hear and to verify that we are being heard. A lack of eye contact can lead to serious miscommunications and social missteps.

Eye contact may be limited for several reasons.

1. *Sensory avoidance:* Students on the spectrum often avoid eye contact for sensory reasons. For some, direct eye contact may feel too intense and may cause anxiety, sensory overload, even pain. Other students may find looking at the eyes of others to be overwhelmingly distracting and disconcerting: Eyes are constantly shifting and darting around, while the up-and-down movement of lashes makes eyes seem to flash and flicker.

2. *Motor control:* Some students do not have the visual-motor control necessary to stabilize their own eyes. They may be unable to focus on and track objects in motion or follow

an object that moves across the center of their field of vision. Consult your school's occupational therapist to see if your students' difficulties with eye contact are a product of visual-motor issues such as crossing midline or visual tracking. If so, the occupational therapist may be able to offer visual training and muscle strengthening strategies.

3. *Social communication:* Some students on the spectrum may not perceive that making eye contact is a component of communication. To them, communication happens through speaking, listening, and writing; eye contact does not seem a relevant or necessary part, and so they don't look for messages you may be sending with your eyes. Check with the speech and language specialist to see if eye contact can be addressed in sessions as a component of social language.

In the natural classroom setting, baseline anxiety among students on the spectrum is likely to be fairly high. They are already very busy with their significant efforts to sit still, listen, process, and make relevant associations, while also refraining from calling out, flapping their hands, grunting, and thinking about batteries. That may be about all they can handle at one time. Making eye contact could be one task too many. In fact, some students may be better able to engage in your lesson *without* the added anxiety or strain of making eye contact.

But in some circumstances, it is essential that students learn to focus their eyes on their tasks. For example, if they are crossing a street or cutting with a knife, they must be taught to look. The next section will describe some strategies you can use to mindfully encourage eye contact in the classroom.

> **Did You Know . . .**
>
> Since students on the spectrum don't understand how your eyes convey information, they also fail to recognize what their own *lack* of eye contact may inadvertently communicate. Do not assume that their averted eyes indicate discomfort or dishonesty. In truth, your students on the spectrum may be more comfortable and forthright when they are *not* giving eye contact than when they are.

Learning to Look: Eye Contact Strategies

For students on the spectrum, eye contact is usually a learned skill—not a natural reflex. Just as a stuttering student struggles to get words out, your student on the spectrum struggles to make eye contact. As is the case for stuttering, the more pressure there is to make eye contact, the more anxiety gets in the way, and the more difficult it is for students to comply. So eye contact should never be required and a lack of it should never be punished. But if you have students who struggle with eye contact, proceed with care and offer lots of gentle opportunities for practice.

Practicing Eye Contact

Lessons on making direct eye contact are best left for one-on-one, low-key moments. Assess a student's anxiety level carefully before encouraging eye contact. Use your knowledge of individual anxiety triggers to help you judge when a student might be able to handle adding eye contact. Try some of these strategies for supporting eye contact:

✴ **Seize the Moment:** Ask for eye contact when a student wants something from you. In these moments, since he has initiated the conversation, he is engaged and highly motivated.

✴ **The Eyes Have It:** Teach students that extra information can be found by looking at people's eyes. Offer verbal and/or visual prompts as needed to support eye contact. The spoken reminder *Look at me* may be all a student needs to remember to turn his eyes toward you. If it helps, you may want to point to your eyes or hold up a *Look at teacher* icon.

✴ **Take What You Get:** Clarify that you do not expect constant eye contact. Be specific that you would like her to look at your eyes *some* of the time, to show you that she is paying attention. Fleeting focus may be as much as these students can give you, but it may be enough.

✴ **Reinforce It:** Explain to him that when he looks at your eyes you can see that he is making a connection with you: *I can tell you're paying attention because you are looking at me.*

✴ **Generalize It:** Give your student specific suggestions as to how to generalize the new skill: *Now you may ask Cindy for the protractor. Try to give her the same great eye contact you just gave me.*

Eye Contact Alternatives

With training and reinforcement, many students can internalize eye contact as a learned response and use it habitually, but it may never evolve to the level of meaningful nonverbal communication. Coerced eye contact can result in an empty success. Some students who have been taught to make eye contact ultimately seem to look *at* and even *through* others rather than genuinely connecting with them. Be open to the possibility that making eye contact may not be the only way students can show you they're paying attention.

> ## Don't Look Now
>
> My own son's most thoughtful and reciprocal conversations happen while he is pacing around the dining room table. Without the burden of eye contact, and with the added proprioceptive input of rhythmic pacing, his sensory system is regulated to its most open, engageable setting.

Ari Ne'eman, president of Autistic Self Advocacy Network, explains, "Eye contact is an anxiety-inducing experience for us, so looking someone in the eye . . . takes energy. We have a saying that's pretty common among autistic young people: 'I can either look like I'm paying attention or I can actually pay attention.' Unfortunately, a lot of people tell us that looking like you're paying attention is more important than actually paying attention" (Padawer, 2014). Consider these alternatives to direct eye contact:

✴ **A Little to the Side:** Allow students to give partial eye contact by looking out of the sides of their eyes rather than looking at you face-to-face.

✴ **As If:** Encourage students to "pretend" to make eye contact by looking at your nose, ears, or forehead, all of which are much more static than your eyes. While this strategy does not avail students of social referencing cues, it does create the more socially agreeable appearance that they are attending.

✴ **Cue Ready Position:** Use the phrase *Get ready* or *Show me Ready Position* with your students, which would imply a set of previously explained expectations such as the following:

> *Ready Position*
> *1. Book on desk*
> *2. Pencil in hand*
> *3. Feet in front*
> *4. Mouth quiet*

Place a *Ready Position* rubric on the desks of students who need it, listing the components of Ready Position and accompanied by visual cues as needed. When you see your students in position, you have a roomful of attentive listeners, even if some of them are looking down or elsewhere.

✴ **Look at That:** There are times during lessons when you will need your students to look—but not necessarily at your eyes. If you are demonstrating an activity, tell them specifically to look at what you are doing: *Look at what my hands are doing,* or *Watch what happens to this sodium hydroxide!*

Looking to Learn

An indirect strategy for encouraging use of eye contact is to use nonverbal prompts instead of spoken words when possible. If a student on the spectrum asks you how many crayons she is allowed to take, hold up three fingers. If she asks you what year the first episode of *SpongeBob SquarePants* aired, look at her and shrug. But implement this strategy gradually. If you notice that she is not seeing your nonverbal signals, get her attention verbally first: *Look at me, Suki. I am going to show you my answer.*

And always check for understanding. If necessary, explain specifically what your nonverbal signals mean. Teach her that your three raised fingers indicate three crayons, that your shrug means you don't know the answer. Over time, this strategy can help a student develop the habit of looking to learn and will enhance engagement in general.

"Elsewhere" on the Island: Exploring Distant Shores

To begin engaging these remote students, you need to first connect with them on their terms. This may be no easy feat. Students on the spectrum may be mired in challenges to engagement that severely limit their availability to participate in learning, socializing, or anything outside the preoccupying inner workings of their minds.

A desire to share experience with others, known as *joint attention*, is often lacking in students on the spectrum. The absence of that social instinct serves to keep these students contentedly secluded on their solitary island, and not necessarily motivated to get off. At the same time, students on the spectrum tend to get locked into repetitive patterns of behavior known as *perseveration*, which protects them from new and overwhelming experiences and satisfies their need for sameness. This next section describes the challenges of joint attention and perseveration, and offers suggestions for what to do when you encounter these obstacles on your mutual journey toward engagement.

Joint Attention

Joint attention is the sharing of attention and experience with another person. An infant seeks joint attention by pointing out an airplane flying overhead because he wants to share the thrill of it with his mother. A toddler taking her first steps looks at her father to see if he noticed. A preschooler takes his teacher's hand and leads her to the easel to show what he colored. Even before they have words, most children seek to share experience.

But, as babies and toddlers, children on the spectrum are not likely to point or pull or seek other ways to compensate for undeveloped language in order to share experience. Even the common *pick me up* gesture, when a baby lifts her arms skyward, is seldom seen among children on the spectrum. This is because engaging another person to share in a discovery or an idea is a social instinct—as if to say, *Let's share this moment together.*

For these reasons, students may not be inclined to embark on any kind of curricular or social journey with you. They may resist your efforts to join with them, and refuse your invitations to participate even in seemingly highly desirable activities. Joint attention does not tend to develop spontaneously among students on the spectrum due to challenges of ability in related areas:

* **Mindblindness:** The inability to take someone else's perspective limits students' ability to share another's experience. (See more on mindblindness in Chapter 8.)

* **Nonverbal Communication:** Most people infer meaning through visual cues. But when you point out an object to students on the spectrum, they are more likely to look, concretely, at your pointed finger than at what your finger is indicating. In order for them to follow the *implication* of your pointed finger they'd have to assume your physical perspective: from *your* eye, down *your* arm, to an object in *your* field of vision. You are asking them to *join you* in your perspective. But they are just looking at your finger. (See more on nonverbal communication in Chapters 8 and 9.)

* **Inference:** Joint attention may require extrapolating from the concrete to the abstract, a skill that is a fundamental autism spectrum challenge. When you say, *Look at our soil pots today!* your students on the spectrum may obligingly look at the soil pots, but will not necessarily join you in inferring why the pots are cause for celebration, despite the emergence of green sprouts.

✱ **Flexibility:** Joint attention also requires flexibility. Even though the sink is overflowing right now, your student on the spectrum is preoccupied with something else. Executive dysfunction prohibits her ability to put her recitation of Pixar movie release dates on a back burner until you have resolved your sink emergency. This kind of inflexibility, or rigidity, is due to another obstacle on the path toward engagement: perseveration.

Perseveration Station

Perseveration is a fixation or repetition of a word, phrase, gesture, activity, or thought, regardless of its relevance to context. Students on the spectrum rely on perseveration to provide themselves a cushion of familiarity and a locus of control over their environment. Perseverative behaviors and fixations help block out sensory threats or other anxiety-provoking stimuli such as unstructured time, noisy activities, or difficult social or academic tasks, effectively insulating these students from the social world. Psychologist Tony Attwood (2009) suggests that one reason that some students on the spectrum perseverate is that they may be afraid of making mistakes. A rigid need to be right and a resultant fear of failure cause them to cling to sameness, to perseverate on what they know for sure.

You'll recognize perseveration as the seemingly endless examination of the same topic, over and over and over again. Perseveration can take any of the following forms:

- rigidly repetitive actions, such as lining up or stacking objects or exhibiting self-stimulatory behaviors (as described in Chapter 4)

- mental and conversational fixation on singular topics, such as air conditioners or the line of ascension to the British throne

- frequent repetition of certain words or phrases, such as *May the Force be with you*, or *My name is Bond. James Bond*.

Some students may use perseverative language or behavior as a way of trying to socialize, although their endless examinations of specific topics can instead quickly become conversation stoppers.

Others appear to zone out when the going gets tough, but in fact they may be zeroing in on a favored topic. Twelve-year-old Tricia knows every stop of every train route in the metro area where she lives, along with what time each train is scheduled to arrive and depart each station. This is her go-to place; it's what she's thinking about when you ask her what effects the ancient Egyptians had on the development of civilizations, or what the value of x is when $2x - 8 = 10$. Train schedules are appealing to Tricia because they are fixed and immutable—they are completely *knowable*. They represent long-standing consistency of system and schedule. Moreover, train times, like school bells, are reliably precise. When else in life can we count on something to happen at exactly 3:04 or 2:58?

Situational anxiety can also trigger perseveration. Some students may settle on a certain aspect of an anxiety-provoking experience to perseverate on—such as what colors the walls are in the testing room, or what time the forecast thunderstorm is supposed to start—just so they can have something concrete to latch onto.

Though spinning and chirping and reciting train schedules may ease certain discomforts inside students, such behaviors will only create and exacerbate other discomforts in the social world. Moreover, students' rigid adherence to repetitive ideas can interfere significantly with their coping skills. Perseveration comes with costs and benefits, as described below. Recognizing both sides of the perseveration equation can help you discern when to step in to try to interrupt the cycle, and when you might want to let it keep spinning.

The Costs of Perseveration: A One-Track Mind

Timothy Pychyl, a professor of psychology observes, "To *persevere* is a virtue . . . to *perseverate* is a problem" (2009). Whereas perseverance is goal-oriented, perseveration tends to be uncontrollable and boundless.

Indeed, psychologist Tony Attwood (2009) perceives typically functioning students as traveling through life in an all-terrain vehicle on an open road. If they find they are headed in the wrong direction, they will say, *Oh! I must be on the wrong track!* and they readily change course. Students on the spectrum, however, ride a train along a single track. When they come upon an obstacle or a road block, or they find themselves on the wrong track, they get stuck. They insist, *This is the right track. Why isn't it working? Why am I not getting anywhere?* They cannot imagine a way around the roadblock or obstacle. These students may be proverbially—or literally—beating their heads against a wall and unable to stop. Students on the spectrum tend to be the last to know and the last to seek help when they are on the wrong track. This extreme rigidity can mean big problems when a student is really headed in the wrong direction.

The Benefits of Perseveration: X-treme Attending

On the other hand, at times this kind of singly focused, inflexible trajectory can have its benefits. Since students on the spectrum can't change tracks on their own, they may not give up trying until they reach their destination, no matter what. Sometimes getting stuck can be useful in terms of persisting and problem solving. These students may be inattentive to *your* agenda, but they are hyper-attentive to their own.

Some theories suggest that lack of interest in or awareness of the social world allows individuals on the spectrum to go much deeper into their chosen topic than others can or do. Unfettered by social concerns such as *What will my friends think?* or *Nobody else acts like this*, or *No one else seems interested in this so I should just drop it*, students on the spectrum have the social freedom to dig deeper and deeper and deeper.

In fact, psychiatrist and autism researcher Laurent Mottron has conducted studies that have shown that, "even autistic people who seem, at first glance, to be profoundly disabled might actually be gifted in surprising ways. And these talents are not limited to quirky party tricks, like knowing whether January 5, 1956, was a Tuesday. Scientists believe they are signs of true intelligence that might be superior to that of non-autistic people." Mottron suggests that the brains of people with ASD seek to focus on and process information that is high-interest, while tuning out more challenging or daunting input, like social cues, for example (Khazan, 2015).

Recent studies have shown complex differences in the neural connections in the brains of individuals on the spectrum. In some regions there may be increased connectivity; in other regions neural connectivity is diminished. These anomalies can make the learning of certain tasks very difficult but also allows for new and different connections to be made. Temple Grandin draws the analogy that when there are fewer connections between Los Angeles and New York, there may be more connections available between Los Angeles and Santa Fe (2008).

Whatever the cause, incredible innovation, stunning artwork, and other exceptional skills can be manifested by individuals on the autism spectrum. Great thinkers such as Albert Einstein, Isaac Newton, Thomas Jefferson, Nikola Tesla, and Dian Fossey, and brilliant artists such as Andy Warhol, Wassily Kandinsky, and Hans Christian Andersen are all thought to have exhibited distinctly spectrum-like qualities throughout their lifetimes. Hans Asperger, who first identified the cluster of strengths and challenges that eventually came to bear his name, recognized nearly forty years ago that, "For success, the necessary ingredient may be an ability to turn away from the everyday world, from the simply practical, an ability to rethink a subject with originality so as to create in new untrodden ways" (1979).

Perseveration Preservation

Stims and other perseverative behaviors can be especially difficult to manage in a classroom because they are exceptionally intractable. Since students on the spectrum can become locked into patterns of behavior, they may develop a physiological and psychological dependence on these behaviors. Even when stimming or perseveration appears disruptive and dysfunctional, it does serve an important, immediate, and specific function for each student who exhibits it. Understanding that specific function can help you and your students *modify* the behavior into mutually meaningful forms of expression. Many professionals try to take an aggressive approach to quickly extinguish what they see as meaningless or disruptive behaviors. But behavior modification strategies are not indicated here; they are ineffective at best and would likely backfire because perseverative and stimming behaviors, like all other behaviors, are coping mechanisms. *Extinguishing a coping mechanism serves only to extinguish coping.*

> "It seems that for success in science and art, a dash of autism is essential."
>
> —Hans Asperger (1979)

Still Stimming

Later in this chapter, you'll find strategies to help you circumvent, rather than extinguish perseveration. But if you feel that a student's stimming or perseverative behavior is dangerous or interfering with social success, then in those cases, of course you need to intervene to modify these behaviors. (See more on modifying behaviors in Chapter 10.)

Getting Engaged on the Island

In practical terms, whether your students on the spectrum are destined to discover a cure for cancer or are spinning in endless circles, they will need to join their attention with yours to engage in learning the curriculum. Indeed, even Marie Curie needed to learn reading and computation skills.

Since students on the spectrum tend to be fixated on their own thoughts, it will be difficult to get them to emerge suddenly and join attention with someone else about something else. It's a huge leap. But if you have students who seem far, far away, try some of these strategies to draw them toward you:

✳ **Keep It Real:** In order to capture engagement, create lessons that are personally relevant and meaningful. Making connections to topics that are of personal interest to students will help them feel more comfortable venturing into new conceptual territory.

For example, near the end of each school year, Gail, a fourth-grade teacher, instructs her students on how to write persuasively. She has them hone their skills by writing a persuasive letter to her on a highly motivating topic: *What would be a better way to organize our classroom, including the seating arrangement, and why?* Gail reads each completed letter aloud to the class, and they discuss which elements are more well-reasoned, respectfully presented, and compelling than others. Together the class selects the letter that is most persuasive and then Gail, while reserving some veto power, rearranges the classroom space according to the specifications in the winning letter.

✳ **Trade Places:** Switch roles with students, giving them opportunities to teach a tiny area of their own expertise. This, too, shifts the energy in the room, and also allows every student to shine, especially those who actually *are* experts in tiny areas!

✳ **Step Out of the Curriculum:** Go ahead and indulge interesting experiential and incidental learning opportunities. When you allow class discussions to veer off into enthusiastic, relevant tangents, lots of practical learning can happen. Because of their personal relevance, these moments can be much more effective and memorable than planned didactic lessons that may feel random and abstract to students.

But when you go off topic, explain clearly what association led you there. Remember that sudden directional shifts can also be confusing to students on the spectrum because these students are probably not making the same cognitive associations that you and others are. So indulge tangents mindfully, and when veering off course, be sure to make the connection and the intention clear.

Try to signal visually when you are pursuing a tangent by actually moving yourself to a different position or location, to literally *step out of the curriculum*. When you move back to a typical teaching position, this is a signal to your class that it's time to refocus on the main topic at hand.

✳ **Alert! Alert!** Students on the spectrum tend to be slow in shifting their attention. Alert students when you are going to tell them something important. Be sure that you have been heard, and then pause for a moment to allow them to shift gears.

A Pensieve Moment

In J.K. Rowling's *Harry Potter and the Goblet of Fire* (2000), fictional headmaster Albus Dumbledore introduces Harry to a "pensieve." A pensieve is a stone basin into which Dumbledore deposits his own memories or thoughts when his mind gets too cluttered or when he needs to focus on something else. He retrieves his thoughts and memories from the pensieve only when he is ready to address and immerse himself in them.

Have your students create pensieves from coffee cans. Cut a slit in each lid and allow every student to decorate his or her own can. As needed throughout the day, your students can jot a note or a quick sketch of their distracting thought and slip it into the pensieve, to be retrieved later with your permission. Keeping the thoughts literally close at hand yet out of sight should create more cognitive space for engagement.

Promise (and deliver) *pensieve time* each day, preferably near the end of the day: a few minutes during which students are allowed to open their pensieves and ruminate on the precious thoughts inside. The knowledge that there will be time allocated for thinking those thoughts will help students on the spectrum curb them at other times of the day.

* **Experts On-Call:** If you have students on the spectrum in your class who are expert historians, spellers, arithmeticians, or similarly skilled, keep them "on-call." Make them aware that they may be consulted at any time. Remind them that this means they must be engaged and paying attention to lessons and conversations, because historical or spelling emergencies can pop up at any time.

* **Make 'em Laugh:** Use humor when you can to relieve anxiety and capture interest in a lighthearted context. Try to keep your witticisms concrete and always avoid sarcasm (for everyone).

* **Jolly Good:** Speak with accents every now and then. But first, know your audience: Though many students on the spectrum find accents endlessly entertaining and engaging, others may find them disorienting or difficult to understand.

* **Define the Time:** Students may not intuit that because you are up in front of the class discussing rules of vowels, it is not also the time to discuss the history of train accidents. Be very specific about what time it is: *This is* not *the time to be thinking or talking about trains. Now it is time for weather systems.* If necessary, give a warning and a time frame to make the adjustment before changing topics: *You may talk about trains for one more minute; then it will be time for weather systems.*

The Hook

A *hook* is a metaphorical connection or link. It's also a great strategy for reaching a student on the spectrum, and grabbing hold of his interest. A hook can be anything familiar that he can glom onto that will help lure him toward new and expanding experiences. Every student's hooks will be different, depending upon his specific areas of interest or fixation. Your mission will be to find the most effective hooks to lure each student off his island.

Finding the Hook

Let's say you have a student who repeats the same fast-food restaurant jingle over and over—it seems to be all he thinks about or focuses on. Ideally, using the ideas for behavior interpretation described in Chapter 3, you have explored what he may be communicating with this preoccupation: What source of anxiety tends to trigger it? What comforts him about reciting it? Maybe it soothes him because it reminds him of family outings. Or maybe singing the jingle helps him stay alert.

And ideally, using the environment-adaptation ideas described in Chapter 4, you have tried to reduce his reliance on singing this jingle. Still, despite your efforts, what if the preoccupation persists? What do you do with it? How do you get around it? Here's a thought: *Use* it.

Using the Hook: Grasping Engagement for Learning

Explore which element of your student's perseveration is most meaningful to him. Suppose you determine that it is, in fact, the food itself—let's say, the french fries—that the student enjoys thinking about. If so, then french fries are your hook. French fries will be the bridge to engagement in the curriculum.

(I have deliberately chosen this somewhat whimsical example in order to demonstrate that regardless of the peculiarity or idiosyncrasy of the student's fixation, there is always a hook that you can use to incorporate your student's interest into any aspect of class work, as needed.)

Adding Individual Flavor

Look for ways to incorporate a student's special interest into elements of his own work and classroom experience. Every time he encounters hints of his favored topic it will boost his feelings of familiarity and comfort and enhance his engagement.

✱ **Behavior:** See if you can find stickers of french fries to use on his behavior chart or create your own icons from laminated paper. Reinforce—or ask his parents or caregivers to reinforce—certain behavioral goals at the end of the week or month with some actual french fries. For older students, offer related screen-time rewards: A quick search of the app store turned up more than 50 apps about fast food and five specifically about french fries!

✱ **Vocabulary:** Sprinkle thematically relevant words on his spelling or vocabulary list at any level, such as *peel, fry,* and *hungry; potatoes, vegetable,* and *delicious;* or *saturated, hydrogenated,* and *carbohydrate.*

Adding Whole-Class Flavor

Try incorporating a student's special interest into whole-class curriculum, to the extent that it engages everyone. Be flexible. Even if you've always taught measurement using blocks, why not try it with real or plastic french fries?

✱ **Math:** Use a student's special interest as a manipulative while teaching basic math skills.

- Measure the length of french fries in inches and centimeters.
- Compare the length of french fries to the lengths of pencils, crayons, and markers, and graph the results.
- Estimate and investigate how many french fries must be lined up end to end to stretch across the room.
- Count how many french fries are in a typical fast food container and multiply how many would be needed to feed the whole class or the whole school.
- Practice dividing one package of french fries among the students in your class.
- Examine nutrition information: What percent of a french fry is actually potato? How much is fat? Salt? Fillers?

✱ **Science:** Integrate learning about the components of a student's special interest into your science unit.

- *What food group do potatoes belong to?*
- *What are the different ways potatoes can be cooked?*
- Make a Venn diagram comparing and contrasting french fries to carrot sticks in terms of shape, length, texture, flavor, nutritional value.
- *What are the effects of carbohydrates, fat, and salt on our bodies?*

✱ **Social Studies:** Examine the popularity of a student's special interest around the world.

- *When and where did french fries actually originate?*
- *In what kinds of climates do potatoes grow best?*
- *Where are french fries most commonly eaten?*
- *Why might they be more popular in certain parts of the world than in others?*

The message to this student is: *French fries can be an interesting topic, but you cannot keep singing about them. Instead, we will use them as part of our learning.* Incorporating your student's favored topic into your curriculum will vastly improve your ability to engage him in the lesson, while the entire class learns as well.

Using Personal Connections to Broaden and Expand

Of course, you don't want your curriculum to be completely, shall we say, *saturated* by fried potatoes, so once you've hooked your student(s) on the spectrum, you will want to use this

hook to broaden his horizons beyond that narrow focus, and to keep the rest of the class engaged and interested. Here are some strategies for moving away from students' special interests and toward your intended curriculum. (Dig into Chapter 11 to collect more strategies for maintaining engagement even as you pursue standardized curricular expectations.)

✱ **Segue:** Now that you have him engaged, use his favored topic as a segue to introduce other topics. For example, in social studies:

> *Where does ketchup come from?*
>
> *Where does beef come from?*
>
> *What's a vegetarian?*
>
> *What major role did potatoes have in United States immigration?*
>
> *Who was president when french fries first appeared in the U.S.?*
>
> *Who was Prime Minister Peel and what did he have to do with potatoes?*

Your student can follow the thread of familiarity through your social studies curriculum, as you expand into related topics such as farming, agriculture, famine, migration, shipping, trade, economy, and more.

A Sign of the Times

In her book *An Inside View of Autism* (1992), Temple Grandin urges teachers to "use fixations to motivate instead of trying to stamp them out." As a fourth-grade student on the autism spectrum in the 1950s, Grandin recalls being attracted to election posters because she liked the feeling of wearing the posters like a sandwich.

Solely because of her fixation on "sandwich board" signs, Grandin became interested in the election. In retrospect, she feels this was a missed opportunity to expand her horizons. She wishes her teachers had seized on and encouraged this oddly acquired, newfound interest and broadened it to facilitate her involvement with the social world. Grandin says, "My teachers should have taken advantage of my poster fixation to stimulate an interest in social studies. Calculating electoral college points would have motivated me to study math. Reading could have been motivated by having me read newspaper articles about the people on the posters. Even if a child is interested in vacuum cleaners, then use a vacuum-cleaner instruction book as a text!" (p. 115).

(Grandin's appreciation of wearing "sandwich boards" actually had a sensory basis. Modern-day occupational therapy recognizes the physiological value of weight-bearing and joint-compressing activities. Therapeutic tools have been created to simulate these effects and also reduce hyperactivity.)

✱ Activate: And now that you have introduced very varied curricular skills via his favored topic, those curricular skill sets are now familiar to your students. Activate what has now become "prior knowledge." For example, tell your class: *Remember when we multiplied and divided french fries? Today we are going to use that same skill with nickels.* Or, *Remember when we made a Venn diagram about french fries and carrot sticks? Today we are going to make a Venn diagram about Buddhism and Hinduism.*

✱ Orient: If your student has trouble using these expanded skills, don't be afraid to invoke his favored topic when necessary. Thinking about it will help him feel safe and oriented and ease his transition to substituted objects. Prompt him to remember and visualize the process of grouping french fries, and then encourage him to visualize grouping nickels instead. But if your invocation of french fries leads him off into his own world again, remind him: *I mentioned french fries just to help you remember, but we are not talking about french fries now. Now we are talking about immigration.* (This might be a good time to have him draw a picture of some french fries and stuff it in his pensieve.)

Make It Stop!

Parents and caregivers may assert that fueling a child's area of perseverative interest is counterintuitive. Gut reactions of impatience and exasperation leave many adults wishing the topic or behavior would just go away. You, too, may not be inclined to encourage further exploration of an already overexposed topic. But by digging a little deeper into it and being creative, you can discover a multitude of useful connections. Trust that these will not only help engage perseverative students and transform their obsessive interests into something productive, but also serve to diminish their reliance on perseverative behaviors.

Read All About It

Read books aloud to your class that you can connect to your student's perseverative interest. Make creative connections. The connections you offer may feel like a stretch to you, but any association will help open up your student to engage in new material. For example, use potatoes as your hook into books such as *Cloudy With a Chance of Meatballs, Stone Soup, Dragons Love Tacos, Robo Sauce,* or *Unusual Chickens for the Exceptional Poultry Farmer.* Movies, television shows, and popular music are often familiar and welcome associations for students on the spectrum. Connections can be found everywhere: Did you know that Miley Cyrus's favorite food is ketchup? Imagine the possibilities. . . .

Exponential Potential

By the same token, new independent reading books may be difficult to introduce because of their unfamiliarity. Of course, students on the spectrum will welcome books that pertain to their favored topic, but this narrow focus is limiting and can keep them isolated on their islands. A more broadening experience can be achieved by introducing a series of books. Start with a book from a series that you can connect to your students' special interests.

When my son's special interest was pirates, I introduced him to the book about pirates from the Magic Tree House series. The word *pirate* in the title and the picture of a pirate on the cover engaged him instantly. Once he had read that book, the main characters were now familiar. Suddenly he no longer needed pirates to help him engage in the other forty or so books in the series because now the series' protagonists, Jack and Annie, provided that thread of familiarity. Then, reading those other Magic Tree House books exposed him to everything from mummies to the moon, from King Arthur to Louis Pasteur, and much more.

Now all of those topics have become familiar and can be used as hooks to even more new experiences. Other engaging series that help hook your students on the spectrum into enjoying reading include The Magic School Bus, Diary of a Wimpy Kid, A Series of Unfortunate Events, The 39 Clues, The A to Z Mysteries, and many others. Each book serves as another link, connecting your students to more of the world, just as every moment of engagement you capture with your students draws them one step closer across the bridge.

(If you would like more information and more strategies to support engagement, hook into www.barbaraboroson.com.)

The iHook: There's an App for That!

Screens, themselves, tend to be very appealing to students on the spectrum. (You'll read about using this to academic advantage in Chapter 11.) Any time you can connect a curricular lesson to an on-screen activity, you are leveraging screen "addiction" to your student's advantage. Moreover, the inherently customizable nature of some apps makes them particularly accessible to perseverative students. Many apps allow students to customize their own avatar or landscape. If a high-interest avatar can lead a student into new curricular terrain, you have found an iHook!

As of this writing, popular apps that boost engagement in these ways include *See.Touch.Learn.* by Brain Parade, *News-o-Matic* by Press4Kids, *Triple Town* by Spry Fox LLC, and *Fun Town for Kids* by Touch & Learn. New apps are being created all the time. Search for "learning games" in your app store. You're sure to find an app for that.

• • • •

Crossing the bridge toward engagement will be a lifelong journey for students on the spectrum. They will need to bring more than a backpack, a water bottle, and a handful of french fries along. They will need their families beside them every step of the way. As you work to engage your students on the spectrum, let's look at why making this journey depends on engaging the family as well.

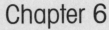

Chapter 6

Meeting of the Minds, Part One

Collaborating With the Family

Collaboration is a buzzword of 21st-century pedagogy. But never is it more important than when working with students who have pervasive special needs and their families.

Collaboration: What's in It for You?

From the very beginning of your relationship with students on the spectrum, collaboration with parents and caregivers will help you gain access to years of historical data including trials and tribulations, failures and successes. This allows you to hit the ground running with tried-and-true strategies, or with your own creative ideas that are based on knowledge of students' past experiences. It also prevents you from falling into the same potholes others before you have fallen into. Don't try to reinvent the wheel; not only would you be wasting time and energy, but the delicate vehicle you are trying to shore up could very well crash and burn while you're putting on those last bolts.

Putting Students in Personal Contexts

Keeping in close touch with families will make your life infinitely easier in the long run. For example, if caregivers have a reliable way to communicate to you that this morning was really tough because Marisa lost her favorite sock or because Peter's toothbrush fell in the toilet, then you'll know why Marisa has arrived at school scowling or why Peter won't get up off the floor. Moreover, because you have previously sought out historical information about these students, you'll know what comforts Marisa when she's scowling and how to get Peter off the floor. You'll know what tends to help and what tends to make things worse.

Who's the Expert Here?

Be confident enough in yourself to recognize that while your expertise is teaching, the parents' expertise is their own individual child. Take full advantage of the fact that they know their *whole child* better than anyone else does. Seeking help from parents or caregivers is not a sign of weakness or failure on your part. It is, instead, a signal of your commitment to maximizing your effectiveness and relationship with this student. Clarify for yourself and for parents that while they know their child best from a historical and holistic perspective, you know him best at school. Remind parents or caregivers, and yourself, that you all share the same goal and that you can all pool your varied expertise to create a productive collaboration that will propel this student toward success across contexts. (Tap into parents' expertise with the parent questionnaire referenced in Chapter 3 and reproducible at www.barbaraboroson.com.)

This chapter will give you ideas for keeping in touch with families in a reliable, maintainable, and meaningful way. Let your emerging understanding of your students on the spectrum, in the context of their pasts and presents, guide your interactions, interventions, and expectations from day to day and across the whole year. And as your relationship with your students deepens, you can offer parents a different view of their child—from the school context. Seamless continuity between the school environment and the home environment will show students that all adults in their lives are on the same page and uphold the same expectations.

Context Clues for You

Consider each student in the context of his or her own history. Parents or caregivers of students on the spectrum may make special requests, asking you to meet Cory at the bus or to call the nurse if you see Kai blinking her eyes rapidly. Try not to disdain or dismiss these requests as the hovering worries of "helicopter parents." Do these parents worry? You bet they do. But they have much to worry about. You can be sure that families of students on the spectrum have a history of intense struggles, littered with crises and traumatic events. Ask questions. You may learn that up until last year, Cory was a runner, and would head for the hills every morning when he got off the bus. Or that when Kai blinks her eyes a lot, she could be on the verge of having a seizure.

For example, Danny was doing fine during the first few days of fourth grade. But then his grandparents approached his teacher, Amir, and asked that Danny be given bathroom reminders every thirty minutes, just as he had been given last year. Amir resisted, perceiving the grandparents as anxious and overprotective: *Bathroom reminders? In fourth grade?*

But when Amir asked why, he learned that Danny had had daily toileting accidents in school right up until his third-grade teacher began reminding him regularly. Now the grandparents' thinking made more sense. Amir regrouped and worked with Danny's grandparents to create a system by which Danny would be supported, but would also begin to take responsibility for his emerging skill. Instead of giving Danny verbal reminders, Amir and Danny created a system whereby Amir would place plain yellow icons at numerous points on Danny's visual schedule, designed to prompt Danny to *assess* his need for the bathroom. With teacher and caregivers working together, along with the support of this visual prompting, Danny became the independent arbiter of his bathroom needs.

Collaboration: What's in It for Parents and Caregivers?

Parents and caregivers of students on the spectrum often have very little access to information about their children's day, yet they have a real need to receive *even more* information than parents of typically functioning children do. Why do they worry so much? Here's why.

What's New? *Nothing.*

Students on the spectrum are likely to be ineffective conveyors of school-to-home information. Compared to typical students, they may appear as follows:

- less organized—forgetting to record assignments in their planners or forgetting even to bring home their planners

- less engaged—tuning out when you present important information

- less intuitive—misinterpreting which of your words are important to relay to parents or caregivers

- less verbal—unable to put their experiences into words

For these reasons, parents and caregivers of students on the spectrum receive much less information about the day and about upcoming events than do parents and caregivers of typical students. Your communications may be their only source of feedback.

What's New? *A Lot!*

Parents and caregivers of children on the spectrum receive scant information but have good reason to worry. Their kids get confused and disoriented, bullied and teased, overstimulated and overwhelmed on a regular basis. They misunderstand and miscommunicate. They lose their stuff and lose control. Their parents and caregivers know, when they send their children off to school, that their kids are in for a struggle because there is no such thing as a typical day for these atypical children.

Further, keep in mind that students on the autism spectrum who are in inclusive classes are being stretched to capacity—and beyond. This is the least restrictive environment; many other settings would offer more support. Though this may in fact be a suitable setting, you can be sure that your students on the spectrum are struggling to maintain their equilibrium in this highly stimulating and challenging social and academic environment.

In order to communicate effectively with parents and caregivers, it helps to tune in to their experience. Remember, their child, who is one of many in your inclusive classroom, is also a powerful force in their family—practically, emotionally, and in other very significant ways, too. The next section will show you that parents face their own host of challenges raising a child on the spectrum.

Parents and Caregivers: Where Have They Been?

As challenging as your journey is with these students, their parents' journey has been all that and more. In addition to coping with the myriad challenges of just getting their children through each day, parents bear a lifelong emotional investment and ultimate responsibility for them, 24/7. By the time they come to you, these families may have traveled a long road of high hopes and dashed dreams.

Practical and emotional challenges abound for parents and caregivers. These "home" issues are neither your problem nor your responsibility, but they are going to manifest in your classroom, during parent-teacher conferences, during impromptu school-home communications, and through the students themselves throughout every day. Being aware of these extracurricular challenges will help you understand the whole child in a family context and will make your own educational efforts more informed and effective across the board.

So stop for a minute and consider the moment in which these parents were told or came to the realization that their *perfect* little child, born with ten fingers, ten toes, and infinite possibility, actually has a pervasive, permanent, neuro-developmental disability. For many parents of children with significant special needs, the diagnosis of a lifelong disability is akin to a death: It represents the sudden shattering of hopes, dreams, and legacy. Often parents go through a lengthy and agonizing grief process that includes intense periods of denial, anger, self-blame, depression, and more, before they can begin to accept what is and what may never be.

Amid those feelings of desperation, these parents had to kick into high gear, rallying on behalf of their child who is on a different trajectory from the rest. Just living with and raising a child on the spectrum day after day can be a physically and emotionally debilitating experience. But despite that, parents must quickly educate themselves about this exclusive society to which they have been appointed but never wanted to join. They must organize a support squad and round up services, squashing any vestiges of parental pride to shout their child's challenges out to the universe in search of help. Obtaining services is time-consuming and costly and rarely well-covered by medical insurance, so a heavy financial burden likely weighs on the family as well. All of this is in addition to attending to the everyday needs of a typical family, including those of the child's siblings who often get lost in the shuffle.

Along the way, they may have encountered assorted professionals who are far less accepting, flexible, knowledgeable, kind, and collaborative than you are. They may have had to fight for services, advocate for equal access, defend against doubters, and more. Following one early evaluation for my son, we were given the following diagnosis by a very seasoned professional: "The only thing wrong with this child is his anxious mother." It took more than a decade for the profound shame I felt then to turn into anger and indignation. Chances are that ever since then, I have dragged the shadow of shame and the armor of indignation with me to every professional encounter I've had.

Given these overwhelming, unrelenting, and painful circumstances, it should be no surprise to you when you come across parents or caregivers who seem highly anxious, depressed, or wary. These parents have good reason to hover and worry or be sad, stoic, angry, or skeptical. Depending on where parents are in their personal journey, some may get teary every time you introduce a new issue of concern while others may flatly deny or reject your interpretations. Some ask that special allowances be made for their children beyond mandated modifications, while others insist that their child be held to the exact same standards as the rest. Just as you do with your students, be mindful of where the parents have been and meet them where they are, as you work together to support their child.

In your journey together, remember that every special adaptation, every accommodation and modification highlights yet again for parents just how *different* their child is. As creative and successful as your sticker charts, weighted vests, and private bathroom signals may be, they are, at best, bittersweet victories for these parents.

Strengths First

The best strategy for establishing a productive collaborative relationship with parents and caregivers is to lead with strengths, as described in Chapter 2. Since their children present so many challenges at school, challenges dominate conferences and other encounters, leaving little or no time for discussions of strengths and successes. If you can open conversations with enthusiastic reports of real progress or relative strength, even if it's small, parents may begin to see you as an ally. Present yourself as someone who sees the whole child, someone who shares not only in the parents' frustrations but also in their pride and pleasure over this child.

Parents and caregivers feel more connected to you if they feel you are seeing their child as more than his challenges, rather than as your "autistic student." Better yet, once you have enjoyed a proud moment together, parents may feel less defensive and more open to hearing about the concerns you need to present next.

Living on the Edge

Just like their special kids, these parents or caregivers may be marginalized among their peers or feel like hangers-on in the school community. They have watched other people's children having play dates, excelling in sports, and getting invited to birthday parties, and they themselves feel the hurt of being left out of those opportunities for social camaraderie.

Plus, parents and caregivers of students on the spectrum may worry about their child standing out or acting up during school events. A school concert is all stress for these parents as they spend the evening gripping the arms of their chairs, braced against hearing the words *Wingardium leviosa!* soar out across the crowded auditorium in the middle of "Ode to Joy."

As you work to create an inclusive community in your class, you are modeling the acceptance of diversity for your students. Ideally, the school administration will follow your lead, taking proactive steps to share general information about Autism Spectrum Disorder with the entire school community. The distribution of generalized, factual information can allay common fears and misconceptions and raise consciousness about the benefits that inclusive programs offer the entire community. An overall atmosphere of acceptance will help all families feel welcome, just the way they are. (Gather more on creating a supportive school community in Chapter 7 and a supportive peer community in Chapter 8.)

Two Different Worlds

The only way school-home collaboration is successful is when it is built on mutual respect, which means acknowledging and accepting the various perspectives and experiences of all parties. Only when teachers and parents accept those differences can we see what we all have in common: namely, the best interests of the children we share.

When you first consult with parents or caregivers of students on the spectrum, you may feel they are describing an entirely different child than the one you see—and it's possible they are. If these differences are not addressed openly and productively from the beginning, you and the parents or caregivers will be pushing against each other all year. But there are often simple explanations for a student's variable functioning across multiple environments, and it will be helpful for both you and the parents or caregivers to explore them together. Sharing this understanding will set the tone for a year of productive collaboration and mutual support.

Challenges at Home: We *Never* Have That Problem at School!

Some students hold themselves together fairly well at school and fall apart when they get home. It's not uncommon even for parents or caregivers of typically functioning children to describe difficult behaviors that teachers rarely or never see at school. You may be surprised to hear parents or caregivers tell you, *She is a terror as soon as she gets home.* There can be a number of reasons for this kind of disparity.

Best Foot Forward

Many students, whether typically functioning or on the spectrum, arrive home from school worn down by the demands of the day. Students on the spectrum, especially, may be firing on all cylinders just to stay on track at school, and may be doing a pretty good job of it. But by the time they get home, they have nothing left; the pressures of the day have left them depleted and irritable, and their already compromised coping strategies are used up.

Reframe this troubling experience for parents or caregivers by pointing out that these students actually have their priorities in order: School is where they *should* put their best foot forward—school is where they need to stretch themselves to meet the expectations of the social world. These students

> **Did You Know . . .**
>
> For every hour of engagement, students on the spectrum need at least another hour of alone time to fully regroup and recover from the stress and stimulation of the social world (Attwood, 2009).

recognize that home is a loving and accepting place in which they can vent their stress and slow their motors. That's a good thing. We all need a few minutes to kick back and recover from the stress of the day; but students on the spectrum, after struggling at school to stay engaged and socialize, after coping with the bright lights and multiple transitions, likely need even more decompression time. Encourage parents and caregivers to allow their children to regroup and retreat for a while after school in ways they find restorative (whether it's doing somersaults, lining up toy cars, playing Minecraft, or rereading the same book for the thousandth time), before having to step up to more demands.

Something's Up

Alternatively, there may be specific problems at school, on the bus, or at home that these students are reacting to at home. Keep an eye out for signs of situations that might jeopardize students' safety or well-being. Remind parents and caregivers to keep in close touch with you regarding any changes in their child's after-school behavior. Since students on the spectrum are often ineffective communicators, they could be at the mercy of a bad situation and unable to report it.

What Now?

Another reason students on the spectrum may demonstrate greater challenges at home than at school is that they crave the structure of the school day. Maybe you have put in place many of the elements of a structured classroom as described in this book—you use visual schedules, verbal prompts with visual cues, organizational systems, transitional protocols, and a consistent behavioral plan—and these students are comforted by these predictable elements of the day.

However, the flexible, low-key atmosphere at home that works so well for other family members may be inscrutable and overwhelming for these rigid, anxious students. At home, rules may change depending on context; every afternoon may present a new commotion of comings and goings; and the dinner menu has not likely been posted a month in advance.

Validate the parents' and caregivers' best intentions in trying to maintain a relaxed environment for their child. But point out that this particular child may actually feel more relaxed in the context of clear and consistent rules and a detailed, time-ordered set of expectations. Many families with children on the spectrum find it helpful or necessary—even if not exactly fun or spontaneous—to run their household on consistent visual schedules. If your families have not considered creating schedules for their children, share with them Chapter 3 of this book, which describes the need

The Picture Communication Symbols ©1981–2010 by Mayer-Johnson LLC. All Rights Reserved Worldwide. Used with permission. Boardmaker™ is a trademark of Mayer-Johnson LLC.

for structure and various types of basic schedules. Parents or caregivers can create visual or written schedules to delineate the more stressful aspects of the day such as the morning routine, the homework routine, and the bedtime routine. Whole weeks or months can be mapped out on schedules. Vacation periods, especially, when all semblance of routine tends to break apart, can be held together smoothly using schedules.

Challenges at School: We *Never* Have That Problem at Home!

On the other hand, some parents or caregivers may get defensive and reject your description of their child's challenging behaviors in your class: *No, Ricky would never do anything like that. He's never done that at home.* Sure, in some cases parents may be "in denial" about the significant issues their child faces, but more likely, they really are seeing a differently functioning child at home than you see at school.

Parents and caregivers may share with you that at home their child does his work independently, shifts gears easily, and plays beautifully with siblings. You're skeptical: You find that at school this same student cannot get through one problem on a worksheet without losing focus, bangs his head against the wall whenever there is a change to the schedule, and is provocative and rigid in social situations. But in truth, many students function much better at home than they do at school.

Bridging the Gap

If you are working with parents who resist your observations, try to frame the discrepant behavior in terms of context. At school, the pressures are immense: There are engagement expectations, social stressors, academic challenges, linguistic demands, multiple transitions, and so much more, all amid relentless sensory stimulation and the chaos of twenty-some unique and unpredictable personalities swirling around in one room. Despite your efforts to structure and modify the environment, these factors can interfere with the functional efforts of a student on the spectrum.

At home, on the other hand, Ricky may do his homework in a quiet, solitary space with soft, ambient lighting. He may shift gears "easily" only because the family allows him to carry his entire Jedi collection with him everywhere he goes. Siblings may have come to terms with the fact that Ricky always needs to be the one who decides what they are all going to build, and that he needs to lick each Lego piece before he adds it to the emerging building.

Reiterate that your mutual goal is to support students' ability to function in *all kinds of contexts*. If Ricky is indeed capable of more than you are seeing in class, consider adjusting the modifications and accommodations you have made to his school program and environment. But also acknowledge to parents or caregivers that as wonderful as it is that Ricky can zip through his multiplication at home, unfortunately it's just not happening independently in the always stimulating and distracting school environment. Remind them also that school is more reflective of the big wide world, in which Ricky cannot make up all the rules and in which licking toys is socially unacceptable.

Some parents may resist the kinds of modifications and accommodations you need to implement, for fear that they will make their child "stand out from the rest." Remind these parents that the very purpose of the adaptations you provide is to help their child to stand out less than he would without them. A visual schedule may prevent him from screaming. A squishy cushion on his chair may prevent him from rocking. A 1:1 aide may encourage him to call peers by name instead of biting them to get their attention. All good things.

Teacher-Parent Communication

To reap the benefits of these varied perspectives, create an ongoing communication system. Share with parents and caregivers your own philosophy about keeping in touch. How much can they expect to hear from you? What kinds of things do you want to hear from them?

Keeping in Touch

✳ **Respect Your Boundaries:** Many teachers, in an effort to demonstrate their commitment, give parents or caregivers their personal cell phone numbers. Although generous in spirit, this is, as a rule, unnecessary and inadvisable. If your cell phone is buzzing while you're spending time with your own family, working out at the gym, or sitting at a movie—when you need to be off the clock—you will grow resentful. Parents and caregivers can and should be expected to limit their contact with you to school hours, via school communication systems. They can leave a phone message for you at school that you will return when you are available. And it's fine for them to send you an e-mail anytime they like; but, unless you choose to respond sooner, they should know not to *depend* on receiving a response outside of business hours. Taking good care of yourself after hours will make you a better teacher between the bells.

✳ **Respect Their Boundaries:** Find out from parents and caregivers where, when, and how they would prefer to be contacted when you need to reach them. Is it okay to call them at work? Is the work number or the cell phone number a better choice during the day? Would they prefer an e-mail? Are they comfortable with texting? What kinds of information can you share with the babysitter, grandparent, or other caregivers?

Creating a Written Communication Log

Here are some suggestions for putting a low-maintenance system into place to ensure that effective school-home communication is seamlessly integrated into every day:

✳ **Check Yourself:** Consider how much feedback is realistic for you to provide. Will you be able to write in the log every day? Once a week? Be honest with yourself and be honest with parents and caregivers; don't set yourself up for a burdensome commitment that you later resent and cannot maintain. Establish a format that feels manageable to you and valuable for everyone. Make it clear that the reason you need to use an effective but efficient system is that writing out detailed notes would take your time away from their child and the rest of the class.

✳ **Use a Template:** To minimize daily effort, use a template that lists categories of functioning across a week and allows space for comments. Categories can include socialization, behavior, attention, engagement, and others. Or list specific targeted behaviors in each relevant area, such as listening, staying calm, staying in a seat, taking turns, or whatever behaviors you and the parents are concerned about. Paste or staple the chart into a notebook and use a checkmark system or other simple notation to indicate how the student performed in each area each day. Update categories and areas to target each week.

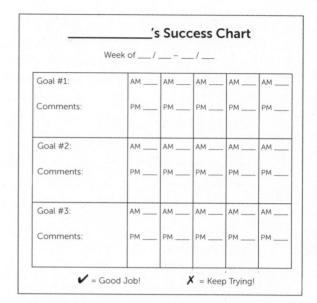

For a reproducible version of this form, please visit www.barbaraboroson.com.

✱ **Elaborate:** When you do indicate a problem on the chart, take a minute to elaborate so parents or caregivers know how to address it at home. Or use stickers to show gradations of problems. For example, a green sticker means *no problem in this area today*; yellow means *minor problem*; and red means *major problem*—which would always warrant elaboration, whether in writing or by phone. Remember that students on the spectrum may be unable to explain what happened; and even if they can, they are unlikely to perceive it and describe it in the way you might. Clarify terms that work best for you and work together with the parents or caregivers to develop a system with which they will feel comfortable as well.

✱ **And Your Point Is . . .?** When you write in the log, try to be very clear about your intentions. Many parents believe that the only reason a teacher would contact them about a problem is so that they will *do something about it* at home. Let parents know that most of the time when you share information, it's only for the purpose of making them *aware* of what happened, and that adequate consequences have already been meted out at school. Remind them specifically that you are keeping them in the loop so that they can discuss the situation with their child, but that no consequence at home is necessary or expected.

However, sometimes you may feel that a certain behavior does warrant some more extensive follow-up at home. Although you can't tell parents exactly how to respond, they will be better able to make sound decisions for their family if they have all relevant information.

Your intention may change from incident to incident, so clarify your intentions every time you communicate in writing or verbally. This will also go a long way toward minimizing defensiveness and misunderstandings, and therefore, maximizing effective collaboration.

✱ **Watch Your Tone!** ☺ So often, in this era of written communication, tone is lost to efficiency, as frequently happens in e-mails, text messages, posts, and tweets. In the case of teacher-parent communication, be mindful that the information you are sharing is highly loaded. Consider your words from the perspective of the recipient who is not a neutral reader, but the parent of a child with a disability. *Did you know that parents of children with special needs cringe every time the phone rings between 8 A.M. and 3 P.M.?* Regardless of the nature of the issue, sensitive buttons are being pressed for the parents every time you contact them with a concern. Your simple comment may inadvertently touch on very raw, underlying feelings of shame, guilt, defensiveness, denial, embarrassment, responsibility, frustration, disappointment, exhaustion, anger, and other powerful responses that undermine their fundamental desire to be supportive.

✱ **Weigh Your Words:** Be careful to use nonjudgmental language and include supportive words and phrases. Suppose you write, *Randall used a racial insult against another student today. Please teach him about respectful language.* Reading that communication, parents may feel chastised and defensive about your unwitting implication that they condone racism or have never tried to teach Randall to be respectful.

✱ **Throw a Crumb:** Always try to intersperse good news and optimism amid your concerns. Take the extra moment to smooth it out a bit: *Randall used a racial insult against another student today. We discussed how bad it feels to be insulted, and Randall did a great job apologizing to his classmate. I'm sure you've been over it with him before, but please remind him again about respectful language. Thanks! I'll keep you posted.*

✱ **Be "In the Know":** Urge parents and caregivers to share with you any concerns they have or events that may have been out of the ordinary or upsetting to the student on any given day. Be sure to check the communication log every morning. Information there may well give you important opportunities to turn down the heat on simmering situations quickly and act preemptively. You won't stand a chance of teaching this student today if you don't know about the broken-shoelace debacle of last night. Seriously.

✱ **Follow Up:** Try to let parents and caregivers know of any news or developments related to what they wrote to you in the morning. And, by the same token, encourage parents and caregivers to write back to you about what transpired at home as a result of your report.

Keeping in Touch: There's an App for That!

Tracking and sharing progress is easier than ever with the use of apps. In addition to districtwide grade portals, teachers and parents can enter into private digital dialogues to share confidential notes, charts, progress, and more.

As of this writing, popular apps that streamline general communication to all of your parents include *Remind* by remind101, *Class Messenger* by Learn Anything, and *BuzzMob* by Chatter Inc. Apps that also offer tools to simplify the tracking, sharing, and reporting of student behavior include *ClassDojo* by Class Twist Inc., and *Teacher's Assistant Pro* by Lesson Portal LLC. New apps are being created all the time. Search for "teacher parent communication" in your app store. You're sure to find an app for that.

Medication in the Equation

Even when the lines of communication are open, medication can be a touchy topic between teachers and parents or caregivers. Many students on the spectrum are treated with prescription medications that help them modulate reactions, sustain attention, and so on. You may also come across students who are on specific strict diets or natural supplement regimens to support their engagement or flexibility. While some parents and guardians swear by their chosen diets, supplements, or pharmaceutical interventions, others are offended, personally or philosophically, by the very idea of psychiatric medication. Many parents have compelling, informed concerns about the short- and long-term systemic effects that can result from medication.

Grin and Bear It

As a teacher, you see your students on the spectrum function in varied dynamic situations for many hours every day. You are on the receiving end of persistently challenging behaviors. And you may find yourself feeling that *your* life would be a whole lot easier if some of your students were on medication.

But under no circumstances should a family feel pressured into providing psychiatric medication for their children. In fact, federal law prohibits schools from making medication compliance a requisite for attending school. Parents or guardians retain the absolute right by law to choose whether or not to medicate their children, and they have varied opinions on this topic.

Please do share your observations, objective data, and resultant impressions. But not being a medical doctor, you are not in a position to recommend that a student try medication. Keep the school psychologist in the loop so that he or she may broach the topic of evaluation with parents or guardians. But *recommending* medication is a hot button that is not yours to press. In fact, most states bar teachers and other school professionals from recommending psychiatric medication.

Your best bet is to maintain an overall non-judgmental, confidential, and open relationship with parents and guardians so that they will feel comfortable sharing and receiving information with you as needed. Regardless of your personal convictions and despite the repercussions of parental choices in your classroom, a prevailing belief that parents and caregivers want what's best for their children will guide you to accept different choices and understand that they are made on the basis of different histories, cultures, and personal experiences.

• • • •

As you work to engage and collaborate with parents and guardians, your collaboration efforts with school personnel should be in full swing as well. Inclusive education must happen not only within the classroom but also throughout a student's day. So let's have a look at how you can support others in the building, and how they can support you.

Chapter 7

Meeting of the Minds, Part Two

Collaborating in the Classroom and Around the Building

You—and your students on the spectrum—are going to need the support of almost everyone else in the school. Some of your colleagues may have plenty of knowledge about and experience with students on the spectrum, while other staff and faculty members around the building may not have the slightest understanding of these perplexingly peculiar kids.

You are now someone who knows a lot about Autism Spectrum Disorder and you're well on your way to becoming a master inclusion teacher. (I happen to know this much is true.) But your students are moving around the building right alongside their typically functioning peers, and you can be sure they need extra support when they're not with you. How will they manage when they're out and about? While it is arguably not your job to help other staff and faculty members make sense of your students, any effort you make to do so will offer multiple benefits—for your students, for your colleagues, and for you. You will enable your students to meet with understanding and have positive experiences all day long. When they return to your classroom, they are more likely to be calm and ready for more learning. Moreover, by helping to build bridges and raise awareness among your colleagues you will bolster a universally welcoming, inclusive environment.

This chapter looks at ways that you and other faculty, staff, and administrators in the school can work together to ease the way for your students everywhere they go. When all adults at school are speaking the same language of prompts and reinforcements, when they all know how to read the messages students on the spectrum are sending through their behavior, when everyone is acting in concert and in the best interest of the students, and when everyone supports each other in support of students with ASDs . . . that's when we're looking at true inclusion.

What Is Inclusion?

The term *inclusion* is used to describe any class that "includes" students with IEPs. In an inclusion model, students with special needs spend their entire day as part of the general education class (with the exception of periodic pull-out therapeutic services). They are fully *included* everywhere and in every way. The potential social, academic, and emotional benefits for both students on the spectrum and their peers are powerful and life-changing.

Several broad models of inclusion for students on the autism spectrum are used around the country. These range from *co-teaching models* (i.e., the full- or part-time collaboration of a credentialed general educator teaching alongside a credentialed special educator) to *consultant models* (i.e., a back-up special educator or team of special educators who provide support on an as-needed basis) to *individual support models* (i.e., a full- or part-time 1:1 aide assigned to a particular student). These models may be implemented variously in different schools and districts depending on student needs, budget constraints, and other factors.

Inclusion offers students on the autism spectrum the opportunity to learn and develop among typically functioning students who can serve as models and mentors for growth and change. In most inclusion classrooms, with added special ed support, the expectations, environment, and curriculum are differentiated somewhat to maximize students' participation and comprehension and enhance their engagement in the general ed experience.

Being a part of a typical classroom supports social and academic progress for students on the spectrum, and can be an enormous boost to the self-esteem of students with special needs who are often made to feel different and less than their peers. (To understand more about the influence of inclusion on typically functioning peers, please see Chapter 8.)

These benefits have inspired the surge of inclusion classrooms in districts across the country in recent years. As of this writing, 40% of all students on the autism spectrum, ages 6–21, spend at least 80% of every school day in a general education classroom (U.S. Department of Education, 2014).

Let's have a look at the roles played by co-teachers, consultants, and individual support providers; then we'll touch base with others around the building.

Co-Teaching

Having a co-teacher usually means that you, the credentialed general educator, are teaching right alongside a credentialed special educator, all day long or for certain periods of the day. Also referred to as "Integrated Co-Teaching," this is an intense partnership that can yield powerful rewards when carefully structured and cultivated. But if you are new to co-teaching, that intensity can also be challenging to negotiate and adapt to. Here are some guidelines to help you adjust to this kind of partnership and make it all it can be.

Check Your Ego

In most cases, your special ed co-teacher is joining you in what was previously your classroom, and yours alone. You may be accustomed to being captain of the ship; in your classroom, you chart the course and keep the ship afloat, singlehandedly. But now you share the helm.

Your co-teacher's role is to consider your classroom and your teaching style from a special-needs perspective. Her comments and suggestions are not criticisms; they are clues from the other side, from a place where the cheerful music you play is unbearable for some, where your convivial group assignments are agony, where your carefully constructed lesson is incomprehensible. Your co-teacher brings alternative ideas and approaches that are specifically attuned to the needs of special learners, and can only enhance the learning of typical learners. Consider your co-teacher to be the spokesperson for your inscrutable students with special needs, helping you take your fabulousness to the next level.

To that end, you need to be willing to adapt your classroom and yourself to meet the needs of the diversity of learners in your class. This may stretch you out of your comfort zone, but that's the very reason you have your co-teacher by your side.

What About *My* Kid?

A thorny issue around integrated co-taught class arrangements sometimes arises when presenting this model to the parents of typical learners. It is not at all uncommon for these parents to fear that students with special needs will detract from their child's learning experience. Some school districts have chosen to deal with this matter by not sharing openly with parents the reason for a second teacher in the class. In those cases, parents tend to assume that their district randomly and generously assigns two teachers to some classes.

But as awareness of Autism Spectrum Disorder and other special needs grows, this rather underhanded strategy feels outdated, as if hiding a shameful secret. The fact is that when integrated co-teaching is done well, *every* student benefits. Find out from your administrators what the district philosophy is about sharing this model openly with parents. Explain to administrators (if necessary) and to parents that having two teachers in the room provides every student the benefit of more differentiated instruction, more options for learning, and, in fact, more continuous learning because an extra teacher is always on hand to intervene with behavioral interruptions.

Best of all, an inclusive class is more reflective of the diverse world in which *all* of our children live. A necessary part of every child's education is learning to accept and work alongside people who are different from themselves. An inclusive class offers creative, facilitated opportunities for shy students to be mentors, for bullies to be buddies, and for everyone to see that we *all* live on a spectrum of diversity, each of us contributing both strengths and challenges. An inclusive class, just by virtue of its existence, sends the welcoming message that everyone belongs—period.

It is possible that your routine of blasting *She Blinded Me With Science* from your classroom speakers every time your students do labwork may have to go. But old routines will be replaced by new ones; as you and your co-teacher get to know each other well, you may find yourselves bursting into spontaneous, gentle duets on occasion: *Do You Want to Build a Snowman?* Indeed, co-teachers often find themselves finishing each other's sandwiches— er, sentences.

You're Gonna Need a Bigger Boat

One of the most important factors in effective co-teaching is the fundamental understanding that you and your co-teacher are equals in the classroom. You need to discuss this and acknowledge it together; and moreover, you need to present this equal and united front to your students and to your students' families. You are not *head teacher* and *assistant*; not *main teacher* and *support teacher*; not even *teacher* and *co-teacher*. If you have a co-teacher, it means that you are *both* co-teachers.

In the classroom, this means dividing the work into equivalent parts. Of course the special educator is there because of her expertise in working with students who have special needs. And your expertise is in working with large groups of broadly typical learners. But the whole class belongs to both of you. It's not *my students* and *her students*. It's *our students*.

Working with a partner presents you with all kind of options. Together you may choose to trade off which of you teaches new concepts, so that one of you is up front teaching while the other walks around and supports all of the students. You may choose to co-teach new concepts side by side, providing different presentation styles simultaneously to enhance comprehension. You may choose to break the class into two mixed groups at times. And you may choose to use different approaches on different occasions. You may choose to be the one who grades the work of your typical learners, while your co-teacher grades the work of the identified students; or you may choose to grade everyone together. Ideally, all of the students in the class view both of you as their teachers, and feel comfortable going to either of you with questions, concerns, or exuberance!

It's important to remember that this role equality must be consistently presented and upheld in all communications related to your class. The sign on the classroom door should have both of your names on it (even if your co-teacher is with you for only one or two periods per day). The listing in the school directory should have both of your names on it. If your class used to be nicknamed with your initial (e.g., "4-P"), it should now be referred to using your co-teacher's initial as well (e.g., "4-PL"). All letters home should come from both of you, regardless of which students' families are being addressed. Make it a priority that both of you speak up at "Meet the Teacher" night, and that both of you attend parent-teacher conferences together. And both of you should be invited to and attend any and all team or grade meetings, whenever possible.

Map It Out

With so many presentation options available, effective co-teaching requires frequent communication between co-teachers. While this may sound dauntingly time-consuming, remember that co-teaching will also save you lots of time: lesson planning, data collection,

Home Is Where I Hang My Hat

Although the terms *inclusion* and *mainstreaming* are often used interchangeably, they are actually different models. In the mainstreaming model, students with special needs are often visitors to the general ed classroom. Many times these students spend most of the day in a special setting, pushing in to the general setting for only certain parts of the day. Even if mainstreaming increases to the majority or all of the day, the classroom is rarely adapted to meet the needs of these students. There may be no special ed support provided in the classroom and the curriculum may not be differentiated to support their different learning styles. Some students on the autism spectrum can function in a mainstream environment, but most benefit more from having more differentiated supports available to them and feeling like an equal member of the general class. That's why inclusion has supplanted the mainstream model in recent years. Whereas mainstreaming had its heyday in the 1980s, today's shift toward inclusion seems more reflective of the diversity awareness and general inclusivity movements of the 21st century (Watson & Skinner, 2004).

When my son was in second grade, he was mainstreamed for part of every day, moving out of his special class and into a general ed class. In his small special ed class, he was an eager participant, but he consistently shut down in the larger general ed class. His teachers assumed, quite reasonably, that the larger class was overwhelming to him. However, because he happens to be quite verbal and can at times be surprisingly introspective, it occurred to me to ask him whether he knows why he acts so differently in the two settings.

He told me, "I don't participate in the big class because the big class isn't really my class."

I assured him, "Sure it is. You are a part of both classes."

"No, I'm not," he insisted. "I'm only a part of the small class, and here's how I know: I hang my backpack in the small class; my name is listed under the small class in the school directory; and my class picture was taken with the small class. I don't have a cubby in the big class, I'm not listed in the big class in the directory, and I'm not in the big class picture. So the small class is my class and the big one isn't."

Can't argue with that logic. His thinking may have been very concrete, but it was also entirely justified *and* utterly avoidable.

To these kids who may not get invited to birthday parties and may not be able to participate on teams or in other mainstream activities, being a part of something means a lot. Whenever possible, look for symbolic and concrete ways to let students know unequivocally that they belong.

behavioral intervention, grading, and other tasks that you used to do by yourself will now be shared. Spend some time upfront getting to know each other if you don't already. Share with each other what you see as your own strengths and your own areas of struggle. What aspects of teaching do you enjoy the most; which do you dread?

And then, play to your strengths! This may be an opportunity for you to get out of teaching that subject or topic that you never felt you were communicating effectively. Perhaps one of you is more comfortable organizing creative activities, while the other enjoys more straightforward instruction. Maybe you can offer to be the data collector in exchange for your partner doing report cards. Or vice versa. Give structure to your roles in a way that is comfortable for both of you and keeps things moving cleanly in the class.

One area that is most important to clarify and structure is that of classroom management. Different management styles and priorities are the most consistently challenging aspects of co-teaching. So get right on top of it. Talk it out. What are your priorities for your students and how do you carry them through? Learn from each other and work out a compromise that you both feel comfortable with. Each of you will have to make some sacrifices in this relationship, so choose your battles.

Equivalent, but Not Equal

Some students with special needs cannot function in a large, loud, bustling environment, regardless of how well supported it is. Don't let the math fool you: A 24:2 student–teacher ratio is not the same as a 12:1 student–teacher ratio. Mathematically those ratios may be equivalent, but for a student on the autism spectrum, a classroom that contains twenty-six individuals in total is a completely different experience than one that contains thirteen individuals. For some, the volume of noise in the room and the number of bodies in motion is way too much. So be ready to remind and caution administrators and parents that when a student makes the transition from a 12:1 last year to a 24:2 this year, it's a whole new ballgame. Even though adding more people to your classroom may not always be your best bet, adding more strategies to your toolbox is always a winning proposition.

Finding Together Time

Consistent communication tends to be more easily achieved in elementary classrooms than in the secondary grades. In most cases, an elementary co-teaching team is together all day, every day. You can even place your desks together to maximize collaborative opportunities, if you like. You share the classroom equally and your schedules and prep periods are aligned, so you have ample time together for planning, debriefing, and problem solving.

At the secondary level, however, special educators often follow the need—traipsing from classroom to classroom and from teacher to teacher. This can make co-teaching much more challenging because your schedules may have very little collaborative time in common.

Thankfully, the digital age has streamlined this somewhat. Via Google Docs, co-teachers can co-create lesson plans, even when they can't sit down together. Moreover, co-teachers can both grade students' documents that have been submitted digitally and shared with both teachers.

Also challenging at the secondary level is the fact that the itinerant special educator is more likely to feel like a guest in your class, since she may come in and out for one period at a time and may not even have a home base (i.e., desk of her own) in the classroom. Make an effort to share the helm and find out what you can do to help her step comfortably into a position as co-leader in the class.

A Permanent Bathroom Pass—and So Much More!

Overall, the potential benefits of integrated co-teaching are many, for students and for teachers. Students with special needs have the opportunity to learn "mainstream" ways while surrounded by models of typical learning and typical socialization. With careful facilitation, they can be fully part of the mix, rather than marginalized into "special" settings. Better yet, you and your co-teacher are (hopefully) a living, breathing, *in situ* model of positive social skills, such as flexibility, teamwork, compromise, turn-taking, sharing, playful humor, forgiveness, and mutuality.

And for yourself, consider these practical benefits: Co-teaching eliminates the solitary-adult aspect of teaching. Now you have someone with whom to brainstorm ideas and share impressions. You can create flexible groupings. You may be able to spend less time on preparation, data collection, discipline, and grading. You no longer have to write out plans for a substitute because your co-teacher serves as the thread of continuity. And as if that's not enough, you can take a bathroom break anytime you need to!

The Key to Co-Teaching

Ultimately, your mutual success will depend less on the extent of your similarities than on how flexibly you blend your differences.

Classroom Consultants

Some "inclusive" classrooms do not include a full-time special educator. Instead, a special ed consultant, or team of special educators, is on call to come in and provide support as needed. Support personnel may include special ed consultant teachers, resource room teachers, school psychologists, school social workers, counselors, or others. Although this type of consultant model is less costly for school districts, it tends to be less supportive for teachers, and unfortunately, for students with special needs, too. Though some students will be able to manage with only occasional, as-needed support, many others need much more.

If your situation is like this, try to clarify the terms of this collaboration right up front. Roles can be unclear, and you're going to want to maximize the effectiveness of this ad hoc style of collaboration.

In one school where I consulted, the classroom teachers called on the special ed team whenever they confronted a behavioral situation beyond their control. The consultants would swoop in like Spiderman to save the day—intervening in the classroom or whisking the troubled student away—and were gone before anyone could get even a good look at them. The classroom teachers shared with me that they resented the special ed team for never observing the class and never staying long enough to share strategies or leave some of their specialized wisdom behind.

Meanwhile, the special ed team shared with me that they resented the classroom teachers. They felt that the classroom teachers were using the special educators as a crutch by calling them in whenever behaviors got out of control in the classroom. They believed that many of these behaviors reflected overall management problems in the classroom. And they resented that their scheduled therapeutic sessions with students were frequently interrupted by behavioral crises in the classrooms.

The problem here was a matter of role definition and communication. I brought the classroom teachers and special educators together and I gave voice to the frustrations of both parties. I reminded the classroom teachers that the special educators do have other responsibilities, and are not actually sitting around, twiddling their thumbs, waiting for emergencies. And I reminded the special educators that yes, the classroom teachers were relying on them as a "crutch" at times, but only because the classroom teachers didn't have the specific expertise that the special educators had! In fact, the classroom teachers had been *specifically told* by the administration to call upon the special educators when the going got tough.

I suggested that the two teams clarify mutual expectations together. I reminded both parties that in order for these students to remain in their classrooms, they're going to need a united team of superheroes and a strong safety net. We worked out a plan through which the special educators would dedicate some time to sharing preventive and interventive strategies, thereby helping the classroom teachers to become somewhat more self-sufficient and not have to call upon them as often. And now the special educators would know that when the calls did come, their expertise was definitely needed. Further, since they would be called upon less frequently, maybe the special educators would be able to add some depth and collaborative planning to their interventions.

This is certainly not the only way consultant support services are handled. In some cases, consultants push in on a set schedule, spending certain parts of every day in the classroom. In other cases, especially at secondary levels, consultants see students only in private or small-group therapeutic sessions, and collaborate with teachers only at team meetings. Regardless of the arrangement, reach out to these specialists for support. While you are the expert on the day-to-day functioning and curricular efforts of your students, these consultants may bring new perspectives and interpretations of behaviors that will make your job much easier.

Individual Support: Classroom Paraprofessionals

Many students on the autism spectrum come to you with a classroom paraprofessional, or aide, mandated on their IEP. Unlike a co-teacher, aides are not credentialed educators. They should not be teaching new concepts or running groups, and are not required or expected to share responsibility for the whole class. An aide is usually assigned specifically to one or several students in your class who need particularly close attention. Also unlike a co-teacher, an aide should adapt himself to *your* teaching style, *your* class rules, and *your* management style.

Although education requirements for aides are somewhat variable across districts, most aides have little or no post-secondary education or formal classroom training. Some districts invite or require aides to participate in general professional development opportunities, but these may or may not address the specific challenges aides face in the classroom. It is a rare school district, in my experience, that recognizes the very specific and demanding nature of the work aides do and provides them with targeted and explicit instruction about their role in the classroom.

Take some time to meet with a classroom aide and let him know what you expect him to do and not do. Be clear in your own mind that aides are there to assist certain students; they are not there to assist you. If aides are able at times to help you out or support other students, terrific—as long as it doesn't detract from their primary responsibility. But don't *expect* them to pass out supplies, sweep up the floor, manage the class while you're at a meeting, or anything else beyond the scope of supporting the specific student(s) to whom they are assigned.

Backing Off

Many aides struggle to find a comfortable balance between hovering and giving a student adequate space. This is a tricky dynamic. Aides often feel that in order to *appear to be doing their job*, they must be interacting with and helping their assigned student at all times. While this level of engagement may make them look and feel vital, it does a great disservice to the student.

Let the aide know that his goal should be to gradually facilitate independence for his student. Clarify that you don't expect or even want him to be on top of his assigned student all the time. This does not mean the aide can be playing on his phone, daydreaming out the window, or going out for coffee. Instead, explain that you expect him to be fully engaged and tuned in to his assigned student *at all times*: supporting her as needed, but also looking for opportunities to fade support, and allowing considered space for supervised independence.

Confidentiality and Discretion

Classroom aides will be most effective if they have access to as much information about their assigned students as possible. However *none* of that information should be shared with aides without a concurrent lesson in confidentiality. Do not assume that aides have had any confidentiality training whatsoever. Also, many aides may be residents of your school's community and may have personal relationships outside of school with the families of your students. Please clarify for them that they are bound by confidentiality. Not only may they not share personal details about *any* students, but they may not even name the student(s) to whom they are assigned.

Up Close and Personal

As time goes by, try to be open to learning from aides as well. Each of them is in the unique position of being able to focus on one or two individual trees while you attend to the entire forest. That means the aide is poised to notice tiny improvements that you might inevitably overlook, as well as subtle patterns of reaction, social provocations, and much more. They offer a whole different vantage point. Let your student's aide know that you value his perspective and encourage his input in terms of the student's minute-to-minute functioning.

The Uncool Factor

Confidentiality takes another turn when aides are working with upper elementary and especially middle school students. By this age, typical peers notice which kids aides spend the most time with. And in some cases, the student to whom the aide is assigned notices that other kids are noticing, too. This can be a tremendous source of embarrassment for those students on the spectrum who may have enough social awareness to feel ashamed. Explain to aides that middle school is the time in child development when everyone wants to fit in by being the same. Students on the spectrum feel different enough already just by having challenges; being singled out in an obvious way for special help is *the worst*.

In the upper grades, this calls for extreme discretion. Suggest that aides not pull their chairs right up next to their assigned students unless a child specifically asks for help. Better if the aide sits nearby and goes to her only when the student asks, or when it's apparent that she's really struggling. Suggest that aides make themselves similarly available to other students, when possible, to diffuse the obvious one-to-oneness of the relationship. Urge aides not to walk into a classroom and yell, from across the room, the name of the student they are here to work with: *Here I am, Casey!* (That happened to my son in seventh grade. *Worst. Thing. Ever.*)

On the Front Lines

Although aides may not have specific training in education or in special needs, they are, by design, placed directly on the front lines of intense behaviors and complex needs. Many aides, caught in the crossfire, do not have the skills to respond productively and, in desperation, resort to their own improvised parenting skills or to their own learned behaviors. Despite their best professional intentions, these responses may be inadvertently angry, resentful, punitive, or otherwise unprofessional in nature.

Help your student's aide to understand why, as professionals, we mustn't take personally any provocative or rejecting behavior from a student who has special needs. Remind the aide that he has been assigned to this particular student because she is not able to control herself or learn independently yet. She does not need to be disciplined, she does not need to be re-parented, and she must never be shamed or humiliated. Rather, she needs to be supported in a consistent, accepting way that, over time, will help her learn more positive and productive ways to function in the classroom and beyond.

Help the aide to understand that a part of his job is to look for patterns and warning signs around problem behaviors. To start, he should get to really know the student, focusing on strengths first (as described in Chapter 2). Explain that this child needs the adults around her to understand what situations trigger her behaviors. She needs someone to help minimize the triggers and their effects, and also to teach her positive new ways of responding. Explain to the aide that he may need to repeat suggestions and instructions over and over again—with patience and encouragement. Share the behavior systems you use in the classroom and how you differentiate them for your student(s) on the spectrum. Also share any specific behavior plans, along with any tried-and-true preventive measures and interventions. An initial investment in helping bring an aide up to speed will be a tremendous boost for both the student and the aide—and will make your life infinitely easier as well.

Nevertheless, being on the receiving end of clinically significant behavioral outbursts day after day takes a toll even on the most seasoned professional. Be sure to share with aides the helpful preventive strategies and interventions you have collected from this book (or lend the book itself!) and always take a few minutes to debrief a challenging behavioral situation with the aide as well as with the student. Check in to make sure the aide is okay.

I worked in a special school with an extremely troubled boy who, on one occasion, slipped into a psychotic rage. A team of building monitors was required to keep him and others around him safe. During this devastating incident, the child became violent and spat out a truly horrifying string of racial slurs, epithets, and obscenities—while surrounded by an intrepid crew of supporters, all of whom represented the very race he was degrading. Their ability to set aside their personal feelings of resentment and continue to remain professional and supportive throughout the incident was nothing short of extraordinary.

The boy ended up being hospitalized, as his condition had taken a dangerous turn. Once the crisis was over, all staff members involved were deeply shaken and angry. We spent hours together afterwards debriefing. First we took time to let the monitors vent their understandable rage and pain about the contempt they had been forced to endure. We then discussed the nature of the child's condition and the fact that psychosis really does have the power to turn a person into someone he's not. We compared the boy we had just been with to the gentle and lovely boy we all knew well. We talked about whether his language necessarily reflected latent feelings of racism, noting that along with the obscenities and racial slurs, came evidence of severely disordered thinking and distorted reality. For example, during the episode, this boy had insisted that the walls were melting around him. We agreed that when not in a psychotic state, he would not believe the walls were melting. In other words, the psychosis was completely altering his perceptions and making him see and say things he did not necessarily perceive or believe when he was in sound mind. In this way, the team was able to set aside their pain and indignation and forgive this afflicted child. We congratulated and thanked each other for holding it together and helping each other through a difficult incident. When he returned to school following his hospital stay, that boy was welcomed back with open arms.

Provide a Cheat Sheet

On pages 233–234, you will find a reproducible ASD fact sheet, created specifically for paraprofessionals. Do your aides and yourself a favor: Copy it, add some student-specific tips on the blank lines at the end, and hand it to them. Ideally it will become required reading for helpers in your classroom.

Your Principal

We all know that principals come in as many varieties as students. Whether your principal is visionary or stodgy, cutting-edge or set in her ways, she must, like you, be ready for the students on the autism spectrum who are coming your way.

Although your principal may seem supportive of your integrated, co-taught class, she may not know as much about this model as you do—especially now that you've already gotten all the way to Chapter 7! As much as she wants you and your students to be happy and successful, your principal is also burdened by sometimes competing considerations, such as budget restrictions, state inspections, time-tested 20th-century strategies, and conventional general education models. Be prepared to defend and explain some of the choices you make in your classroom for the sake of your students on the autism spectrum.

Many teachers feel pressured by their principals to decorate every inch of wall space in their classroom. Explain to your principal why clean, clear surroundings are crucial when it comes to decorating a classroom that includes students on the spectrum. (And if you don't remember why, check Chapter 4.)

Many teachers worry that principals will frown upon seeing a student's desk positioned apart from the rest, turned partially away from the action, or even partitioned off. Explain why spending a portion of the day in a less stimulating position can be helpful or even necessary for students on the spectrum. (And if you don't know why, take a look at Chapters 4 and 8.)

Teachers also worry what a principal will think if she peeks into the classroom to find a student pacing back and forth, wearing headphones at his desk, or stretched out on a beanbag during math. Explain why certain students need their sensory environment to be modified in ways to meet their individual needs. (And if you don't remember why, check Chapter 4.)

Don't be afraid to ask for special, building-level accommodations for your students on the spectrum. For example, if you feel your student needs a more contained version of recess, ask for it, and show your principal this chapter and Chapter 8. If you feel your student needs special tools or assistive technology to supplement his writing or reading, ask for it, and show your principal Chapter 11.

Remember, as the classroom teacher, you are the one who sees your students on the spectrum in action, so you have the best sense of how they do and what they need.

Therapeutic and Other Support Providers

Many students with Autism Spectrum Disorder receive supplementary services, as mandated on their IEPs. These may include speech and language therapy, occupational therapy, physical therapy, counseling, reading support, resource room instruction, and the like. Most of these supports can be provided as either push-in services (i.e., within the classroom) or pull-out services (i.e., outside of the classroom).

Therapeutic supports provide numerous benefits for students on the spectrum. Each addresses specific areas of challenge that need the more intensive guidance that can be provided by a specialist. It's important to remember that the challenges your students face in these areas may not be readily apparent to you. Students who speak and articulate beautifully may still require intensive speech and language therapy to help them with pragmatics—i.e., the social use of language (as described in Chapter 9). Students who seem perfectly capable with both fine and gross motor skills may need intensive occupational therapy to help with sensory discrimination or visual tracking issues (as described in Chapter 4).

Even though having students and/or specialists coming and going in your classroom throughout the day poses a disruption for you, the skills they work on in those sessions are vital to students' overall functioning.

Historically, most of these sessions have been provided in small offices, outside the classroom, where students benefit from individual or very-small-group attention and the work is highly focused. An added benefit of pull-out services for students in inclusive classrooms is that the quiet, small-group setting serves as a respite from the challenges of the larger, louder environment of the inclusive classroom. In this sense, pull-out therapeutic services can be very grounding and comforting for some students.

Over time, however, educators have noted that since students on the autism spectrum have difficulty generalizing information, the skills learned in therapeutic environments were not necessarily being transferred to the classroom or elsewhere.

Another difficulty that emerges around pull-out services is missed class time. When students are pulled out, they may miss important or fun goings-on in the classroom. Teachers are forced to either plan around these scheduled appointments or help these already-struggling learners catch up on what they miss. Therapists can seem rigid about pulling out a student, even when it's a bad time for you, but remember, they have mandates to meet. And if they are collecting students from other classes at the same time, they cannot push in or change their schedules on an impromptu basis.

In recent years, more and more districts have been moving toward push-in models. When students have the opportunity to work on their social skills, motor skills, sensory responses, mood regulation, and so on *within their natural environment*, new skills are assimilated in more meaningful and broadly applicable ways. This kind of learning is highly beneficial for students on the spectrum.

Another benefit of the push-in model is that both you and the therapist have access to each other's language use, coding, and prompts. The therapist can see that when you say *Think again*, Jeremy understands that he's on the wrong track. You can see that when the therapist says *Read the room*, Miriam has learned that this means her behavior is poorly suited to the situation. When you and the therapists use *consistent language* across contexts for prompts and reinforcements, the development and generalization of skills grows exponentially.

An ideal scenario, when possible, may be one in which a student has a particular service mandated at least twice per week, and sessions are divided between pull-out and push-in models. First, the therapist pulls a student out to teach a new skill in a very focused and directed way. Then, the next day or later in the week, the therapist pushes in to help the student apply that new skill in the natural environment, facilitating that all-important generalization piece. This approach also cuts missed class time in half.

To further enhance the effectiveness of therapeutic supports, remember to include all therapeutic providers in team meetings or other discussions about the students you share. Pool your knowledge and everyone benefits.

Special Area Teachers

Special area teachers are in a uniquely challenging position. Like you, they may not be specifically trained in the intricacies of special education. However, unlike you, they rarely get specific support or operating instructions when students with special needs arrive in their classrooms. In many cases, special area teachers are not provided copies of IEPs; nor are they briefed on students' challenges, triggers, unique needs, or special learning styles. Worse, when they go to art, music, library, or phys ed, elementary students are outside of their comfort zone (your classroom). Their transitional anxiety is elevated, so their functioning may be compromised even before they walk in the door.

And if that's not difficult enough, let's take a moment to consider the significant challenges embedded in the special areas.

Sensory challenges can be extreme. In music, symphonies and jazz riffs may feel like cacophonously screeching tires to students on the spectrum. Bongos and tambourines may make their heads throb. In art, there are tactile challenges (immersing hands in clay or fingerpaint or papier maché) and olfactory challenges (paints, magic markers, pottery dust). In phys ed, the sounds of bouncing balls, cheering children, and skidding sneakers reverberate across the cavernous space. Plus, students' comfort with proprioceptive and vestibular activities are regularly put to the test. And in library, the sudden and extreme shift to near-silence can feel overwhelming. (See more about sensory issues and shifting gears in Chapter 4.)

And common to all of these special areas is an expectation of group work. Whether it's called a *collaboration* in art class, an *ensemble* in music class, a *reading group* in library, or a *team* in phys ed, collegial social and learning skills are assumed and expected, but pose a tremendous obstacle for students on the spectrum.

You may be very eager for a well-earned break from your students on the spectrum while they are in their special area classes. But if you don't take a little time to ease their transition and pass along a few tips to their special area teachers, you'll receive much more stressed and stressful students back afterwards. Here are some simple ways you can help:

✱ **The Gift of a Visual Schedule:** While you're printing out icons for your students' visual schedules, print out an assortment related to art, music, and phys ed. Pass these icons along to the special area teachers, and let the teachers know how to use them and how helpful they are for your students on the spectrum. Truly a gift that keeps on giving.

✱ **Send a Care Package:** If you think it would be helpful, send your students on the spectrum off to their specials with a transitional object or comfort anchor. If they don't have such an object that they bring from home, find something from the classroom that is specifically comforting for them. Be sure to let the special area teacher know that yes, you are aware that it's hard to sculpt a clay pot with an Obi-Wan Kenobi figure clutched in one hand. Go on to explain that this student needs the Force of Obi to be with him, or else the clay pot wouldn't be possible at all.

✱ **Don't Be Stingy With the Wisdom:** If you know the kinds of situations or activities that are triggers for your students, please: Pass that knowledge along! If you know exactly what will happen if Rhenecia is seated next to Elias, raise a red flag.

✱ **Provide a Cheat Sheet:** On pages 227–228 of this book you will find a reproducible autism fact sheet, created specifically for art, music, and library teachers and another just for phys ed teachers and coaches on pages 229–230. Do your colleagues and yourself a favor: Copy them, add your student-specific tips on the blank lines at the end, and hand it out. Done, done, and done.

Building and Bus Staff

Your students on the spectrum interact with many staff members around the building outside of your classroom. Their contact with secretaries, custodians, bus drivers, hall monitors, cafeteria workers, recess aides, and the school nurse tends to happen during transitional times, so anxiety is up and coping skills are down. The bus, the cafeteria, and the playground are consistently sensory and social nightmares. The custodian may come around only when something highly disconcerting has happened, like a spill or vomit. The nurse is needed only when something is physically amiss, like a fever or a stomachache.

So these staff members may be seeing your students on the spectrum at their absolute worst—and yet typically receive no training to support their interactions with them.

Since we cannot anticipate every single situation or emergency that will arise, the best strategy here for supporting your students around the building is to arm these staff members with some basic information to help them adjust their expectations a bit. Let the custodian

> **Did You Know...**
>
> Students on the spectrum are one-and-a-half times more likely to have sleep problems and at least three times more likely to have stomach afflictions than their typical peers (Polimeni, Richdale, & Francis, 2005; Molloy & Manning-Courtney, 2003).

know why, for example, when she helps your student on the spectrum clean up the juice that spilled all over his pristine lunch, a "Thank you" may not be forthcoming until later. Tell the secretary that a proper "Good morning, Mr. O'Connell" may be low on the student's list of things to remember in order to deliver the attendance sheet. Alert the nurse that just because Katie cannot describe or differentiate whether the discomfort in her throat feels more like scratchy or more like swollen, it does not mean her throat doesn't hurt.

When you can, encourage building and bus staff to be supporters of your students' efforts. Assure them that you are working on manners and self-calming strategies and expressive language skills along with all of the academics you pursue in the classroom. Since these students are so complex and varied in terms of strengths and challenges, try asking building and transportation staff members to refrain from instructing, correcting, and scolding and instead aim for encouraging, supporting, and reassuring—whenever possible.

In a professional development workshop that I provided for bus drivers and other building staff, a man sauntered into the session and introduced himself to me and to the group by announcing, "I'm Frank, and my job is to terrorize small children into behaving on the bus." He was kidding, but only sort of.

A bit later in the session, when I spoke about sensory issues and explained that the bus can be a sensory nightmare for students on the spectrum, he interrupted, challenging me sarcastically: "So what are we supposed to do? Give them *earplugs*?" I immediately responded, "Absolutely! Great idea!" He was completely taken aback and right then I could see something shift in him.

As the session proceeded, his swagger and cavalier attitude gradually dissipated as he learned about the many intense challenges students on the spectrum haul with them onto his bus and everywhere else. At the end of the session he asked me, in front of the whole group, "Hey, is it possible for adults to have autism? Because listening to you, I'm starting to wonder whether I might have it, too. I don't always know the right thing to say or do . . . I always need my coffee cup to sit a certain way in the cup holder . . . and I can't stand it when my bus is too loud."

I was certainly not in a position to offer this man a diagnosis. But I am sure that, at the very least, the session had raised his awareness about a whole spectrum of issues and behaviors he had already been in contact with every day. It provided him with the notion that a little help and support can go a long way, and had even opened him up to some powerful self-reflection. I'd say that was a good day's work: enlightenment for him, gratification for me, and a kinder, gentler bus ride for a whole bunch of students.

Provide a Cheat Sheet

On pages 231–232, you will find a reproducible autism fact sheet, created specifically for building and bus staff. Add some student-specific tips about your students on the blank lines at the end, and pass it on.

Take It to the Next Level

Since inclusion really includes not only all students but all faculty, staff, and administrators in the building too, the best outcomes for students are often seen when the entire school community comes together. In addition to the ways described in this chapter, many schools schedule multidisciplinary inclusion brainstorming sessions; community awareness activities; panel discussions with experts, family members, and even students; trainings for classroom paraprofessionals, building staff, and transportation staff; and professional development for special area teachers—and for you, too! As you collaborate with others in your building on behalf of your students, consider suggesting autism in-service trainings for *everyone* from parents to crossing guards to the superintendent. You are in the perfect position to be a voice for your students, to be their champion, and to spread understanding around the school.

●　●　●　●

As you develop reciprocal and collaborative relationships with parents and caregivers and with your professional colleagues, the effort to bring all hands on deck continues within your classroom. You have students who learn and function in ways that may be radically different from others. The next chapter describes the social challenges that confront *all* students in an inclusive class, and guides you to coax a cohesive classroom community from a collection of very diverse participants.

Chapter 8

Something for Everyone

Socialization and Self-Esteem

The most compelling reason for placing students on the autism spectrum in inclusive classrooms is so that they can benefit from the social examples of typically functioning peers. The presumption is that by immersing them in a typical social environment they will absorb social savvy and emerge, well, *socialized*. However, social skill instruction is not commonly part of classroom curriculum. Instead, this hypothetical social awakening is often expected to happen by osmosis.

But students on the autism spectrum do not learn by osmosis. Unless new ways of functioning are specifically taught and reinforced, new skills will not spontaneously develop. Instead, students may go on carrying years of hurt and rejection, vestiges of failed social interactions from which they have learned nothing. These painful experiences chip away at students' self-esteem, leaving them less and less likely to risk venturing into the social world. The more they turn inward to avoid social rejection, the less practice they get interacting. And soon, what were already compromised social instincts have turned into rusty, clumsy efforts to be part of the social world. Some students stop trying altogether.

The No Child Left Behind Act left lots of children behind in terms of socialization. Enter the Every Student Succeeds Act (ESSA)! And what innovative standards does ESSA bestow upon us when it comes to socialization? None. Social skills are still not taught or standardized as a part of college and career readiness, so students on the spectrum are still being left behind and, worse, left out.

Your creation and maintenance of a differentiated, supportive, and instructive social environment in your classroom can break the painful cycle of rejection and withdrawal. Before your students on the spectrum will be able or even willing to risk social participation, they will need to know that you believe in them. They'll need to know that you *get* them, that you will help them through difficult moments with patience and understanding. They'll need you to model optimism, acceptance, and forgiveness. The safer the environment feels and the more positive experiences you create, the more motivated your students will be to risk social encounters.

Circuit Safety

In *Look Me in the Eye* (2007), his memoir about growing up on the autism spectrum, John Elder Robison describes the strain of socialization as compared to the safety of his favored private world: electrical circuitry. He recounts, "I got along well with my circuits, and they never ridiculed me. They presented me with tough problems to solve, but they were never mean. [Interacting with people forced me to move] farther away from the world of machines and circuits—a comfortable world of muted colors, soft light, and mechanical perfection—and closer to the anxiety-filled, bright, and disorderly world of people" (p. 210).

This chapter will show you how to teach and reinforce rote social skills in order to bolster self-esteem and arm your students on the spectrum with tools to bring to the social scene. You'll learn to support social thinking, scaffolding all the way, in order to encourage social savvy. And you'll find strategies to create a caring and accepting classroom community that will spark all kinds of *social* circuits.

The Hidden Social Curriculum

The terms *social skills* and *social interaction* refer not only to casual chatting and socializing; they also refer to social behavior, which is behavior that meets with conventional approval. Social behaviors at school include:

- following the rules of the classroom and other environments
- respecting the rights, space, and belongings of others
- responding to varied situations with flexibility
- acting in consideration of the feelings of others

All of these skills are necessary parts of effective functioning in a social world.

The unspoken messages of social interaction have been described as a *hidden curriculum*. In every aspect of life, students are expected to know or intuit "appropriate" behaviors without being taught what they are. Every context has its own set of unspoken expectations. For example, the specific demeanor that students use with the principal is not necessary or appropriate to use with peers—and *vice versa*. *Good behavior* in the gym is completely different from *good behavior* in the library. What's right in one place can be very wrong in another.

Gaps in intuition often cause important chunks of information to be missed by students on the spectrum. Eight-year-old Max was taught the rules of the playground at his new school. He was told, *Take turns on the equipment, no cutting lines, and no jumping off the top of the slide.* It didn't occur to anyone that Max would need to be *taught* that walking in front of a moving swing would be dangerous, or that when an out-of-bounds kickball rolls near him, he can't just pick it up and walk off with it. Those matters of inferred sensibility are part of the hidden curriculum.

Other aspects of hidden curriculum vary from moment to moment. Although five minutes ago you were available to listen attentively to Candace's detailed description of her favorite movie, now that the hamster has gotten out of its cage and is headed for the classroom door, you are no longer available to listen. This turn of events has not been scripted for Candace, so the changed expectation for her behavior is not apparent to her. She rigidly clings to her role as speaker and sees no reason to stop talking.

Absent are these students' abilities to read nonverbal social cues in others, such as facial expressions and body language, as well as gestures, tone, and emotion. And, accordingly, absent is a sense of how others will interpret *their* words or actions when they walk away in the middle of a conversation or laugh when someone gets hurt. (See more on interpreting nonverbal and paraverbal communication in Chapter 9.)

Given their challenges in the areas of engagement, emotional regulation, flexibility, and communication, the constantly changing social landscape is a minefield to students on the spectrum. Teachers often assume that students are being oppositional when they do not perform social or behavioral skills that seem age appropriate or that they have been taught before. But students on the spectrum need social behavior to be specifically taught and retaught many times before it sinks in.

Teaching the Hidden Curriculum by Rote

At the beginning of the school year, you probably review rules with your class. You support compliance with these rules by discussing them with the class, exploring their implications and applications, and displaying them for easy and frequent reference.

For students on the spectrum, social expectations must be taught much the same way. Social rules must be broken down into specific components, then prompted, rehearsed, and memorized.

Alone Together

During the preschool and early elementary years, typical peer interaction is in the realm of parallel play; that is, students play alongside each other without necessarily communicating or collaborating. As typically developing students move through the elementary and into the secondary years, communication becomes more reciprocal and sophisticated. Conversation becomes layered with implication and innuendo.

While peer socialization becomes increasingly nuanced and abstract, students on the spectrum remain rigid and grounded in concrete. They find no way to neatly apply a rigid rubric to the unpredictable twists and turns of socialization. Conversations among typically functioning students veer off on inexplicable tangents. Tones shift from sincere to sarcastic to sardonic and back with no prompts, no visual cues, no graphic organizers. Peer relationships change from day to day, moment to moment. Interactive play meanders freely through the wild fields of peers' imaginations, allowing a block to become a boat, a castle, an alien, a bird. But for students on the spectrum, whose thinking is grounded in the concrete, a block is a block is a block. (See more on conversational challenges in Chapter 9.)

✲ Script It: Before students on the spectrum enter a social situation, try to brief them as to what they should expect and what social behaviors you expect from them. Whether they need help joining in on activities with peers, participating in a group project, or passing out the graduated cylinders, lay out expected social behaviors.

You might ask the school counselor, resource room teacher, or speech and language specialist to write a Social Story. First developed by educator Carol Gray, Social Stories are short, highly individualized, fact-based stories that guide students through specific challenging social situations, such as waiting in line, doing homework, staying calm, taking turns, and many others. Gray has created a specific formula for writing these stories that includes starting with the student's perspective, expanding to include other perspectives, and leading to a positive outcome. Social Stories vary in style and content according to a student's age, functioning style, and specific reaction to a given event, so they are most successful when written with a particular student in mind.

These stories can be written for—or with—students who need them. They can be posted in the classroom, stored in individuals' desks or in designated folders, copied and sent home, reviewed every day, or consulted as needed. A Social Story might look like this:

Going to an Assembly

When I go to an assembly, I always want to dance or sing along with the music.

Lots of kids like to dance and sing.

Some assemblies are noisy, and it's okay for kids to dance and sing along.

Some assemblies are quiet, and kids need to be quiet.

When the other kids in the audience are being quiet, I need to be quiet, too.

At quiet assemblies, I will try to sit still and keep my mouth closed.

When the other kids start clapping, I can clap, too.

✲ Unpack Innuendo: Deconstruct social rules, even the ones you've never consciously considered; discuss them with your students on the spectrum and check for understanding. If your student is having trouble sitting quietly, unpack what sitting quietly means. Show him a photo of what "sitting quietly" looks like and explain, *Sitting quietly means mouths closed, hands and feet still. No clapping, stomping, talking, or any other noise until the show is over. Can you show me how you will sit quietly?*

✲ Drill Social Skill: Review social rules the way you might drill the multiplication tables. New behaviors can become learned responses, such that when you give the prompt, *Georgie,* *what will you do when you are at the assembly?* Georgie will learn to respond instantly, *Sit quietly.*

✱ **Create Social Contracts:** Make individualized contracts with students as needed, modifying or adding new goals as targeted skills become assimilated. Here's an example:

Dana's Friendship Contract

If someone drops a pencil near me, I will pick it up and return it to the person who dropped it.

When someone near me is working, I will stay quiet.

When people say hello to me, I will look at them and say hello.

Ensure that each term used in the contract is understood by the student. Discuss how Dana can recognize what someone working looks like. Be sure she has learned specifically what *stay quiet* means. If not, those details should be broken down further in the contract. Alternatively, depending on each student's favored learning style, you may choose to present these goals in tactile, photographic, pictorial, or digital form, and reinforce them with verbal reminders.

Prompt students to review their social rules periodically or just before embarking on interactive tasks. Revisit them together often.

Social Stories: There's an App for That!

Digital Social Stories make for concrete and compelling teachable opportunities. Social Story apps allow you to add photos, videos, and voice recordings, inviting students to realistically see themselves in the described situations. As of this writing, popular Social Story apps include *StoryMaker for Social Stories* by *HandHold Adaptive* (created in consultation with Carol Gray) and *Pictello* by AssistiveWare. New apps are being created all the time. Search for "Social Stories" in your app store. You're sure to find an app for that.

Social Thinking: Variations on a Theme

The strategies discussed so far in this chapter teach students rote responses in scripted situations. With adequate practice, these skills alone can give students quite a leg up. Rote memorization will help them through the precise situations you have scripted. So, the next time someone drops a pencil near her, there's a good chance Dana will pick it up and return it to its owner.

But you will need to teach the generalization of these skills as well, because your concrete, rigid students on the spectrum will not generalize them spontaneously. When a pen instead of a pencil drops near Dana—forget it. When it's a paper clip—no chance.

Taking social know-how one step further means being able to generalize and apply those rote skills flexibly, across a variety of situations that may not have not been specifically scripted. That is *social thinking*, a much more complex skill that often requires taking the perspective of others.

A Theory of Social Relativity

Dana's teacher tried to facilitate rule generalization and empathic understanding by teaching Dana an axiom: *Dana, your classmates are your friends. Friends help each other out.* Dana listened, but then, after some consideration, responded, *Why?*

Difficulty taking someone else's perspective may be the single greatest impediment to students' successful social interaction. Many of the same challenges that keep students disengaged are the ones that render them socially inept.

Why Should I?

Students on the spectrum may need immediate incentives to boost their motivation to participate socially. Of course, the ultimate motivator for pro-social interaction is that it fosters good feeling between people. But that concept requires abstract social thinking and your students may not have access to that. (See Teaching Social Thinking, below.) For now, these students need to learn to comply with their social contract simply because that is your classroom rule. Remember that most students on the spectrum welcome rules and structure—as long as you ensure that the rules are unequivocally clear to them.

Mindblindness

The ability to understand that another person's internal experience is different from one's own is called *theory of mind*, or, more familiarly, mind-reading. A deficit in this area is called *mindblindness*. Students with mindblindness are unable to decode how the actions or demeanor of other people reflect their respective states of mind (Baron-Cohen, 1995, 2001). This significant interpersonal gap restricts students' abilities to interpret other people's perspectives and accounts for the inscrutable nature of the hidden curriculum.

For example, although Carolena is doubled over, having a coughing fit to the point that her eyes are watering, Wesley insistently repeats his question about whether she likes to play Frisbee: *Do you, Carolena? Do you?* **Do you?**

Can You Feel What I Feel?

In addition to mindblindness, students on the spectrum also struggle with joint attention (as described in Chapters 5 and 9) and executive function (as described in Chapter 4). Together, these challenges render students on the spectrum quite limited in their ability to understand others and respond in socially expected ways.

In ideal circumstances, these skills all add up to a kind of theory of social relativity; that is, the recognition that every individual's actions and reactions are relative to his or her own experience. But students on the spectrum, who lack these skills, are often seen as rude, selfish, inconsiderate, or stupid.

Tony Attwood (2009) points out that students on the spectrum tend to notice and understand objects and facts more than they do thoughts, feelings, and intentions. They can be highly observant when it comes to certain aspects of their environment while simultaneously oblivious to others. For example, a student on the spectrum is likely to notice a single book out of place on the bookshelf. But that same student won't notice the cries of the classmate whose fingers she steps on while going to reshelve that book.

Stay Where You Can See Me

When outside or on a field trip, teachers often tell students, *Stay where I can see you*. This is actually a very challenging instruction for students with mindblindness, as it requires them to adopt your personal and visual perspective. How can they know what *you* can see?

Much clearer for all students and more effective, too, is this directive: *Stay where you can see me*.

Honesty: Such a Lonely Word

Students on the autism spectrum very rarely lie or use manipulation or guile. With their rigid adherence to rules, limited capacity to take another's perspective, and minimal awareness of social pressure or expectation, they are likely to answer questions directly.

This unmitigated honesty does not tend to curry social favor with peers. When seven-year-old Simon is asked by a classmate if he likes her shirt, he quickly responds, *No. I hate green. It's gross.*

When twelve-year-old Yi Chen is asked to walk Joel to the nurse to get an icepack, she declines: *No. I didn't hurt him, and I'd rather go to band.*

The nuanced skills of *being polite, telling part of the truth,* and *being a friend* require social thinking skills, mind-reading, and the flexibility to bend the rules of honesty just a bit now and then. But by teaching rules and algorithms, social thinking can develop, and even the nuances of honesty can be taught.

Teaching Social Thinking

Given these profound gaps in social understanding, it is easy to see why students on the spectrum are commonly thought to lack empathy. Their apparent disregard for the feelings of others implies a lack of caring. But the little-known fact is that students on the spectrum often care very deeply for and about others. The problem is not that they don't have empathy. It's that often *they cannot read the signals* of another person's distress. And, even when they can read the signals, they do not necessarily know how to respond.

A spontaneous recognition of the feelings of others may never happen organically for students on the spectrum. But they can learn to *think* their way through to what someone else might be feeling, using context clues and other cognitive strategies. And they can learn to respond in generous and suitable ways, using memorization and debriefing. If you want to encourage social thinking and the generalization of skills toward empathic behavior, here are some strategies to try:

✱ **Reach for Reciprocity:** When appropriate, try joining students where they are and expand from there. If a student's preferred topic of interest is guitars, join him in a lively discussion of guitars. But throughout the discussion, prompt him to interact with you and respond to your contributions to the discussion. Prompt him to ask you questions about guitars and to listen and respond thoughtfully to your answers. Ask him questions that are related to guitars but that encourage him to stretch slightly off subject: *What other kinds of instruments are there? How are they similar to guitars? How are they different? What do you like better about guitars? What might be better about the others?*

✱ **Role-Play:** Give students the opportunity to role-play problematic interactions by setting up groups of students to practice these skills together. Play out real situations that went badly and then try practicing them in better ways. Challenge students to try portraying each character in a scene and debrief every time: *How did you feel when you were the one who got left out? How did you feel when you were leaving someone else out?*

✱ **Study Facial Expressions:** Much of the hidden curriculum is encrypted in the facial expressions of others. Spend time studying facial expressions with students.

- Most educational supply catalogs, stores, and websites sell emotion posters that show photographic faces revealing various labeled expressions. These posters are perfect for students on the spectrum who cannot interpret facial cues and may not even realize that facial expressions carry meaning. Have a mirror on hand and challenge students to try to match their own facial expressions to those on the poster.

- Play feelings charades, in which students act out emotions and peers have to guess what they're feeling.

- Take photographs of students' facial expressions and create a matching game with the photos.

✱ Practice Body Language: In addition to facial expressions, consider the many signals that we use subconsciously throughout the day that pose challenges to students. Students can memorize nonverbal communications and attribute generalized meaning to them. Teach them what shrugged shoulders mean. Teach them the difference between a head shaking horizontally (*No*) and a head nodding vertically (*Yes*). Teach them what *thumbs-up* means, what breathlessness implies, what *busy* looks like. (See Chapter 9 for more about nonverbal and paraverbal communication.)

> ## Social Interaction: There's an App for That!
>
> Many apps help students learn interactive strategies and skills, including how to recognize and interpret intonation, facial expressions, body language, and the perspectives of others, and how to initiate conversations.
>
> As of this writing, popular apps for these purposes include *Between the Lines* by Hamaguchi Apps; *Social Skill Builder: My School Day* by Social Skill Builder, Inc.; *Model Me Going Places, Model Me Conversation Cues,* and *Model Me Friendships* by Model Me Kids, LLC; *Conversation Builder* by Mobile Education Store LLC; and *The Social Express II* by The Social Express. New apps are being created all the time. Search for "social skill development" and "conversation starters" in your app store. You're sure to find an app for that.

Debriefing

When a student on the spectrum is involved in a troublesome social situation, always debrief it with the student afterward. Since students on the spectrum will not spontaneously reflect upon or learn from their mistakes and missteps, the effect of their behaviors on others needs to be made overt, and a replacement behavior or reaction must be developed. Consider this example as a guide for debriefing challenging behavior with students on the spectrum.

> **Scenario:**
> Jamal was removed from the lunchroom by an aide for shoving his sandwich in Chandra's face.

1. **Listen:** Simply doling out consequences for their misdeeds will neither help students on the spectrum learn what they did wrong nor will it change their behavior in the future. Instead, educate yourself about the situation so that you can educate the student about

what went wrong. Ask neutral questions that show that your mind is open to your student's interpretation of what happened.

> Jamal's teacher, Oscar, recognizes that chastising Jamal for his misdeed will close the door on a teachable moment. So instead of approaching with anger, Oscar asks Jamal a question calmly and openly: **What happened in the lunchroom?**
>
> Jamal responds, *Chandra said she was still hungry. I was giving her some of my lunch.*

What had been seen as a hostile or aggressive act is now revealed to have been an extremely empathic and generous act, only very poorly executed.

2. **Mirror:** By mirroring students' words back to them, you demonstrate that you are listening and that they have been heard.

> Oscar tells Jamal, *You wanted to give Chandra food because she said she was still hungry.*
>
> Jamal, who has no idea why he's gotten in trouble for his actions, now knows he has been understood and can let down his guard a bit.

3. **Acknowledge Intentions:** The good intentions of students on the spectrum often lead to bad outcomes. Because they don't know how best to respond to a situation, their good intentions may go unnoticed, misconstrued, or even negatively reinforced. Look for opportunities to positively reinforce good intentions.

> Oscar recognizes this as a golden opportunity to grab hold of a terrific social instinct gone awry and reframe it as a strength. He tells Jamal, *You wanted to be helpful because Chandra is your friend. Good idea!*

4. **Introduce Another Perspective:** Guide students on the spectrum to put themselves in the shoes of another person. (But don't use those exact words, or you can bet they'll start untying their laces!) This kind of mind-reading will not happen spontaneously, but powerful epiphanies can be realized as you guide students to make the connection between their own feelings and the feelings of others.

Oscar talks to Jamal without accusing him: *Let's see if we can figure out why Chandra got angry. How do you think you would feel if someone suddenly pushed food into your face?*

Because Jamal is now feeling less defensive, he is more open to learning. Oscar helps Jamal understand that because he thrust the sandwich in Chandra's face and didn't use words, Chandra did not recognize that he was trying to be nice.

Oscar goes on to confirm that Jamal understands what the other student might actually have felt in the situation: *Chandra thought you were being mean because you shoved the sandwich right in her face. That didn't feel to her like you were being a friend.*

5. **Reteach:** Once students on the spectrum begin to understand how their actions are perceived, they can begin to explore new approaches. State clearly the new skill that should be generalized from this experience.

Oscar gives Jamal a rule to remember: *Putting food in other people's faces is rude and disrespectful.*

Oscar asks, *How do you think you could do it better next time?* He and Jamal rehearse different ways Jamal could handle that situation in the future, such as holding his food out in a friendly way and accompanying his gesture with words.

Oscar summarizes for Jamal, *So from now on, when you want to share your sandwich, you will hold it near you and ask the other person, "Would you like a piece of my sandwich?"*

6. **Expand:** Students on the spectrum will need to be taught exactly how much to generalize this new skill. Push the boundaries of their rigidity by exploring variations on the situation.

Oscar guides Jamal to apply his new skill to other, slightly different situations: *I think it's great that you like to share with others, Jamal. That's being a good friend. How would you offer to share other things besides your sandwich? How would you offer to share some grapes? How would you share a cookie?*

Over time, as different teachable moments arise, Oscar coaches Jamal to expand the application even more broadly:

- *Would you use the same words if you wanted to share a book?*
- *How would you offer to share a ball?*

- *What would you say if you wanted to share an idea?*
- *What will you do if someone does not want what you are offering to share?*

7. **Make It Meaningful:** Describe what's in it for your students by adopting these new behaviors.

> Oscar encourages Jamal: *Other kids will be happy when you offer to share with them, as long as you offer in a respectful way. Sharing respectfully is a great way to be a friend.*

8. **Practice:** Be prepared to practice and review this new way of thinking many times before it becomes assimilated into daily behavior. Prompt students ahead of time, coach in the moment, and look for opportunities for practice.

> Oscar keeps an eye on Jamal in class, watching for natural opportunities: *Jamal, I see that there are not enough markers at Table 4. Why don't you respectfully offer to share some of your markers, using the skills we talked about?*

In the context of your busy classroom, and given varied communication skills among students, social learning will rarely proceed as systematically as it does in this example, but keep these elements in mind as a framework to guide and inform your social interventions. In this case, a situation that would have left Jamal reprimanded, confused, and patently rejected, instead has now provided him with praise, support, and a way to act on his empathic inclination to be a friend.

Simply Sympathize

Listen carefully and without judgment. A student's experience is his experience. You cannot begin to know what it feels like for him to be at the mercy of his impulses, sensory reactions, preoccupations, social ineptitude, speech limitations, and anxiety. So if he was devastated by the fact that the pizza was rectangular today instead of triangular, then so it is. Don't disparage his distress as nonsense, because it's not. It's unbearable to him and is therefore a real force affecting your classroom community.

You don't have to empathize—chances are, you won't feel his pain. But try to sympathize with the fact that a situation is deeply meaningful to him and move forward from there.

Socialization: A Two-Way Street

While students on the spectrum struggle to make sense of their peers, their peers certainly struggle to make sense of them. Collaborative work and play require flexibility, spontaneity, sharing, turn-taking, patience, inferential thinking, and more—each of which poses another challenge to students on the spectrum as they try to apply rules and systems to this frenetic, improvisational dance.

When rules fail, these students may dig in their heels, wander away mid-conversation or mid-activity, refuse to take turns, misinterpret information, change topics abruptly, interrupt, fall behind, overreact, underreact, resort to aggression or destruction, or slip into perseverative behaviors such as rocking, chirping, grunting, or using repetitive phrases. Or they may try to insist that others conform to their own sets of rigid rules.

The alternately inscrutable, unavailable, and exasperating social operating systems of students on the spectrum require more patience and forgiveness than typically functioning peers may be prepared to give. It takes work to befriend these students. Typical peers need to go *much more than halfway* to make a connection, which many peers are unwilling or unable to do.

Meanwhile, for better and for worse, many children on the spectrum develop some insight on their limitations. During the later elementary years and beyond, they may begin to notice that they do not fit in. They don't get invited to parties. They are not part of the "jockocracy" that rules the playground. They feel the sting of children laughing at them—even if they have no idea how to respond. They know they are missing cues, missing social rules, missing the joke, missing something. They just don't know what to do differently. And often their attempts to make a situation better only make it much worse.

For example, in his memoir, John Elder Robison recalls his efforts to make friends:

> *At recess, I walked over to Chuckie and patted her on the head. My mother had shown me how to pet my poodle on the head to make friends with him. And my mother petted me sometimes, too, especially when I couldn't sleep. So as far as I could tell, petting worked. All the dogs my mother had told me to pet had wagged their tails. They liked it. I figured Chuckie would like it, too. . . . It never occurred to me that Chuckie might not respond to petting in the same way a dog would. The difference between a small person and a medium-sized dog was not really clear to me.*
>
> Smack! *She hit me!*
>
> *Startled, I ran away.* That didn't work, *I said to myself.* Maybe I have to pet her a little longer to make friends. I can pet her with a stick so she can't smack me. *But the teacher intervened.*
>
> *The worst of it was, my teachers and most other people saw my behavior as bad when I was actually trying to be kind. My good intentions made the rejection by Chuckie all the more painful . . . I never interacted with Chuckie again. I stopped trying with any of the kids. The more I was rejected, the more I hurt inside and the more I retreated (2007, p. 9).*

You Can't Unring a Bell

The lasting effects of disrespectful actions and disregarded feelings may be rather abstract concepts for some students on the spectrum to fully grasp. They may believe that once they apologize, all prior offenses are both forgiven and forgotten. After social missteps, my son is fond of saying, "Let's all just pretend that never happened." But, for the sake of their peers, students on the spectrum need to recognize the cumulative or lasting toll their repeated behaviors may take on others.

Try this concrete activity to help them understand. Give your student on the spectrum a fresh piece of plain looseleaf or printer paper. Prompt her to note how clean, clear, and smooth it is. Now have the student crumple it tightly into a ball in her hand. Explain that crumpling the paper is like disrespecting someone's belongings or hurting their feelings.

Now prompt the student to make it better. Encourage her to smooth out the paper; to try to get it back to the way it was before. Point out that even though the paper may be flattened out a bit now and even usable again, it's not the same as it was before.

Use this paper exercise as a metaphor to bring home that every time we put someone down or damage their work, we are hurting them in a way that we can't entirely take away. We can smooth things over by helping to fix the problem or by offering nice things, but the relationship isn't smooth anymore. Ultimately, the lesson is: Let's all try to make sure this doesn't happen again. (See Perseveration Exasperation on page 163.)

The next section will show you how to bring all of your students closer together by drawing both ends toward the middle: bolstering skills and confidence at one end and raising consciousness at the other.

Building a Classroom Community

Typically functioning students have enormous potential to influence the lives of their peers on the spectrum. They have the potential to be friends, supporters, and champions, or bullies, provocateurs, and antagonizers. They learn, from lessons and by example, to celebrate differences and stand up for what's right or to smirk and look the other way. Harness the potential for peers to develop and practice new attitudes about kids who are different from themselves. Help them respect and appreciate the strengths of their classmates on the autism spectrum.

Kathleen Seidel, a disability rights advocate and parent of a child with ASD, draws this analogy: "A Cray supercomputer is used for really complex, intense computing that involves the manipulation of massive amounts of data. It runs so hot it has to be kept in a liquid cooling bath. It requires a very special kind of TLC. And is the Cray defective because it requires this kind of nurturing environment for its functioning? No! It kicks ass! That's what my kid is like. He needs support, needs attention, and is amazing" (Solomon, 2013).

Your example and your efforts can imbue your typical students with generosity of spirit and empower them to become conscientious citizens throughout their lives.

Tapping Peer Potential

In younger elementary classes, students are likely to be kind to each other because you tell them to be, because being kind is *cool*. These are the rules of school and friendship, and the platitude *In this class, we are all friends* still has some traction.

But in the upper elementary and secondary grades, students begin to notice differences more, and gaps in development may become more glaring. Students begin to branch off into groups of friends with common interests and reject others.

By utilizing some of the affirming activities suggested below, you can ensure an *It's cool to be kind* dynamic in and beyond your classroom.

> "In elementary school, it's 'cool' to be kind. In middle school, it's 'cool' to be cruel."
>
> —Tony Attwood (2009)

Setting a Tone: Creating a Classroom With a Conscience

From Day One, your open acknowledgment and acceptance of differences will help set the tone for the year. As you demonstrate the importance and relevance of acceptance, be sure to weave all kinds of diversity into your curriculum. This means expanding beyond differences of race, to include culture, class, religion, gender and sexual orientation and identification, ability, and more. Being in an inclusive class provides all of your students lifelong lessons in understanding, empathy, and community consciousness.

Models of Courage

Back up your inclusive words by filling your classroom library with biographies of people who exemplify courage in the face of discrimination, such as Malala Yousefzai, Ruby Bridges, Jackie Robinson, Anne Frank, Billie Jean King, Susan B. Anthony, and Cesar Chavez. Include biographies about individuals who have triumphed over physical challenges, such as Bethany Hamilton, Helen Keller, Stevie Wonder, and Franklin Delano Roosevelt.

Different Like Me: My Book of Autism Heroes by Jennifer Elder offers brief biographies of influential people who showed signs of Autism Spectrum Disorder, including Albert Einstein, Thomas Edison, Lewis Carroll, Hans Christian Andersen, and many others.

Choose books to read in class that happen to feature characters who are different, such as the Joey Pigza books by Jack Gantos, which feature a feisty protagonist who has ADHD; *Out of My Mind* by Sharon Draper, which features a brilliant protagonist with severe cerebral palsy; and *Wonder* by R.J. Palacio, which features a determined protagonist who has a facial deformity. (Please visit my website, www.barbaraboroson.com, for a list of recommended books, organized by theme and reading level, all of which send quiet messages of inclusivity and acceptance.)

Affirm Acceptance

Where does intolerance begin? Try to raise awareness of social injustice among your students. Is it right to treat people differently because of the way they look, act, or learn? Try to ground these concepts by encouraging students to look around themselves. Who is being treated unfairly because they are different? How do we feel about that?

Since the goal is to move beyond tolerance toward actual acceptance, we need to incorporate meaningful explorations of differentness into the general curriculum. Celebrate diversity at all grade levels.

✱ **Grades K–1:** Use basic lessons of *same and different* to expand into conceptual differences such as religion, race, and ability. For example: *Everyone has different abilities. What activities come easily to you? What do you find more difficult?*

✱ **Grades 2–4:** Connect conversations about differences to intolerance and bullying: *What is bullying all about? Why do some kids bully? Why do some kids get bullied? What can you do about it?*

✱ **Grades 5–8:** Use the social studies curriculum to connect historical examples of persecution to discussions of diversity and discrimination, courage, and acceptance. *Have you ever felt you were being discriminated against? Has anyone in your family ever suffered discrimination? Have you ever judged anyone on the basis of what he or she looks like without knowing who the person is on the inside?*

Encourage "Goodmouthing"

Since the spontaneous social efforts of students on the spectrum may be clumsy at best and disruptive, intrusive, provocative, or destructive at worst, all members of your classroom community may need incentives to work cooperatively and gently together.

Rules of Comedy

Jed Baker (2009), an expert on social skills training, synthesizes the nuances of humor into clear rules. His list is a useful guide for all students, so you may want to post it in the classroom.

- It's never okay to make fun of the vulnerable: many jokes are put-downs. But putting down someone who is already struggling is not funny—it's just plain mean.

- Blurting out random thoughts is not funny. And those impulsive comments are often the ones that get you in trouble.

- Making fun of yourself is never okay.

Chapter 8: Something for Everyone: Socialization and Self-Esteem

✱ **Modified Marble Jar:** At the elementary level, try modifying the classic Marble Jar system. Instead of awarding marbles for following classroom rules, use them to reinforce acts of kindness and inclusiveness. Add a marble whenever you catch a student being a good friend and reward the class when the jar gets full. Prompt students about what *being a good friend* looks like; for example, offering to help someone clean up a mess, taking turns, using kind words, including others in their play, and so on.

✱ **Put Down Put-Downs:** Have a class discussion, at all grade levels, about what put-downs are and how they make us feel. Many times students do not realize that what they think they are saying only in fun really cuts to the quick. Let all students know that teasing is *never* funny and that saying, "I was just kidding" afterwards—or "No offense, but" beforehand—does not erase hurtful words. In an inclusive class, it is vitally important to make your classroom a *Put-Down-Free Zone.*

✱ **Put Up "Put-Ups":** As opposed to put-downs, "put-ups" are comments that make people feel good about themselves. Elementary classes can brainstorm some great put-ups, then put up a Put-Up Chart. Explore together how put-ups can also be communicated without words: through a smile, a thumbs-up, a high-five, and so on. Feed the Marble Jar when you hear or see spontaneous put-ups. Consider doing a whole-class keepsake holiday project in which your students make Put-Up Books for each other. A week or two before the holidays, give each student a small notebook with his or her name on it. Pass the books around the class so that every student can write a personalized, signed entry into every other student's Put-Up Book, such as: *You're so good at the times table!* or *You have a nice smile!*

When all notebooks have made it around the whole classroom and back to their owners (and you've looked them over for propriety), have every student add a put-up about him- or herself. As important as it is for us to bolster each other, it is equally or more important to affirm ourselves.

✱ **Cultivate Kindness:** In middle school, my daughter launched a Kindness Matters campaign, in which students were given incentives to catch their peers being kind. Kind acts were noted on sticky notes and hung in the school lobby, gracing the school entrance with garlands of kindness.

Out and About

Since students' experiences at school extend well beyond the walls of the classroom, supports must be in place to help them through those times when the structure and predictability you have tried to create within the classroom suddenly vanish and it's every kid for herself. What follows is a description of two of the most socially challenging times: lunch and recess. After that, you'll find suggestions for how your school might create a network of peer support around students who need it. (And be sure to bring lunch and recess aides on board, using the ideas in Chapter 7 and the fact sheets on pages 227–234.)

Love It or Hate It: Lunch and Recess

The time of day that is most anticipated by many students can be the most challenging for students on the spectrum. Nothing at school is as unstructured as recess. The very purpose of recess, for most students, is to grant them a reprieve from structure: *Here's some free time! Get up and go!*

But for students on the spectrum, a break from structure is no reprieve; it's sensory assault and social agony. Lunch and recess tend to be wildly unstructured. There are no assigned seats, no inside voices, no designated partners, no activity schedules, no clear or fixed rules. Carefully calibrated student–teacher ratios evaporate as all kinds of students are thrown together in large numbers. Supervision is usually inadequate. This is prime time for bullies, and your students on the spectrum—with their blatant idiosyncrasies and social naiveté—are especially vulnerable. In the environment where these students commonly need the most support, the least support is provided. These periods are fraught with confusion, hurt feelings, and rejection. Lunch presents all kinds of sensory overload, as described in Chapter 4. And recess is a social free-for-all. It's no wonder that many times students on the spectrum can be found hovering around the periphery during recess, trying to keep away from the hub of noise and chaos, possibly feeling left out, or perhaps relishing the peacefulness of a quiet corner.

Anything Goes

Recess activities are often organized and mediated only by students. While a valuable exercise for some, this dynamic can create a multitude of challenging situations for others—especially for students on the spectrum.

At one school where I consulted, four square was a popular recess game with endless variations. At any given moment, four square might be played according to "Old-School Rules," "New-School Rules," "Regular Rules," even "No Rules." The rules of the game changed constantly—even mid-game. How could a student who relies on the stability of rules play a game in which the "rules" change abruptly or vanish without warning?

Kwan, a fourth grader on the autism spectrum, wanted to participate but struggled to make sense of the game. I created a system for him: If most of the kids in the game and in the line say he's out, he should get out of the game—even if he doesn't agree. But for Kwan, that rule was not specific enough. Since the number of students judging the game could vary, the word *most* was far too abstract: Exactly *how many is most*?

Fortunately, Kwan was able to understand the idea of majority rules. I explained to him that if *more than half* of the kids say he's out, he's out. If *fewer than half* of the kids say he's out, he should stand his ground and state that most of the kids agree with him. If equal numbers disagree, he should request a do-over.

This plan created a rubric of expectations for Kwan. He likes to play the game. He still does not understand the overall rules—who would?—and he doesn't have the flexibility to roll with the changes, but now he has his own set of functional rules, his own local coherence, that he can cling to and apply consistently to an otherwise incomprehensible situation.

Recess Required

Never, ever take away recess.

Some students may need to have recess modified to meet their sensory and social challenges, and that's fine. But if you're tempted to remove recess for behavioral reasons, don't do it! If necessary, take away access to a particular activity at recess (and debrief why the student has temporarily lost that privilege). But never withhold the opportunity to burn off energy. You and that student are guaranteed a rocky afternoon if you do.

Lunch and Recess Strategies

If lunch or recess seems to be a hot spot for your students on the spectrum, take a little time to put a plan like one of these in place during this period.

* **Monitor Monitors:** Have a word with lunch workers and recess monitors. Alert them that certain of your students may need some extra support and ask them to keep an eye out or intervene gently when necessary. If you think they might need some strategies, offer them a copy of the fact sheet for building staff, found on pages 231–232.

* **Push-In Support:** Ask speech and language therapists or occupational therapists if they can schedule push-in sessions with these students during lunchtime or recess. Therapists can use the sessions to set up interactive group games or other activities on the playground. These activities can then be supervised by lunch or recess aides on non-therapy days.

* **Get a Jump on the Lunch Crunch:** If the lunchtime crush is overwhelming, consider allowing your students on the spectrum to go to the lunchroom five minutes before the lunch rush, to avoid the line and find seats in a calm environment.

* **Out of the Fray:** If lunchtime is overstimulating, look for quieter, calmer places for students on the spectrum to eat. If indoor recess is over-crowded and noisy, look for indoor recess alternatives. On indoor recess days, my ten-year-old son had a permanent pass to be a kindergarten helper, where he always felt safe and welcome and had the opportunity to demonstrate his relatively mature, big-kid skills.

Peer Support

Most elementary schools do not offer formal, facilitated social skills groups, but these can be enormously helpful. The school counselor and speech and language specialist might be able to organize a small social skills or social language group or a support network around socially needy students. If you have students on the spectrum who are friend-deprived, here are some avenues you or the therapists in your school may pursue to recruit peers for support.

A Circle of Friends

Ask the school counselor, speech and language specialist, or special education teacher to create a circle of support around students who are socially challenged. As described by special education teacher Mary Schlieder (2007), a Circle of Friends participates in supervised lunch and activity groups with the target student(s) at least once a month, playing games and practicing social skills, such as making conversation and taking turns.

With the consent of the parents or guardians of all students involved, a Circle of Friends works like this:

- Socially savvy students who have interests in common with the target student are invited to be members.

- Circle members must be informed about the social needs of the target student. They are taught that it is their responsibility to respect this student's right to privacy and confidentiality by not confronting him with what they have learned about his specific challenges and by not ever sharing that very personal information with others.

- These structured groups offer students safe opportunities to practice socializing and to feel like a part of something. Moreover, the skills developed and relationships formed during these structured activities tend to carry over beyond lunchtime and recess, creating new circles of friends and supporters for all students involved.

All In

Consider the various potential incarnations of peer support networks:

- Students who may have the potential to be bullies should be considered as peer supporters if they are highly social. The lessons in empathy that develop within this supervised relationship can expand the value of the experience in numerous directions.

- When possible, also invite students who struggle with learning or physical challenges but are socially capable to act as models of social behavior. Imagine the pride they will feel by being hand-picked to be a helper—and the benefits for your students on the spectrum who can help these peers with *their* needs.

- What better put-up can you offer students on the spectrum than an opportunity for them to help or mentor others? Maybe students on the spectrum can turn the jump rope, play catch with the kindergartners during recess, or carry books for a peer with a broken arm. Perhaps they can quiz peers on their multiplication tables or help them locate books on the library shelves.

Look for ways for every student to demonstrate his or her strengths.

Facilitated games can include the following, among many others:

- *Telephone*, which encourages listening, turn-taking, and flexibility
- *Twenty Questions*, which encourages thinking in categories and reasoning
- *I Spy*, which encourages joint attention
- *Charades*, which encourages joint attention and nonverbal communication

A Circle of Friends can also serve as your eyes and ears in the hallway, on the bus, in the cafeteria, or during other times that your student is having a problem or is acting in a way that might get him or her into trouble.

A Smattering of Friends

If your school cannot set up a true Circle of Friends, you can try implementing elements of it, taking whatever proactive steps you can to ensure that all students feel safe and included, even during the less structured, more challenging times of the day.

✱ **Daily Double:** Appoint companions-of-the-day to partner up with specific students for small-group projects, walking in the hall, or any other suitable activities.

✱ **Lunch/Recess Buddies:** Designate student volunteers to seek out any students who are alone. Volunteers can offer to sit with them at lunch and engage or join them in activities on the playground. Give volunteers some strategies to engage reluctant peers. But remind them that even though their identified classmate struggles with challenges, he is still an individual and, like everyone else, has feelings and opinions that must be respected. Despite peers' best efforts, this student may not always be receptive to social overtures. He may prefer to be alone or with someone else sometimes, just as we all do, at times. Teach them to respect his right to make his own choices, and to try again at other times.

Bullying

Students on the spectrum are prime targets for bullying. Their awkward or "clueless" social behaviors leave them vulnerable to teasing, aggression, and rejection. Plus, their limited self-regulation makes them likely to get upset in dramatic ways that are gratifying and encouraging to bullies. Given the many challenging issues in your classroom, it will be important for you to be especially attuned to and proactive about what's going on behind your back and behind the scenes.

Help all students understand exactly what bullying is. Since bullying can take many forms and be quite subtle, keep these three facts in mind as you work to help students on the spectrum recognize what is and is not bullying:

- *Bullying is intentional.* True accidents do not count as examples of bullying. Bullying is done on *purpose* to be mean.
- *Bullying is repeated.* Bullying is a *pattern* of ongoing intimidating or hurtful behavior.

- *Bullying usually includes a power imbalance.* This means that one student is leveraging his or her age, height, strength, popularity, ability, or even racial, religious, or cultural majority status against someone else to gain an advantage. With students on the spectrum, it is frequently social savvy that is leveraged.

Remind students that bullying isn't just the mean things they do; it's also the nice things they never do, like inviting someone to join them instead of letting her sit alone at lunch, or being friendly even to people they are not friends with. "Bullying survivor, expert, and activist" Jodee Blanco calls these subtle rejections acts of "aggressive exclusion," and they can be among the most chronic and insidious examples of bullying (2008).

Battling Bullying

If your students on the spectrum are being bullied, offer them concrete strategies they can access when necessary. Teach them the following:

✽ **Steer Clear:** *Steer clear of kids who bully.* Make this point specifically; students on the spectrum may not intuit that proximity increases the likelihood of negative interactions.

✽ **Stay in View:** *Stay where you can see an adult at lunch, recess, or anytime you feel at-risk. Or find a buddy to stick with during these times.* Support students in this effort by recruiting peer buddies, as described in Peer Support beginning on page 159.

✽ **Look Brave:** *When you do have an interaction with a bully, try to look brave, even if you don't feel brave. Being brave looks like standing tall and staying calm. Save your upset feelings inside until later and then speak to an adult privately about them.*

✽ **Think Proud:** *Find ways to feel good about yourself. Focus on what is special and wonderful about you. What are you an expert at? Do not let a bully take away your pride and your confidence.*

✽ **It's Not You:** *Always remember that it is the bully who is misbehaving and doing the wrong thing—not you. You have not done anything wrong. Lots of kids get bullied, but no one deserves to be bullied* (Baker, 2009).

Encourage Courage

Often the best protection from other kids is other kids. Harness elementary students' innate drive to do good and their basic desire to please in order to cultivate conscientious objectors and model citizens. By middle school, some of those generous instincts get buried under the desire to fit in and look cool.

Teach students that they all share a collective responsibility to combat bullying and that bystanders are expected to take a stand against bullying whenever they see it. Younger elementary age students usually do plenty of tattling, but as they move through the upper elementary years, tattling becomes unpopular and peer pressure drives that sense of righteous indignation underground. Explain that *tattling* is something done for the sole purpose of getting someone *in trouble*, whereas *responsible reporting* is done to get someone *out of trouble*. Grab hold of righteous indignation when you see it and honor it; demonstrate to students that it is those who speak up for what's right who make this world a better place. *That's* cool.

Perseveration Exasperation

Occasionally, the impulsive or perseverative behaviors of students on the spectrum may result in others feeling bullied. Eight-year-old Mark became focused on experimenting with peers' names. He arrived at school one day insistent on calling his peers by their full names: "Theodore," "Stephanie," "Jacob," "Vincent," and "Margaret." When Mark was told to stop but didn't, Teddy, Steffie, Jake, Vince, and Maggie felt exasperated and disrespected.

Rather than simply issuing consequences, Mark's teacher, Rochelle, took him aside and asked him why he was persisting in this behavior. Mark was able to explain that he was curious about nicknames since he did not have one himself, and wanted to *hear* how full names become nicknames.

Rochelle praised Mark for this spontaneous course of study, and pointed out the signals of displeasure that Mark had not recognized in his peers. She then taught Mark that every person gets to choose what he or she wants to be called and that we must respect those choices.

Rochelle helped Mark create a way to explore the nickname phenomenon using people who were not part of the class. Mark made a chart comparing nicknames, starting with famous Johns: John Adams, Jonathan Livingston Seagull, Johnny Depp, Jack Black, and so on.

I Can't Even

Offer all of your students a place to vent their frustrations by creating a *Classroom Concerns* depository. Hang a large envelope on the wall. Students can write down their frustrations or worries at any time and deposit them in the envelope. Retrieve them on a regular basis and discuss your students' feelings with them privately. Try to listen openly to students' reports of their own experience, which may be quite different from your own. Often these discussions will lead to simple solutions such as a change in seating arrangement or addressing a certain behavior with another student.

Beyond Restitution

The perseverative and impulsive nature of students on the spectrum may take quite a cumulative toll on classmates. Day after day, classmates may be subject to the same disruptive or destructive behaviors. Here are three steps to guide provocative students toward making things right:

1. **Apology:** Even if an apology is uttered by rote, the words *I'm sorry* are crucial to effective socialization. Over time, those words may become spontaneous and heartfelt. For now, they are just compulsory and need to be stated whenever appropriate. But that's not enough.

2. **Restitution:** If Dion knocked over Kelly's block castle by being impulsive, careless, or inconsiderate, he should provide restitution by helping Kelly rebuild, thereby restoring her castle to its original glory. With your support, this can serve as a valuable opportunity for Dion to practice collaboration, flexibility, and empathy: Right now, he cannot build *his* way; he needs to build *her* way.

   - If, however, the castle was the casualty of an emotional or physical outburst by Dion, then now may not be the time for restitution. Dion may be in no condition to "help" Kelly. And Kelly may not be especially receptive to "help" or anything else from Dion. If restitution feels unrealistic, consider reparation as an alternative.

3. **Reparation:** Even with mumbled apologies, and with or without restitution, it is unquestionably a strain on classmates to spend the day in an environment in which their block structures get demolished without warning, or they get poked, interrupted, and intruded upon all day long. Reparation goes beyond restitution. It's a way of making up for anguish, pain, and suffering.

   - In this example, as reparation, Dion could be encouraged to find a way to do something extra nice for Kelly to make her happy again. Kelly deserves that.

   - Chances are, Dion will suggest something generous but egocentric, such as, *She can borrow my Dictionary of Aircraft Engines!* If Kelly declines Dion's proposal, guide Dion to consider Kelly's interests, so that he can offer something that would be meaningful to her. This is a good opportunity for Dion to practice taking another person's perspective: *What would Kelly like?* Maybe Dion could offer to give her his computer time today or take over her classroom job for the rest of the day or week.

   - Now Kelly has been more than compensated for her loss. And Dion has taken several steps closer to social understanding.

Addressing the Class

If you find that members of your class are struggling with the inclusive dynamic, despite your efforts to foster an accepting community, you may consider asking the school counselor or an outside expert to facilitate a class-wide or school-wide discussion about ASD. (Please see Chapter 7 for ideas on educating and inspiring a supportive school-wide community around students on the autism spectrum.)

Using these strategies, a supportive classroom community is within reach, but it is not a one-shot deal. Long-term maintenance will require your consistent modeling and positive, proactive energy. What an example you will be setting at the helm of a truly heterogeneous society, an inclusive environment in which all individuals are welcome and accepted. The next chapter will take this one step further, describing what can make communication so difficult and how to create a classroom that is responsive to the communication needs of all students.

Chapter 9

Say What?

The Spectrum of Communication

Communication includes spoken and unspoken interaction. Among students on the spectrum, communication can be compromised by a wide variety of challenges, some readily apparent and others more subtle.

By definition, students on the spectrum exhibit challenges with the interactive or social aspects of language. Some may deliver highly complex and well-articulated declamations but be robotic in their tone. Others may be articulate and animated, but repeat the same expressions over and over or only quote movies or television shows. Others may speak persuasively, but only on a topic of their choosing. Still others have memorized rote conversational fragments that they sprinkle handily into common dialogues but cannot deviate from. Some students on the spectrum may also have challenges with word production that manifest in every encounter. These students may be nonverbal or inconsistently able to produce conventionally meaningful sounds or words. For some, coherent thoughts or words may form in their minds but get tangled or garbled on the way out of their mouths.

This chapter describes the wide-ranging challenges of both spoken and unspoken communication that students on the spectrum may face and offers strategies to help you create a classroom that is responsive to all kinds of communicators.

Challenges of Spoken Communication: Expressive Language

Expressive language skills reflect the cognitive process involved in formulating and transmitting information through spoken words. Expressive language challenges may include articulation, fluency, pronoun reversal, semantics, and echolalia.

Articulation

In typically developing children, speech, by age four, should be 100% intelligible, across contexts, even if there are still some articulation errors. For example, the sentence *I saw a wabbit on my birfday* contains two articulation errors, but is still intelligible. By age seven, however, a typically developing student should have mastered articulation of all speech sounds.

Significant or persistent errors in articulation could signal a variety of dysfunctions including:

- *Dyspraxia,* which is a problem with motor planning, can cause students to be unable to figure out how to shape their mouths around the words that are clear in their heads.

- *Dysarthria*, which is a neuromuscular impairment causing poor muscle control and coordination, can cause students to be physiologically unable to manipulate their mouths to form the words that are in their head.

Speech and language specialists and occupational therapists should be consulted to assess the etiology of the difficulty and recommend intervention.

Fluency

The rhythm and flow of speech, known as fluency, is most commonly affected by stuttering, stammering, or other disruptions in speech. These *dysfluencies* can include inadvertent repetition, elongation of sounds, or prolonged silences during speech production.

Stuttering can also be characterized by interjections, which are grammatically irrelevant interruptions to one's own speech. Sometimes we use interjections deliberately to decorate language, as in *poof!* or *bada-bing, bada-boom.* But frequent inadvertent interjections such as *uh* and *um* can be indicative of a processing delay, wherein the concepts are slow to develop in the student's mind or slow to form themselves into words.

Over time, dysfluencies can become intractable, so intervention by a speech and language specialist must be provided promptly in order for a student to benefit from new strategies. Stuttering can cause shame and stress for students, and also worsens under stress. You can help by being reassuring and by encouraging dysfluent students to take their time with speech. In this way, you are also modeling patience and acceptance for your other students.

Pronoun Reversal

The confusion of subjective pronouns is known as *pronoun reversal*. Most often, this manifests as the use of *you* to mean *me* and *me* to mean *you*. For example, when admiring a peer's toys, a student might offer a convoluted compliment, such as, *You like my toys*, when, in fact, she means to say, *I like your toys*. Or, if someone asks a her, *Do you have any pets?* she might reply, *You do have pets! You have a dog and a bird!*

In some cases pronoun reversal can be an extension of echolalia, in which case a pronoun that is already in use gets repeated. (See more on echolalia below on page 170.)

But pronoun use is inherently complicated because pronouns are inherently subjective; the words *I, me,* and *you* refer to different people within the same conversation, depending upon who is speaking. These are called *deictic forms*—their meaning changes depending upon the context of their use. These fluid early elements of language development are highly confusing to rigid, concrete learners.

Worse yet, to understand that *I* means something different to each person who says it requires taking the perspective of others, or mind-reading, which is especially challenging to students on the spectrum. (Read more about the challenges of mindblindness in Chapter 8.)

Semantics

The rules that govern the meaning of words are known as *semantics*. The use of practical semantics is a particular trouble spot for students on the autism spectrum for several reasons.

Abstraction

Conceptual and abstract words such as *value* or *culture* or *personal* are difficult for concrete or visual learners to fully grasp. Similes, metaphors, idioms, jokes, proverbs, and sarcasm are commonly lost on students on the spectrum as they struggle to understand even direct statements. This challenge extends well beyond the literal interpretation of basic proverbs

---

How Sarcastic Can You Be?

One day, a group of fifth graders was being particularly loud and unruly. Their teacher, Arthur, used a sarcastic question to chastise his class: *Can you be any louder?* Malik, a student on the spectrum, ever eager to please, promptly raised the volume of his voice. Arthur did not realize he had inadvertently invited this result because he was not even aware that he had used sarcasm. He sent Malik to the principal's office.

Consider carefully how you use language in your classroom. Subtle idiosyncrasies of speech, such as sarcasm and idioms, that you may use casually with your peers, are neither advisable nor appropriate in an inclusive classroom—or really in any classroom.

---

such as *The early bird catches the worm*. It means that the allusions of poetry may be inscrutable. And practically speaking, being mired in the concrete world can have catastrophic social implications.

Multiple Meanings

Another semantic challenge faced by students on the spectrum is fluidity of meaning. Fluidity is not a comfort zone for rigid students on the spectrum. When students first learn the meaning of the word *bark*, for example, they learn that it refers to the sound a dog makes. That definition becomes fixed in their heads, like a rule. So when they are told, *Please do not peel the bark off of that tree*, they are utterly baffled. They cannot automatically accommodate or generalize this new usage.

Idiosyncrasies and Neologisms

Other semantic challenges result in a tendency for students on the spectrum to use idiosyncratic language and neologisms.

- *Idiosyncratic language* is the use of common words or phrases in unusual ways, as in *The weather is blurry today*.

- *Neologisms* are invented words. In recent years, many neologisms, such as *blog* and *cyber* have been accepted into common parlance as we develop Internet vocabulary. However, when students on the spectrum create their own neologisms, though sometimes clever, they rarely carry shared meaning and instead serve mainly as further impediments to communication.

If a student uses similar sounds or words consistently, you may come to recognize that *mim*, for example, always means something affirmative. In the context of your classroom, then, *mim* serves as language because it is communicative. Chances are, your student's family will have been conversant in *mim* for a long time. The family may have adapted to and adopted some of this student's words into their own family-speak, enabling *mim* to become a part of their agreed-upon language conventions.

Idiosyncratic language and neologisms reflect the gross approximateness of language use among students on the spectrum. As stated above, these students may not entirely grasp a specific concept or connect what they see before them to what they've already learned. They may not be able to access or retrieve the precise word for a concept, or they may not have heard or assimilated the pronunciation of the word correctly. They just try to come as close as they can.

Echolalia

The repetition of the speech of others is called *echolalia*. When you ask a student, *Are you finished?* and he responds, *You finished,* he is exhibiting echolalia. While echolalia can occur to a small extent in any child's development, it is more common and persistent among students on the spectrum. Echolalia can be immediate, as in the repetition of words just heard, or delayed, as in the repetition of words heard long before, including those heard in movies or television commercials.

Though echolalia may seem uncommunicative or indicative of a lack of comprehension, it may in fact be an important communication tool for students on the spectrum. Sometimes students may use immediate echolalia as an intentional effort to maintain social interaction in the face of having no spontaneous response at their disposal.

Delayed echolalia, also known as *scripting*, may serve a more specific communicative function when used consistently. For example, a student who has read or seen *Diary of a Wimpy Kid* may have learned that the nonsensical phrase *Zooey Mama!* is a way of expressing humor or enthusiasm. Your student may adopt that phrase into his repertoire as a script, and use it every time something strikes him as funny. Another student may use the expression *May the odds be ever in your favor* from *The Hunger Games* to demonstrate that she is feeling anxious.

While these kinds of expressions may *appear* to be meaningless, it will be helpful to all when you make the effort to decipher their origin and their meaningfulness to the students who use them. If the students themselves cannot explain these expressions to you, their parents and caregivers are the next best resource for this kind of background information.

A Word Is a Word

Of course, a long-term goal is acquisition of conventional communication that can be understood out in the world. But it is important to consider that, depending on your students' histories and current levels of functioning, an incomprehensible grunt from one student may be a magnum opus from another. A student may have gone from being completely nonverbal for many years to using one sound consistently in a meaningful way. If students use any sound or word to convey a consistent meaning, they are using at least primitive language. Be sure to acknowledge their contextually successful effort to communicate, even as you prompt the use of conventional responses.

Chapter 9: Say What?: The Spectrum of Communication

Because echolalia can serve different functions for each student, your response to echolalia must be differentiated. Consult with a speech and language specialist who can determine whether a student's echolalia is productive and how best to respond to it.

Creating a Communicative Classroom: Supporting Expressive Language

If you have students in your class who have mild to moderate expressive-language challenges, this section offers some communication strategies to support them. Later in this chapter, we will look at tools that can be used to support the efforts of students who need a little more assistance.

✴ Sending Up an SOS: Create a system or signal that individual students can use to communicate with you without words. Whenever students' ever-present anxiety builds, their limited word retrieval skills may fail them altogether. They may become too anxious to organize the words to tell you they need to use the bathroom or that they don't know what page you're on. Work individually with these students to formulate some simple, private signals they can use to let you know they need help or need a break. They can pass you a card, hold up two fingers, and so on. Five minutes to regroup can buy many hours of engagement and expression.

✴ Better Than Ever: Students who struggle with expressive language may have fully formed thoughts in their heads but can't necessarily translate those thoughts into words. These students may be reluctant to participate in language-based activities, may raise their hands and then forget what they were going to say, be unprepared when called on, or use more immature language than their peers. But remember that perfect language production may be an elusive goal, and current language levels may reflect many years of hard work and progress. Try to acknowledge and celebrate even the tiniest steps forward.

✴ Note to Self: Allow students to jot down or quickly sketch their thoughts on a sticky note or index card during a lesson. They may have an easier time putting their idea into words if they can see it manifest before them.

✴ Greetings and Salutations: Use classroom routines to encourage language use. Depending on your students' communication needs, create systems that require the use of routine language. Perhaps your daily morning meeting can require each student to greet a peer on either side using one of several possible greetings. The routine of this ritual will quickly become familiar to students and increase the likelihood that they will be able to participate.

✴ Talking on the Job: Create daily jobs in the classroom that encourage interactive language use: Perhaps your appointed attendance monitor can call the roll, or your designated equipment distributor can take a survey each day to see who needs to borrow a classroom ruler or compass. Prompt the use of social skills (such as not interrupting, addressing others by name, saying *Thank you*) when performing these tasks.

✳ **To the Point:** Keep your questions very direct. Remember the old joke in which one person asks a passerby, *Excuse me, do you know what time it is?* The passerby looks at his watch, answers *Yes, I do,* and keeps walking. In that instance, the response actually does fit the question. The problem was that the question was not specific enough. With language-challenged students, consider the directness and specificity of your questions and statements. When you ask, *Who can tell me today's date?* your expectation is not as clear as it is when you say, *Manny, please tell us what today's date is.*

✳ **Making Group Work Work:** Look for creative, structured opportunities to support language. Small collaborative groupings can help reinforce academic lessons as well as increase the likelihood that your anxious students will participate, since they may feel less intimidated sharing in a small group than with the whole class. Small groupings may also bolster a feeling of connectedness among students. On the other hand, group work poses significant social and flexibility challenges to many students on the spectrum. Try these small-group strategies to support success:

- Group work is a discrete skill. Teach a class lesson on group work. Teach students how to perform each of the different roles in a group; how to set goals and prioritize tasks; what it means to compromise; what to do when there's a problem; strategies for resolving conflicts; and how and when to get help.

- Assign roles within each group, such as reader, scribe, facilitator, and reporter; but add in some concrete jobs that might suit your students on the spectrum, such as timekeeper, materials manager, even fact-checker. Carefully chosen roles are helpful in that they create boundaries around communication expectations, reinforce students' special strengths, and simultaneously stretch their skill and language base.

- Keep groups small and kind. Choose members mindfully.

- Present a written set of expectations that you can place on each table to supplement your verbal instructions.

- Provide an example of what the expected outcome should look like.

Challenges of Spoken Communication: Receptive Language

Receptive language skills reflect the cognitive process involved in the comprehension of language. Imagine being in a country where everyone speaks a language you don't understand. The words come quickly, and you have no time to translate or process the words before responding. Students with receptive language challenges may have that experience in their own classroom. If they cannot keep up with the language swirling around them, they tune out, and then tuning out becomes a learned behavior.

Central Auditory Processing

Difficulties with discrimination of sounds, filtering of sounds, or synthesizing auditory information may be due to central auditory processing challenges. Among other complications, central auditory processing difficulties can cause students to:

- hear and learn sounds incorrectly, impacting speech development

- miss critical information, which compromises comprehension and capability across all aspects of school and life

- overlook meaningful auditory input while tuning in to background noise, or be unable to differentiate among stimuli. This confusion impedes focus and interaction. Sometimes students with central auditory processing difficulties may seem to be ignoring you, but in truth, their auditory focus is somewhere in the distance at that moment and they truly cannot hear you.

- focus more on the mechanics of language than the actual content. Students may get so distracted by words that accidentally rhyme or are alliterative, for example, that they miss what's actually being said.

Creating a Communicative Classroom: Supporting Receptive Language

If you have students who have mild to moderate receptive-language challenges, this section offers some communication strategies to support them. Later in this chapter, we'll look at tools that can be used to support the efforts of students who need additional help.

✳ **Less Is More:** When students on the spectrum don't understand what's going on, more words can equal overload. Their language and auditory processing systems can get overwhelmed or shut down completely. Explanations sometimes require the use of many words, but for these students, those words will run together as noise and be blocked out. So take it very slowly, and offer little bits of information, allowing plenty of time along the way for processing.

✳ **Echo Check:** Check for comprehension often to ensure that students' verbal responses are not simply echolalic reproductions. Try rephrasing your question or asking students to answer using different words so that you can verify conceptual understanding.

✳ **A Work in Process:** If possible, when you first want to ask a question, call the student's name or touch her desk to get her attention, and wait to be sure you have engaged her before proceeding. (Try to avoid tapping the shoulders of students on the spectrum, as unexpected touch may be misperceived or jarring.) Once you're sure you have her attention, then ask the question. Patiently give her the time she needs to process the question and formulate an answer.

For example, you just asked Carla to name a local mountain range. Your question is greeted with silence. Though she appears to be ignoring you, she may be slowly processing your question. Try to give her the time she needs.

Often, in an effort to be helpful, a teacher will gently repeat the prompt: *Carla, did you hear me? I asked you to name a local mountain range.* Unfortunately, Carla—who had been working on tuning in to your request and then struggling to remember what the words *local* and *range* mean, and was beginning just now to consider what local mountain ranges she knows and retrieve and express the names of them—has been thrown completely off-course by this interruption to her process. Now she has to process your *new* question: *Carla, did you hear me?* Then she will have to start all the way back at the beginning of her effort to come up with a mountain range.

Try not to interrupt the process; just be patient. But if a student asks for help or seems truly lost, try reframing the question in a simpler way. Perhaps the wording of your question was challenging. This time, reword it: *Can you think of any groups of mountains near where we live?*

✷ **Read and Repeat:** Read aloud books that will be welcome and accessible because of their predictable, repetitive qualities.

✷ **Don't Do This:** Since some students may miss the beginnings of your communications while they reorient their attention and process your words, try to frame instructions in the positive. Tell students what *to* do, rather than what *not* to do, so that they do not miss the critical word *Don't* at the beginning.

> Instead of telling Rita: *Don't poke Fernando!*

> Try this: *Rita?* (pause) *Please keep your hands to yourself.*

An added benefit of positive instructions is that embedded in the instructions are specific behavioral alternatives which might not otherwise be inferred. Now Rita knows what to do with her hands when she stops poking Fernando.

✷ **Pre-teach:** Preview books and chapters with the class, outlining what they can expect in the upcoming pages. This will support students on the spectrum by making new information predictable, which will bolster active listening and comprehension.

Creating a Communicative Classroom: Tools for Students Who Need More

If you have students on the autism spectrum who have little or no functional expressive language and very limited receptive language, consider these tools that can bolster their abilities to participate fully in classroom communication.

Visual Communication Systems

Visual communication systems enable students to initiate and engage in communication using picture-based communication symbols. Here are some ways to use them:

✱ Visual Symbols for Expressive Language: Using cards, students can "speak" by showing picture-based communication symbols. At any time, they can select one or several that convey the message they are trying to communicate. Some icons are photographic, some pictorial, and some offer only written words. Some support the expression of basic concepts such as *All done* or *More, please*; others convey whole sentences, such as *I need a break, I don't understand,* and many more.

✱ Visual Symbols for Receptive Language: You can supplement the meaningfulness of your own spoken words by pairing your words with visual cues. You can use the cards to do the following:

- add visual cues to your curriculum by lining them up for storyboarding or for laying out the elements of a unit

- demonstrate concepts such as *Same/Different, First/Then,* or *Cause/Effect*

- supplement your spoken instructions and facilitate transitions by using symbols such as *Hands down, Eyes on me,* or *Line up*

Picture-based communication symbols can be as simple as words and pictures you draw on index cards, or photographs you take in the classroom or cut out of magazines. They can also be printed from professionally developed software programs. At least twenty thousand downloadable icons are available through a variety of sources, including Boardmaker by Mayer-Johnson, one of the most longstanding sources of icons and display systems for educators. (Links to many sources of icons can be found at www.barbaraboroson.com.)

Picture-based communication cards can be organized by category and stored for easy viewing and access in a three-ring binder with plastic sleeves. Affix a Velcro strip across the front of the binder to display cards currently in use. Alternatively, they can be purchased in a Velcro-lined flip book with a shoulder strap that you and your students on the spectrum can carry and access easily throughout your day.

First	Then
Put toys away.	Play on computer.

The Picture Communication Symbols ©1981–2010 by Mayer-Johnson LLC. All Rights Reserved Worldwide. Used with permission. Boardmaker™ is a trademark of Mayer-Johnson LLC.

Assistive Technology for Communication

Assistive technology, including text-to-speech and speech-to-text software and word processors, can help students whose communication needs significantly interfere with their ability to function in class. Such supports do not diminish students' efforts to use conventional communication. Instead, assistive technology devices help communication-challenged students begin to perceive themselves as communicators, which inspires them to continue working on developing their conventional communication skills.

Picture-Based Communication: There's an App for That!

Although digital picture communication systems lose the tactile element, there is much to be gained from digital communication supports. Not only are endless numbers of icons available at the touch of a finger, but apps also provide voice output, reinforcing for students consistently what their intended message sounds like when spoken.

As of this writing, popular picture communication apps with voice output include *PECS IV+* by Pyramid Educational Consultants, *Compass* and *Sono Flex* by Tobii Dynavox, *Look2Learn* by MDR, *ProLoQuo2Go* by AssistiveWare, and *GoTalk NOW* by Attainment Company, Inc. Additionally, the GoTalk Pocket device by Attainment Company, Inc. provides compact portability. New apps are being created all the time. Search for "communication symbols" in your app store. You're sure to find an app for that.

Assistive technology in the form of text-to-speech programs can be used to support students with expressive speech or language difficulties. Nonverbal students or those with expressive challenges can type their communications into speech-generating devices, which then produce synthesized speech, giving voice to the typed communications. Other programs offer speech-to-text technology so that students who have difficulty writing, typing, or spelling can allow their words to be transcribed just as they rush out of their mouths.

Word Processors

Many classrooms today provide all students with technology resources that open up new worlds of learning and communication for everyone. Assistive technology, designed specifically for students with special needs, takes these supports even further. Specialized word processing devices, such as *Forte* by Writer Learning Systems, provide a variety of features, including:

- oversize keyboards, high-contrast screens, and combination keystrokes (that can be activated by pressing one key instead of holding two at once) to support fine motor and sensory motor challenges

- word retrieval and Smart word prediction to support expressive language challenges

- natural-sounding voice technology that reads students' words aloud for communication purposes and/or to provide auditory feedback

- automatic instant-save features and on-screen templates to provide organizational support

If you think you have students who might benefit from assistive technology, ask your school administrator or the district's evaluative team for an Assistive Technology Evaluation to assess the students' needs in these areas. (Gather more data about assistive technology in Chapter 11.)

Beyond Words: Challenges of Social Communication

Effective communication depends on more than the verbal elements of language. The subtext of social communication, also called *pragmatics*, poses an enormous challenge to students on the spectrum, leaving them mystified and quite inept. When nine-year-old Monique flubbed the ball in a kickball game, her teammates rolled their eyes and groaned, *Oh, great kick.* Monique's enthusiastic response—*Thanks!*—was as sincere as it was socially devastating. This section will work to demystify these challenging elements of communication and show you how to support more meaningful communication in your classroom. Pragmatic competence depends on facility with nonverbal and paraverbal communication, as described below.

Nonverbal Communication

Nonverbal communication, commonly known as *body language*, refers to gestures, facial expressions, body position, and body posture. Crucial implication lurks in conspiratorial winks, meaningful kicks under the table, rolled eyes, and more—especially in the secondary grades. All of this information may be completely overlooked or misread by students on the spectrum. Casual banter is incomprehensible, and students on the spectrum are left lost and confused, teased and bullied.

Paraverbal Communication

Paraverbal communication, commonly known as *prosody*, refers to the tone and inflection behind our spoken words. Prosody is *how* we say what we say. Elements of prosody include pitch, volume, intonation, rate, rhythm, and emphasis. These elements are essential to conveying a speaker's feelings and intentions and are critical components of social language. Most of us use prosody subconsciously to convey the mood of our words, indicating happiness, sadness, frustration, humor, politeness, wariness, anger, and so on. Typically, listeners construe meaning from our words on the basis of both what we say and how we say it. Without adequate prosody, many well-articulated verbalizations can be grossly misunderstood.

As typically functioning students move through the elementary and secondary years, language becomes layered with unspoken innuendo such as sarcasm, impatience, kindness, disdain, anger, and more. Words are used in ways that don't match their definitions. Suddenly *Great kick* means *You blew it*, and *Yeah, right* means *No way.*

Prosody is a profound area of challenge among students on the spectrum as they cannot interpret—and often aren't even tuned in to the existence of—unspoken messages. For this reason, they may overlook or misconstrue the inflections in others' speech. Combined with their mindblindness and limited joint attention, a lot of information gets lost in translation, and the interactive and social implications are devastating. Students on the spectrum often cannot

> **Did You Know ...**
>
> As much as 93% of information about feelings and attitudes is communicated paraverbally or nonverbally (Mehrabian, 1980).

R U 4 Real?

Words all by themselves are highly subject to interpretation. Communicating without the benefit of those unspoken clues is like trying to decipher the tone of a terse text message. Words alone do not communicate the mood behind a typed message like *Thanks a lot*. Sincere or sarcastic? Who knows?

Exclamation points and emoticons are the written equivalents of tone, facial expression, and other body language. All are used to ensure that our message is read in the way we intend: *Thanks a lot!!* ☺

Not coincidentally, the neologism *emoticon*, a word created specifically for e-communication, is formed by the two words: *emotion* and *icon*. Just as emoticons help us decipher the emotion behind the words, actual pictorial icons help students on the autism spectrum understand and express facts, instructions, interests, needs, ideas, and, indeed, emotions. Pictorial icons have been helping students on the spectrum express and organize themselves for decades.

tell the difference between a sincere comment and a sarcastic remark, a sad sentiment and a cheerful expression, a compliment and a reprimand, or a suggestion and a command.

Little Professors

Challenges with prosody can go both ways, in that students on the spectrum who have trouble *interpreting* typical prosody may also have trouble *speaking* with typical prosody. This gap is particularly striking among those students on the spectrum who are very verbal and articulate. These students may have had little or no delay in speech development, yet in some cases their speech develops with a monotonous, robotic quality. They are often known as *little professors*. While this nickname is largely due to their pedantic tendencies, it may also reflect the flatness of their affect and tone—devoid of emphasis and emotion.

Pragmatics

The ability to interpret nonverbal and paraverbal cues is called *pragmatics* or social language. This composite skill is necessary for students to be able to use language in a natural context—i.e., to make conversation. No component of language is more dynamic than conversation because it is, by definition, interactive, and therefore dependent on the unpredictable, spontaneous input of others. This is why pragmatic language is one of the most challenging aspects of language for students on the spectrum, even when their speech skills are strong.

Nonversation

Communication challenges in combination with social limitations make conversation rather one-sided with students on the spectrum. Interactions are not exactly *inter*active, and conversations seem, well, more like *non*versations.

Many articulate students on the autism spectrum possess a wealth of knowledge on a very singular subject. What can first seem like a highly sophisticated level of conversation can quickly become peculiar, if not annoying, to listeners as students reveal their poor pragmatic know-how. A conversation devolves into a nonversation as these students doggedly pursue their own conversational agenda, oblivious to a listener's lack of interest and unaware of any expectation that they stop talking or refocus their attention elsewhere.

In the later elementary and secondary years, when conversation among peers becomes nuanced and loaded with social implication, the ability to interpret unspoken meaning is a litmus test for peer acceptance. Fitting in socially is all about reading between the lines, getting the joke, and so on. Social communication is more complex now, and students need to comprehend the words and implications coming at them as well as the receptivity of peers toward their own contributions.

Give It to Me Straight

Students on the autism spectrum often feel more comfortable interacting with adults than with peers for a variety of reasons:

- Familiar adults are more likely to be accepting of differences in conversational style, such as self-centeredness or lack of give-and-take.

- Familiar adults tend to be straightforward and friendly. Students can or should be able to trust that you will say exactly what you mean and that you are not being sarcastic or disdainful.

- Adults may be more patient awaiting word retrieval and will accept linguistic approximations and use context clues in order to support a child's efforts. In other words, supportive adults will pick up some of the slack in a challenging conversation.

- Conversational content with adults tends to be linear, whereas peer topics and responses can be wildly unpredictable and loosely connected.

What's That Supposed to Mean?

When talking with peers, on the other hand, students on the spectrum never know what to expect. For example, when eight-year-old Kameron steps off the bus at school, his peers greet him with a seemingly simple question: *What's up?* Obligingly, Kameron looks quizzically at the sky, and everyone laughs. What is so funny about that?

Without social intuition, students on the spectrum can't tell when to laugh along and when they are being laughed at; they don't know how to join a conversation and when to stop talking. Without the ability to read nonverbal and paraverbal cues, they struggle to make meaning out of words alone. Without flexibility, they get left behind when conversations meander inexplicably and take sharp unexpected turns. Without joint attention, they don't engage in the conversational topics of others. These pragmatic challenges compromise students' ability to use language in a natural, interactive context. Like so many other skills that many of us develop intuitively, effective use of pragmatic language must be taught to students on the spectrum.

Pragmatic Pitfalls

Here are some common pragmatic challenges among students on the spectrum:

- joining into existing conversations
- modulating language use according to context
- knowing when to stop talking
- taking turns speaking and listening
- considering the interests and needs of others
- initiating socially expectable topics
- reading between the lines
- interpreting non-literal language
- utilizing gestures and facial expression to support verbal communication

These challenges are very apparent to others and can be quite off-putting, especially to peers. They pose a dramatic impediment to socialization.

Lost in Translation

A particularly challenging conversational dynamic happens when children on the spectrum converse with non-native language speakers. Both students on the spectrum *and* non-native speakers need their conversation partners to pick up some of the conversational slack, decode their linguistic approximations, and use context clues to compensate for limited fluency. When both parties need that kind of accommodation from the other, and neither is capable of providing it, a lot of critical meaning gets lost in translation.

Creating a Communicative Classroom: Supporting Social Language

Effective pragmatic language use takes practice. If you have students who struggle with social language, start by consulting the speech and language specialist in your school for support. Often speech and language specialists have specific curricula and strategies to support social language and pragmatic skills.

Practicing Pragmatics

Beyond the help speech and language specialists can provide, here are some strategies you can use to facilitate conversational competence.

Initiating Conversation

Many students on the spectrum long to interact with peers but have no idea how to initiate, join in, maintain, or end conversations. Try laying out some guidelines.

Who Is Available for Conversation?

Encourage students to assess a situation before moving in. A good candidate for conversation would be the following:

- someone who is standing alone
- someone who has finished working
- someone who is not involved in another activity

Topics for Conversation

Review effective topic openers such as these, categorized by psychologist Jed Baker (2009):

- Past topics: *How was your* _____*?* (week, weekend, day, vacation); *Guess what I* _____*!* (something you did)
- Present topics: *What are you* _____*?* (doing, reading, eating, playing)
- Future topics: *What are you going to do*_____*?* (after school, this weekend, over vacation)
- Interests: *How is* _____ *going?* (sports, projects, activity); *Do you like* _____*?* (sports, television show, music, movie, book)

Look for natural opportunities to practice identifying conversational topics during collaborations, morning meeting, read-aloud time, assemblies, and so on.

Getting to Know New People

Give students strategies for branching out to make new friends:

- Name: *What's your name?* (pause and listen) *Mine is* _____.
- Age: *How old are you?* (pause and listen) *I am* _____.
- Fun: *What do you like to do in your free time? Do you like* _____*?* (television, movies, games, sports, places)
- School: *What school do you go to? What grade are you in?*
- Family: *Do you have any brothers or sisters? Do you have any pets?*

Joining In

Students on the spectrum often struggle to know when and how to join in with a conversation or play activity that is already in progress. Some may join simply by playing alongside the others without ever interacting; some may barge right in and try to take over; others may stand nearby and watch but never approach; and others will simply steer clear. Their rigidity and difficulties with impulse control make interaction especially challenging.

Jed Baker (2009) breaks the joining-in process into comprehensible steps that can be taught:

1. Watch and listen to what the other kids are doing. Decide whether you want to join them in what they are already doing.

2. If you want to join them, walk up and wait for a pause in the play.

3. Say something nice, such as, *You're good at that!* or *That's cool!* or *That looks like fun!*

4. Ask if you can join them: *Can I play?* or *Can I help?*

5. If they say *No,* move on and look for someone else to play with.

"Close Talkers"

Personal space, also called *proxemics*, is another aspect of nonverbal communication that can be very loaded socially. Know any "close talkers"? Surely you've had students who barge right into your area of comfort when they speak to you, or others who keep an impractical distance.

We all have individual standards for our own personal space, and it can change from context to context. But there is a generalized personal space rule that students should learn to respect. Try teaching them to keep an *arm's length distance* from anyone they interact with. This is a consistent rule that students can apply to all situations, whether interacting with peers or with the principal.

Some students who come too close may be seeking sensory input. Ask the occupational therapist to explore this issue. A weighted vest or other input-providing device might help resolve this problem.

On the other hand, some students on the spectrum may require a greater personal space around themselves than you might expect. Grant that space in order to allow them to be at ease, especially when you are approaching students who are anxious, agitated, or sensorily defensive. Stand in a position that would not cause them to feel cornered or trapped. Turning slightly sideways and maintaining a generous personal space may feel less threatening to anxious students. Occupational therapists may also be able to use brushing (as described in Chapter 4) and other strategies to help desensitize these students.

Maintaining Conversation

Students on the spectrum often have difficulty knowing how to build on existing conversations. Here's where the waters get really murky. Even when they ask peers good questions like, *What are you playing?* or *Do you like Justin Bieber?* there's no telling what kind of response is going to come back at them. How can they plan what to say next when it's all unpredictable, it's moving so fast, and none of it seems to make any sense?

Listen Up

Often students on the spectrum are so preoccupied with what they want to say next that they do not listen to or even hear the words of others.

✱ **Stop, Look, and Listen:** Remind students often to *stop, look,* and *listen.* Post that prompt on their desks in words or in icon form.

If necessary, teach them a visual cuing system so you can convey this message, as needed, even from afar. For example, students can learn that when you call their name, they must look at you for a cue. If they see that your finger is up, that means they need to stop talking. If they see you touch your eye or ear, that means they should be looking or listening.

You can use this kind of signal system to support students whenever you notice them monopolizing conversations, intruding on others, or interrupting classroom lessons or activities. (This kind of system offers the added benefit of showing them that nonverbal cues are important vehicles of communication. It reminds them that they need to look in order to learn.)

✱ **Cross Fingers:** Gail, a fourth-grade teacher, encourages all of her students to cross two fingers when they have something to say but must wait their turn to speak. When their turn to speak finally comes, the tactile prompt of crossed fingers helps them remember what they were going to say. This simple strategy is especially helpful to students on the spectrum because once they learn to trust this technique, they may be better able to put their compelling comment on a back burner—temporarily—to focus on another speaker's words.

✱ **Active Listening:** Teach students to *show* that they are listening. Explain that even though *they* know that they are listening, others need to know it too. This is an especially important strategy for students who have limited eye contact and may appear inattentive. Remind students on the spectrum specifically that it is not enough to ask a polite question; they must also listen to the answer. Encourage students to use verbal indicators such as, *Wow!, That's cool!,* or *Really?* when they hear something interesting, to provide evidence that they are engaged.

Staying on Topic

Even once students on the spectrum can identify a topic of conversation and demonstrate listening skills, more skill is required to respond meaningfully. Due to difficulties with focus, impulse control, flexibility, organization, processing, perseveration, pragmatic language challenges, and other issues, students may not recognize the conversational threads or unspoken associations that lead from one topic to another.

✱ **Look for Connections:** In his memoir, John Elder Robison recalls that as a child he was so used to living inside his own world that he answered peers with whatever he had been thinking about. He writes, "If I was remembering riding a horse at the fair, it didn't matter if a kid came up to me and said, 'Look at my truck!' or 'My mom is in the hospital!' I was still going to answer, 'I rode a horse at the fair.' The other kid's words did not change the course of my thoughts" (2007, p. 20).

Encourage students to look for connections between what was just said and what they will say next. Introduce a card game such as Uno or Blink to visually illustrate that connections can be made in different ways. In these games, players add cards to a pile by matching them on the basis of color, number, suit, or picture. Teach students that words connect to other words on varied bases as well. Words can connect to others by being about a similar experience, by seeking more information about a topic, by offering an opinion about a topic, and more.

Teach stock connective phrases such as these:

>*That reminds me of . . .* or *Speaking of . . .*
>
>*What was your favorite part?*
>
>*That sounds fun! Can you tell me more about it?*

Questions that begin with *Who, What, When, Where, Why, How,* and *What else* are also useful "wildcards" for students to play as a way of demonstrating their interest in the speaker's topic.

Constructing a Conversational Tower

Many students are able to relate to maintaining conversation if we compare it to building a Lego tower. In order for a conversation to keep going, the various pieces (i.e., sentences and ideas) must connect and fit together tightly. If they don't, the tower will become unstable and fall down (i.e., the conversation will collapse).

For example, suppose Erin and Tanya are having a conversation. Erin starts off by saying, *This science unit is confusing.* Explain to both girls that Erin has put down a foundation, or a base to begin building a conversation. Now, if Tanya wants to build a conversation with Erin, Tanya must choose a conversation piece to add that will fit onto Erin's base.

If Tanya puts out the piece *I have a chocolate cupcake in my lunch today!* then Tanya's conversation piece does not connect to Erin's conversation piece. Like a Lego tower, the conversational tower will fall apart. Erin may look for someone else to talk to.

Instead, Tanya might try to put out conversation pieces like these:

>*What part do you think is confusing?*
>
>*Really? I think it's okay so far.*
>
>*Do you want me to help you?*
>
>*Yeah, I'm confused, too.*

Any of those pieces would attach neatly to Erin's conversation base. Erin will then add more pieces to this sturdy tower and, lo and behold, a reciprocal conversation is now under construction.

In Uno and Blink, eventually the time comes when no one has a card in hand that can connect with the pile. At that point, game play pauses while each player selects a new card from the deck. In conversation, students on the spectrum can be taught that when they can't find anything to say that connects to the conversation, they can essentially "draw a new card from the deck" with this handy question: *Do you mind if I change the subject?*

Taking Turns

Conversational skills also rely on the ability to take turns, including the subtle skills of knowing when to start talking and, often more important, when to stop. These skills are difficult to script because conversations vary in terms of length, topic, pace, expertise, formality, and other characteristics. But to some extent, students can practice turn-taking skills with instruction and guidance.

✱ **Learning to Listen:** If you have conversation monopolizers in your class, incorporate structured conversational skill-building elements into class activities such as morning meeting or smaller group discussions:

- Provide a toy microphone, wand, empty paper-towel roll, or a *My turn to talk* card that will delineate whose turn it is to talk. Explain that only the person holding the "microphone" may speak; everyone else must be quiet listeners. Practice this technique in pairs first, expanding into small and then whole-class groupings as skills develop.

- Challenge the speaker to make a connection between what he or she says and what was said just before. Dissect connections together and encourage students to name them. This will help students recognize that a topic is the thread that weaves and holds a conversation together. Redirect topics as needed.

- Offer strategies for recognizing when it's time to pass the microphone. Quantify time limits, as appropriate, such as a certain number of sentences or minutes. Use a gentle bell or chime, if necessary, to delineate the end of a speaker's turn.

- Acknowledge the patience and effort of the listeners. Curbing impulses to blurt out thoughts can be quite a challenge in itself. Some students on the spectrum worry intensely that they will forget what they want to say. They may focus all of their attention on holding that thought, and miss out on everything else being said around them. Suggest that they cross their fingers or jot down a quick note to themselves to help them remember what they are waiting to say. Some students on the spectrum like to keep a tiny notebook in their pocket for moments like these.

Quitting Time

Outside of this kind of structured conversation, students on the spectrum may expound endlessly on their topic of interest. Ultimately, they'll need to learn to read the interpersonal signs of disinterest, without a wand or timer, and infer independently that it's time to stop talking:

- Remind students to look at faces and body language to get information about the listener's level of interest.

- Teach them the words that imply that a listener has had enough, like: *Okay, thanks* or *Got it* or *Well, I've gotta get going.*

- Teach them to read the nonverbal cues from others that indicate that it's time to stop talking, such as someone looking at the clock, standing up, moving toward the door, and so on.

- Have them practice talking *a little bit* about a subject.

- Teach polite ways they can end a conversation:

  Well, I have to get back to work now.

  I think the teacher wants us to be quiet now.

  I have to get my stuff. The bell is about to ring.

- Remind them to follow those up with a *Bye* or a *See you later.*

● ● ● ●

Regardless of the types of communication challenges you and your students face together, a truly communicative classroom can allow many different communication styles to be developed and accepted. Nevertheless, students' efforts to communicate very often take the form of intense behavior. The next chapter will address behavioral communication, and ways to be responsive—and effective—when the going gets tough.

Chapter 10

Boiling Up and Over

Turning Crisis Into Opportunity

You may be wondering why this chapter comes so late in this book when behavior is such a pivotal classroom issue. Here's why: If you have taken the time to understand all of the issues and challenges addressed in the preceding chapters, and if you have implemented some of the suggested preventive strategies, you have already warded off many crises. Many, many times you have kept the pot cool by avoiding triggers and respecting anchors, by creating a predictable classroom routine, establishing a smart sensory environment, maintaining positive, supportive relationships, and so much more. And many, many times, when the pot began to heat up, you read the signs and intervened quickly, confidently, and effectively, providing soothing sensory tools, social supports, comfort objects, and more. Congratulate yourself and your students because together you have kept things simmering along much more smoothly than they would have without your preventive and responsive efforts. Trust that this is true.

If you have not read the preceding chapters but just jumped to this chapter for a shortcut to help with challenging behaviors, the ideas here won't amount to much. They will get you through a tough moment or two, but they won't help you get to the source of the problems and cannot sustain you or your students on the spectrum. Please take the time to read through the other chapters; that's where you'll find most of the answers you need to head off crises and maintain equilibrium.

Still, in spite of all of your effort, the peace you have facilitated is admittedly a fragile one. You simply can't plan for everything. Potential anxiety triggers lurk everywhere for students on the spectrum. Comfort anchors that are critical to their functioning get lost or wet or broken. Their internal security systems are at Code Red at all times. Every interaction, every transition, poses the terrifying threat of unfamiliar terrain; every moment is fraught with the possibility that they will have to deviate from the comfort of their individually scripted guide to life. If it's off their script, they're not prepared for it, and feelings of panic and desperation can be instantaneous and overwhelming.

Disruptive and destructive behaviors have the potential to escalate into crisis situations or trauma, or to transform into opportunities for growth. This chapter will show you how to help students grow from each experience so that when on occasion the pot does boil over, no one will get burned.

Temperatures Rising

Given all the factors at play, it is no wonder that students on the spectrum sometimes lose control. They work at least twice as hard as typically functioning students at everything they do. While your whole class is learning the rules of a new game, students on the spectrum are also trying to maintain focus and eye contact, comprehend instructions, wait their turns, keep their hands from flapping, and not talk about Minions. While your whole class is taking a test, students on the spectrum are also trying to tolerate the glare on the paper, organize the sea of words swimming on the page, keep intrusive thoughts at bay, and avoid chewing their collars. This is hard work at best, and when all other things are not equal, the pot may boil over.

When circumstances feel overstimulating or overwhelming, students on the spectrum try to block out the offending input. Most often they either retreat into themselves to seek order internally, or they act out.

All in a Minute

Consider this example: When Jelani puts on his coat at home before walking out the door of his house every morning, he begins a tense transitional period between home and school. From that moment, his anxiety is elevated, and he takes comfort in repeatedly reminding himself that as soon as he gets to class, he will take off his coat, hang it up on his trusty third hook from the left—the one with the red knob—and then be able to settle into his day at school. Jelani relies on this daily routine of going directly to the coat closet to hang his coat on his hook. Even if it will be 85° and sunny today, Jelani may need to wear his coat to school simply because he cannot begin his school day without seeing this routine through from start to finish.

But one day he arrives to find that something unthinkable has happened: His hook has fallen off the wall. Or the red knob is missing from his hook. Or Ava has accidentally hung her coat on his hook. Or the coat closet is closed altogether because someone just vomited in there. Or no one's hanging up their coats this morning because you're all leaving for a field trip in ten minutes.

Any of these scenarios violates Jelani's script. He can't possibly settle into a new day without hanging up his coat. Hanging his coat on his hook is one of the anchors that allows Jelani's day to proceed. It's part of his routine: He can't improvise around it, and he can't let it go.

He doesn't know if he is allowed to hang his coat on another empty hook—that information hasn't been scripted for him. He doesn't have the language or social know-how to ask Ava politely why her coat is on his hook or if she might move it. He can't possibly keep his coat on until the field trip because that's just not how a day is *supposed* to begin. And worst of all, he doesn't know how to adapt internally to this unexpected change. His fragile balance is toppled.

Now that anxiety is brimming, whatever limited expressive language and impulse control Jelani may have had access to before is seriously compromised. He may fly into a rage, knocking his coat, or Ava's, or everyone's to the floor. He may yell at Ava. He may start growling. His hands may start flapping. He may curl up in a quiet corner of the closet and cry. He may keep his coat on—zipped up to his chin, hood on tight— and shut down completely by refusing to participate in the morning activities. Or he may come out of the closet and simply take his seat, looking as if everything is just fine, while inside he is reeling with anger, panic, and confusion. And most notably, he may not understand or be able to explain what is causing his breakdown.

By the time he comes out of the coat closet, he is in a dysfunctional state, unavailable for learning, and you may have no idea what's happened. You ask him, and he cannot respond. Your other students can only offer: *He was just sitting there crying!* or *Jelani just started screaming at me for no reason!*

Now Jelani's anxiety is way up, and his coping skills are way down. And it's only 8:01 A.M. When Jelani emerges from the closet, he may find that his desk has been moved. Or the book he set carefully on top of his desk yesterday is not there now. Or the classroom clock has stopped. Or the reading center is now in another corner of the room. Or, potentially worst of all, his teacher is absent. His anchors are floating away, and with them his self-control.

Whether he says it with words or by sitting down on the floor, by pulling his hat down over his face or by knocking his desk over, Jelani's unspoken message is this: *I am not joining Morning Meeting unless I can hang my coat on my hook first. That's how I always do it. That's the only way I know how to do it. The rule is: Morning Meeting always comes after I hang my coat on my hook, and that's how it has to be, because if it isn't like that, I have no idea what to do or what will happen next.*

Turning In and Tuning Out

As described in Chapter 3, some students try to cope with anxiety by going deep into their world of lists and systems. They far prefer to confine themselves to the structure and predictability of rules than to face chaos or disorder. So they try to maintain sameness by insulating themselves from the unexpected and clinging to the familiar. You ask Jelani, after he emerges from the coat closet, *Why did you knock all the coats to the floor?* His anxiety is high now, and getting higher all the time: It's bad enough his hook fell down; now he is in trouble too. This is a place of sheer panic. If he can answer at all, he may respond, *The longest dinosaur ever was the Seismosaurus, which measured more than 43 yards long. That's as long as two school buses in a row. The Seismosaurus was a relative of the Diplodocus, which. . . .* He is not showing off. He is not being provocative. He is not trying to be funny or a wise guy. He is giving you all he's got. He is operating straight from anxiety. The situation around him is out of control, so he retreats into his head to what he knows, what will not change (what, in this case, has been the same for millions of years).

Other students on the spectrum may be unavailable for conversation as they are putting all their energy into coping. They tune out their surroundings and tune in to a place of comfort in their minds. They scroll through the daily train schedule or visualize the disk drive operating inside their computer.

Acting Out

Some students on the spectrum have physical ways of modulating stress. As described in Chapter 4, they may resort to behaviors that regulate their senses and are comforting in their familiarity, even if they appear bizarre to others. These students may find comfort by spinning, hand-flapping, rocking, making noises, toe-walking, head-banging, biting, grinding their teeth, and more. In so doing, they soothe or stimulate their senses while refocusing their energies on something repetitive so that the offending stressor fades into the background. To the extent that you can, grant students time to regroup and restore in these ways, even as you look for signs that they may be ready to rejoin the class activity. But occasionally physical reactions take the form of destructive behaviors, which can be overwhelming to everyone involved.

Acting-out behaviors can represent a crisis for students on the spectrum and/or the people around them. Take comfort in the knowledge that crisis and trauma are very different things. Whereas *trauma* connotes sustained injury or pain, *crisis* signifies a point at which change occurs, for better or for worse. A badly handled crisis can certainly result in trauma to the student and to others around him or her. But with some prior knowledge and strategies at hand, you can help a student through a crisis in a way that is transcendent. New learning and growth can emanate from a crisis that is gently supported, carefully considered, and thoughtfully debriefed.

Crisis Management Strategies

Here is a quick guide for how to respond productively in the moment of a crisis. Familiarize yourself with these approaches now so you'll be prepared for sudden eruptions. Then read on to see what comes after the crisis; that is, how to interpret behavior and make the necessary modifications to head off recurrences.

Crisis—Step 1: Safety First

* **Isolate the Situation:** To the extent that you can, move the acting-out student out of the classroom or clear the other students out of the room in order to maintain the safety of anyone who may be in danger, whether that's you, other students, your colleagues, or the student herself. Also keep in mind that calming down amid a sea of gaping onlookers is not only humiliating but next to impossible. Even if it is not a dangerous situation, try to isolate the student who is in crisis to preserve his privacy and so that he can recover with dignity.

* **Call for Help:** Recruit help from other adults to cover your class while you are occupied with this student. Rely on your co-teacher, classroom aide, hall monitor, or neighboring teacher to fill in for you while you handle the crisis.

✱ Find a Safe Space: Identify, in advance, a soothing place of respite, such as a sensory room, therapist's office, or other quiet place in which a student in crisis can calm down. If the therapist can be available on-call, her office might be the best place to go, if possible.

Crisis—Step 2: Defuse the Situation

If you do not know right away what the behavior is communicating (and you probably won't at this point), that's okay; simply try to ease the situation in the moment. You'll analyze it later. (See "Interpreting Behavior" in the next section.)

Access information you have previously obtained from this student's history regarding how best to help him calm down. You should know in advance what helps to calm him when he's upset and what makes things worse. (To get information, use the family questionnaire referenced in Chapter 3 and reproducible at www.barbaraboroson.com.)

✱ Restrain Yourself: Before you face any crisis situation, find out what your school or district's policy is regarding the physical restraint of students. It can be tricky to protect yourself from liability while protecting your students from imminent danger. Alert school administrators that you may have volatile students in your class, and ask them what alternative strategies they endorse and recommend for those times when students are physically out of control.

✱ Shush: When trying to defuse a situation with a student, use as few words as possible.

- Since this student's sensory system is already overloaded, any excess verbiage will exacerbate the crisis, so keep it soft and succinct. Often during a crisis, a student's logic and rationality are inaccessible. When you perceive that, just stop talking.

- Instead of talking, offer visual cues, such as writing down a message to the student on a piece of paper, or picture cards directing him to begin a predetermined calming sequence. Show the student the *Calming Down* card that you have placed in his coolbox, as described in Chapter 3. Silently offering this card to the student provides him not only a basic list of calming strategies that work for him, but also the familiarity and visual input he may need to help him break through the crisis.

✱ Don't Engage: If you think the student is able to hear and listen, demonstrate *supportive non-responsiveness* to the behavior:

When you use a calm voice, I will listen to you.

I cannot understand you when you're yelling.

When you stop kicking, I can come closer and help you.

✱ Distract: If you have a volatile student, get in the habit of keeping comforting samples of your student's special interests on hand, such as an action figure, a sticker, or a train schedule. Don't worry that this will reinforce the tantrum—these are comfort objects. As long as you don't present the very item a student is tantrumming about, you are not rewarding the tantrum. It's not okay to give in to what set students off, but it can be okay, periodically, to distract them with something they love.

✱ **Respect the Moment:** Do not confront a student with ramifications or threaten consequences in the moment. If you point out to him, *Do you see Morgan's papers all torn up on the floor? That's what you did. You are going to have so much to clean up,* you will be increasing anxiety and fueling the continuation or exacerbation of the outburst. Now is not the time.

✱ **Give It Time:** Do not try to debrief the incident with the student right away. His sensory system will be raw from the offending event and the ensuing outburst. He is very likely frightened; it's terrifying to lose control of oneself. And depending on his social development, he may be embarrassed by his out-of-control behaviors.

> *"Yesterday ended last night. Every day is a new beginning. Learn the skill of forgetting. And move on."*
>
> —Norman Vincent Peale (1996)

Take time also before having the student rectify whatever may have gone awry as a result of this incident. If others were wronged by the student's behavior, apologies, restitution, and reparation may be called for, as discussed in Chapter 8—but only when the student is ready.

✱ **Oh, Hey:** Once the student is calm, allow him time to regroup and gear up before rejoining the rest of the class. When he does, try to restore routine as quickly as possible. Returning to the class will be emotionally challenging, so try to make it as smooth as possible. Now is not the time for a big greeting or a round of applause; nor is it the time for chastising or consequences. Now is the time to let those raw nerves recover and let the student's system reset. Welcome the student back into the fold quietly, warmly, and without fanfare.

Exude Calm

When students lose control, they depend on the adults around them to maintain control and restore equilibrium efficiently. If your tone reflects that you are out of control and overwhelmed, your students are likely to become even more frightened and overwhelmed. Use the strategies in this section to help you regulate your own emotional temperature as you dig deep to discover the heat source. Calmness and confidence in adults are great predictors of a smooth outcome and also serve as excellent modeling behaviors for all students.

Crisis—Step 3: What Happened?

When you can, begin to work through what happened. This next section will help you make use of behavior as communication so that both you and your student can learn from it. Without this next step, nothing will have been learned and crisis behaviors will recur.

Taking Care of You

Acknowledge to yourself the toll this experience may have taken on you. Find your own trusted person with whom you feel comfortable venting whatever anxiety, fear, frustration, self-doubt, anger, resentment, or any other strong feelings you may experience as a result of this incident. Or find another outlet for your feelings. Get in touch with your own comfort anchors. Crises can be exhausting and demoralizing for anyone involved. Expressing your energy and venting your professionally pent-up true feelings will enable you to renew, regroup, and return to school with fresh energy tomorrow.

Understanding Behavior as Communication

Working to extinguish a student's negative behaviors will not get you to the root of the problem. At best, it's like offering only a cough drop to someone who has strep throat. It may help for the moment, but, really, it's missing the point and ultimately will allow things to get much worse. Instead, this section will show you how to dig a little deeper to address the origin of disruptive and destructive behaviors and work to prevent them. As we discussed in Chapter 3, *it all springs from anxiety*. So the route to diminishing challenging behavior is recognizing and heading off or relieving the antecedent anxiety.

Remember that a behavior and its triggers may have no apparent connection to each other. Jelani's behaviors, such as perseverating about dinosaurs or knocking his desk over, do not appear to be connected to his coat room crisis. We might infer that he's lost his favorite toy dinosaur. We might assume, when we see that desk go flying, that Jelani has encountered a problem with the desk itself—maybe the desk is wobbly or something insulting has been scrawled on it. But most often, we need to go deeper than that. This section will show you how to look beyond difficult behaviors by putting them in the specific context of the whole child, and then to intervene effectively.

The Last Glass

When considering the accumulation of assaults a student on the spectrum may face, Lenore Gerould (1996) compares it to balancing a tray of water glasses on one hand. Each student seeks to keep her own tray balanced, but every upsetting event is like another glass of water added to the tray. Some glasses are heavier than others, and the student must constantly try to adapt and cope as the tray wobbles. In the end, it takes only one more glass to topple the tray and send everything crashing down. That last glass may not have been the heaviest or the fullest; it was just the one that came right before the fall.

Every student on the spectrum needs someone who really knows her and her triggers to notice how heavy and unstable her tray is getting. For example, suppose you have a student who can't tolerate her clothes getting dirty. Even if she seemed composed when she returned from art class with paint on her shirt, that paint adds another glass to her tray and may contribute to her edginess this afternoon. Help keep every student's tray light and steady by maintaining a watchful eye, soliciting information from other adults in the building, and by maintaining the preventive strategies discussed in Chapter 3.

But when that tray tips, and it will, you'll need to know how to read what's going on and how to help.

Interpreting Behavior: Finding the Heat Source

Occasionally, after she's calmed down, a student on the spectrum will be able to tell you why she thinks she lost control, but more often than not, she will blame whatever event immediately preceded the crisis: *I couldn't get my shoe tied, so I threw it.* It's very unlikely that the student will be able to recognize that the uncooperative shoelace was only the last glass on the tray.

If your students on the spectrum exhibit disruptive or destructive behavior, take a look at these strategies to help you interpret the meaning of the behavior so you can turn the heat back down and keep it down.

Learning Together

When possible, as you come to understand exactly what a challenging behavior was communicating, collaborate about it with the student if you feel she is capable of insight. Most students on the spectrum, however, are not able to engage in much self-reflection. Not only are they unlikely to make these connections themselves; they cannot be expected to apply an abstract cognitive-behavioral theory to their sensory-oriented, anxiety-fueled, impulse-driven systems.

But they can and must begin to make concrete connections between cause and effect, and they can learn to substitute certain behaviors for others in an environment that supports their needs. (Chapter 4 offers strategies for modifying the sensory environment, and Chapter 8 offers strategies for debriefing behaviors and teaching social thinking.)

For those students on the spectrum who are capable of some degree of metacognition, helping them to realize why they do what they do is a crucial first step in developing behavioral self-control. (But keep in mind: It's a first step on a very long journey.)

In a calm and quiet moment, help her to make the connection between an accumulation of small upsets and an out-of-control reaction, or between a big trigger and a big reaction. Ask her what she thinks. Let her digest your suggestions and respond on her level. What is her interpretation? Does she agree with your analysis? Does she have any other suggestions to make it easier next time?

This next section will help you uncover those connections for yourself, using your own knowledge and experience, the feedback you get from parents or caregivers, and the input of students themselves to try to determine what triggered a problematic behavior.

Pattern Protocol

To help you note antecedents, put the problematic behavior in context by looking for patterns.

Who: Does this behavior tend to happen in the company of certain people?

- Might specific teachers or aides have different ways of interacting with the student or different expectations?
- Is everyone who works with this student educated about how best to support her?
- Do certain peers tend to be in the mix when behaviors escalate?

When: Is there any pattern or cycle related to the timing of the behavior?

- Does this behavior happen more during anxiety-provoking transitional times, such as first thing in the morning, just before or after lunch, or near the end of the day?
- Does this behavior arise more often on transitional days, such as Mondays, Fridays, or right before or after vacation?
- Does it tend to happen before lunch when he might be hungry? Is it usually after lunch? What does he eat and drink for lunch?
- Does the behavior always happen before a certain activity that feels overwhelming to him?
- Does the behavior happen so that he will get time in the cool-down room where he can have a much needed break from the classroom?

Where: Is there a consistent place where this behavior tends to occur?

- Does it usually happen in the classroom, in the lunchroom, in the hallway?
- Is it often during a certain subject?

What: What is the context of the challenging behavior? What else is happening? What are the warning signs or indicators that she is escalating?

- Was she refusing to participate?
- Had the volume of her voice increased?
- Was she stimming (flapping, pacing, humming)?

Why: As you examine possible triggers, try to figure out why those contexts are triggering challenging behaviors. Contexts that are often agitating include factors of the following:

socialization and self-esteem

regulation and sensation

health or medication

anxiety about what's missing

anxiety about what's next

Interpreting Behavior: Significance

Before you go too far, consider the *significance* of a behavior, and assess whether or not it truly constitutes a problem. Take a moment here to look at this radical possibility: *Is the behavior objectively problematic or might it be, simply, different?*

For example, sure, you don't expect students to stand up when they speak up in class, but is the fact that Karina always stands up every time she participates really a problem? Is the fact that DeShaun needs to tap his foot while reciting the Pledge of Allegiance really disturbing anyone?

Stretch yourself to think outside the box whenever possible and be open to allowing differences to the extent that they are not disruptive or dangerous to others. If an unusual behavior is non-problematic, leave it alone. Students on the spectrum have enough to work on and you certainly have enough on your plate, too. Whenever possible, let it go.

Interpreting Behavior: Function

Consider the *function* of the behavior: What is the student trying to communicate with this behavior? Look for patterns. (See box, "Pattern Protocol," on page 195.) Consider how this incident connects to prior incidents and what may be the antecedent for these reactions. Be sure you are familiar with the specific anxiety triggers and comfort anchors of students on the spectrum: Only then will you be able to assess accurately what may have contributed to this reaction.

When challenging behaviors persist for any student, call on school counselors or school behavioral specialists. They are specifically trained in managing difficult behaviors and can organize an action plan for assessment and intervention.

A Token Example

Jorge, a second-grade teacher, used a token reward system to help his student, Kayla, stop chewing on crayons. Jorge was very pleased to see that his system quickly extinguished this disturbing behavior.

> *"Fear is the main emotion in autism."*
>
> —Temple Grandin (2008)

But within a few days, Jorge noticed that Kayla was exhibiting new repetitive behaviors. Now she was leaning her chair back until she crashed to the floor, repeatedly. Trusting in the now-proven effectiveness of his token system, Jorge used the same system to extinguish the crashing. Sure enough, within a week, Kayla was no longer leaning back and crashing to the floor.

Meanwhile, Kayla's classroom personality had begun to change dramatically. She had become restless and reckless, constantly bumping into objects and classmates, and, on more than one occasion, bit a classmate.

I was called in for a consult because Jorge was exasperated. He felt that he and Kayla were taking one step forward, two steps back. We reviewed the chronology of events and invited the school's occupational therapist in to join us. Through our discussions, Jorge came to view Kayla's behaviors in a new light. The chewing and crashing and biting behaviors all served the same sensory function for Kayla; they all provided her with proprioceptive input (i.e., input to her joints and muscles). When Jorge had extinguished chewing, Kayla started crashing her chair. When crashing was extinguished, she resorted to biting. All of Kayla's seemingly disparate behaviors were actually communicating the very same message: Her system needed that input and would obtain it, one way or another.

We worked together to address Kayla's behaviors from a brand new proprioceptive perspective, customizing a sensory diet just for her:

1. We noted that Kayla's challenging behaviors seemed to be less prevalent on days when she had phys ed or occupational therapy because her joints and muscles were getting lots of good input from the physical activity. Therefore, the occupational therapist switched Kayla's session schedule to ensure that Kayla would have either phys ed or occupational therapy on almost every day of the week.

2. The occupational therapist provided a small squeeze ball for Kayla to keep in her pocket so she would be able to access input, discreetly, through her arm and shoulders anytime she felt she needed it.

3. Jorge incorporated a "Jumping-Jacks Jam" into his class's daily morning meeting. He also agreed to give Kayla the option of doing some of her daily work standing up and leaning against a wall, rather than sitting so she would get input into her feet, legs, and hips while working.

4. Jorge encouraged Kayla's parents to send her crunchy and chewy snacks, such as raw carrots, hard pretzels, granola bars, and dried fruit. On difficult days, Jorge agreed to allow Kayla to chew gum.

These socially benign strategies gave Kayla ready access to the proprioceptive input she craved and the psychic comfort of feeling sensorily balanced and supported. That comfort provided the added benefit of reducing her anxiety and making her better able to go with the flow of the external world. She no longer needed to seek sensory input; sensory input was now built in to every day. Her destructive and disruptive sensory-seeking behaviors faded away.

The Other Side of Biting

Students with limited social skills or minimal language may also use negative behaviors as poor attempts to interact with other students. By biting peers, Kayla had indeed been making a personal connection of sorts, albeit a very unfortunate one. The same goes for students on the spectrum who hit, shove, poke, tap, bump, interrupt, and so on. We need to recognize that when we eliminate those negative behaviors, we may inadvertently be eliminating all social interaction.

So be on the lookout for social effort. Teach students socially welcome ways to greet peers. For example, instead of alienating and hurting peers by biting them, Kayla was taught to greet peers with high-fives, which was a great solution for her: High-fives encouraged her efforts to socialize while simultaneously supplying her even more of that much needed proprioceptive input.

By the way, Kayla enjoyed this new greeting so much that she began high-fiving students repeatedly throughout the day until Jorge had to set a clear limit of one high-five per peer, per day. Given all the other input that was now built into her schedule, twenty-four high-fives per day was enough, even for Kayla.

Modifying Behavior

Even after you have identified the triggers and adapted the environment or expectations, remember that students on the spectrum may still be highly reactive. Limited executive function severely restricts their ability to stop and think before reacting. Modifying the environment in ways described throughout this book and using incentives, reinforcements, and other behavior-modifying strategies described in Chapter 3 will help. But this section will describe strategies, along the lines of positive behavior support, to follow if challenging behaviors persist in spite of your preventive and responsive efforts.

Measuring Progress

When working to ameliorate persistent challenging behaviors, it's helpful to view them in terms of three basic, measurable elements: frequency, duration, and intensity. Gather data to help you compare these elements over time. This will help you see and celebrate progress where it might otherwise have been easily overlooked.

Frequency: How often does the behavior occur? Track how many times a particular behavior happens in a day, in a week, in a month.

Duration: How long does it last? Note how long the behavior persists each time it emerges.

Intensity: How bad does it get? Consider the behavior on a scale of 1 to 10, with 1 indicating a mildly disruptive behavior and 10 meaning a frightening, destructive, or dangerous behavior.

I consulted at a school where Conor, a first grader, was having harrowing tantrums every day, lasting up to ten or fifteen minutes. Working together, his team, teacher, parents, and I were able to understand the function of his behavior, modify his environment, and implement a new behavioral plan. (See Functional Behavior Analysis below.) Conor's teacher, Carmen, began to track the frequency, duration, and intensity of the tantrums.

When I returned to the class a few days later, Carmen was discouraged. She said, "It didn't work: Conor is still melting down every day."

Carmen and I sat down together and compared the frequency, duration, and intensity of Conor's outbursts to what they had been before our first meeting. We realized that although the frequency of outbursts had not diminished (yet), they were now lasting only about five minutes—less than half as long as before. And they were no longer escalating to the point that Carmen was concerned for Conor's safety or the safety of the other students. So our plan had made a significant positive impact on the duration and intensity of the tantrums. We had more work to do to reduce the frequency, but we were definitely on our way.

By breaking the plan into measurable components and comparing them over time, Carmen was able to note real progress in not-so-obvious places. This recognition gave Carmen something to celebrate with Conor and gave them both a reason to be hopeful. And hope, of course, is one of the best predictors of success.

Functional Behavior Analysis

A Functional Behavior Analysis (FBA) is a systematic means of understanding ongoing challenging behavior in light of its context and function, and using that information to map out a plan for positive change. School counselors or behavioral specialists are directed (according to the Individuals with Disabilities Education Improvement Act) to utilize an FBA approach when addressing ongoing problematic behaviors.

An FBA is usually developed by a school psychologist or other behavioral specialist in collaboration with the interdisciplinary team members, parents, and, when feasible, the student. An effective FBA has three parts: a description of a challenging behavior, an interpretation of the behavior, and a behavioral intervention plan.

1. **Description of Behavior:** The school psychologist or behavioral specialist may ask you to track the frequency and details of a problematic behavior and record a brief description of what it looks like—before, during, and after. If you are asked to provide this kind of information, it may help to look at it from an "ABC" perspective:

   A = Antecedents: Look for possible antecedents of the problematic behavior.

   - How had the day been going overall for this student?
   - What may have upset her before this behavior occurred?
   - How was she acting before her behavior became problematic?
   - Where was she? Who was she with?

   B = Behavior: Describe the behavior itself.

   - What happened? When and where did it happen? Who was present?
   - How did staff respond? What helped? What made things worse?
   - How long did it last this time? How bad did it get?

   C = Consequences: Examine what occurred as a result of the behavior.

   - How did the situation resolve?
   - How did the student react and recover?
   - What were the effects of the behavior on others?

2. **Interpretation of the Behavior:** The school psychologist or behavioral specialist will work with you to interpret patterns around this behavior. Since FBAs are designed to be broadly applicable rather than specifically for students on the autism spectrum, your input will be

especially valuable. Chime in with specific patterns you have observed and antecedents you have identified (as described earlier in this chapter). Be sure to contribute those all-important sensory components, because otherwise they could be easily overlooked during a standard FBA process.

3. **Behavioral Intervention Plan (BIP):** With the support of the interdisciplinary team (including you, all specialists, and the student's parents or caregivers) the school psychologist or behavioral specialist can craft a plan to prevent and respond to similarly challenging behaviors in the future. To formulate a BIP, the school psychologist or behavioral specialist studies the descriptions and interpretations of the behaviors and uses them to recommend new environmental and behavioral modifications. An effective BIP relies on clearly delineated target behaviors and objective means for assessing change.

   When appropriate, the student can collaborate and sign off on the plan as well. All members of the team should agree to support the plan's implementation and have a copy of it to refer to. Continuity across environments will maximize success.

   Be patient with your students as this process unfolds. Remember, some of these behaviors have been locked in for many years; it could take nearly as long to unlock and unlearn them. Note subtle signs of change and celebrate them.

Behavior Analysis: There's an App for That!

Life is hard enough for you when you have students acting out in dramatic ways. Functional Behavior Analysis should help make your life easier, not harder. Now, with a few clicks, you can upload and chart behavioral patterns; track antecedents, behaviors, and consequences; graph frequency, duration, and intensity; share data with your team and with parents; and export data into spreadsheets or IEP programs.

As of this writing, popular apps for behavior analysis include *Behavior Tracker Pro* by Marz Consulting Inc., *Class Dojo* by Class Twist Inc., *Teacher's Assistant Pro* by Lesson Portal LLC, and *Easy Behavior Tracker for Teachers* by TicTapTech, LLC. New apps are being created all the time. Search for "school behavior" in your app store. You're sure to find an app for that.

● ● ● ●

By now you've read about establishing an optimistic environment, heading off anxiety, soothing the senses, collaborating with family and colleagues, capturing engagement, creating a responsive classroom, building a classroom community, and responding to challenging behaviors.

Now, at last, in the next chapter, you'll see that it's time to activate this knowledge and put it all together so that you can effectively engage your whole class in a dynamic curriculum.

Chapter 11

Info In, Info Out

Making Curriculum Happen

Being the dedicated educator that you are, your most pressing question may be, *How do I teach curriculum to students on the autism spectrum*—especially in the context of the Common Core and other rigorous state standards?

Well, guess what: Most of the answers to that question are in the chapters that come before this one. The fact is, if you have read the preceding chapters, then you have been laying the groundwork since page one. Ideally you understand now that you couldn't possibly have taught academic curriculum to students on the spectrum until you first implemented new strategies and new ways of thinking. Most likely, you've come to see that these students can't be available for curricular learning until you have addressed their anxieties, settled their sensory systems, hooked them into engagement, facilitated friendships, cultivated a collaborative community, coaxed communication, interpreted their behavior, and all the rest. That's why this chapter on curriculum comes at the very end of the book. And that's why this chapter all by itself would be woefully inadequate! If you haven't already read the chapters that come before this one, please go back and start at the beginning. I promise that you will find strategies you can implement *right away* to help you break through to these students and create a productive learning environment for your entire class. Once anxieties are alleviated, senses soothed, and minds opened wide (or at least, *ajar*), then this chapter can help you help students on the spectrum access curriculum and demonstrate what they've learned.

Differentiating in the Era of Uniformity

As classrooms have become increasingly diverse, curricular standards have become increasingly uniform. Since the Common Core State Standards (CCSS) and other new, rigorous academic standards began to take hold across the country in 2010, the national agenda has become firmly focused on college and career readiness for all students. Inclusivity is not a buffet; students on the spectrum in inclusive classrooms are being held to all of those standards right along with everyone else. And while college and career readiness is something we clearly want for all students, actually getting everyone there—especially students with significant learning differences—is a murkier prospect.

You've got your work cut out for you, for a couple of reasons. First, the new standards emphasize the very skills that tend to be the most elusive for students on the spectrum. The goal of turning students into critical readers who use metacognition and who analyze author intention or bias, for example, requires prerequisite abilities like self-reflection and theory of mind—both skills that may be beyond the concrete conceptual capacities of students on the spectrum.

Second, unfortunately the new standards offer little support to general educators like you who face an influx of non-standard learners into their classrooms. While the Common Core standards are extremely specific in terms of curricular expectations, they offer only a brief addendum regarding the education of students with special needs. The addendum, entitled "Application to Students with Disabilities," primarily reinforces the basic assumptions of special ed best practice, namely, provide support and related services, follow the IEP, and ensure quality education by qualified personnel. Hopefully, in your classroom and district, those practices have been firmly in place since long before standardized learning goals took over. So how do we bridge the gap between where we were and where the standards say we all need to be?

Without a doubt, the Common Core and other higher academic standards have made the general curriculum in the inclusive environment even more challenging for students on the spectrum—and therefore more challenging for you, too. As Dr. Katharine Beals, a professor of education, points out, the word *remediation* actually appears nowhere in the CCSS. Beals explains:

> *Now that general curriculum is being shaped by dozens of grade-specific Common Core standards, and that teachers (including special-ed teachers) are increasingly expected to align each day's lesson with one or more of these standards, there's even less room for remediation. . . . Sample texts must 'exemplify the level of complexity and quality that the Standards require all students in a given grade band to engage with.' So, while one might supplement a text, say, with glossaries and storyboards, one can't adjust the text itself to match the student's reading level (2014).*

Advocates of CCSS might disagree on the question of whether the standards allow less room for remediation. Perhaps, instead, remediation takes a different form now than it did in the pre-Common Core era. Though leveling the content itself in an inclusion classroom is not acceptable under the new standards, teachers are welcome to scaffold content with as many external supports as they can find. And as you scaffold ever higher, a lifeline stands at the ready in the form of Universal Design for Learning.

Universal Design for Learning

The CCSS addendum about disabilities refers educators to Universal Design for Learning (UDL) for guidance and support in differentiating instruction in inclusive environments. Originally conceived in the 1990s by Anne Meyer and David Rose, co-founders of CAST (the Center for Applied Special Technology), UDL has evolved into a framework for teaching and learning that is intended to reduce barriers to instruction while maintaining high achievement expectations for all students. UDL is based on the notion that rather than force students into a one-size-fits-all learning style, we must provide varied and flexible options for learning, along with appropriate supports and accommodations. The goal is to meet students where they are and as they are and lead them to become resourceful, knowledgeable, strategic, goal-directed, purposeful, and motivated learners.

UDL also supports the idea that by teaching to the margins of your class, ultimately everyone benefits. Consider, for example, that curb cuts were originally created for the specific benefit of individuals in wheelchairs. However, as a result, navigating the sidewalks has gotten much easier not only for folks in wheelchairs, but also for people pushing strollers or riding bikes. In the classroom context, expanded styles of instruction wake up the whole class and facilitate learning for all students.

UDL is built upon three essential principles:

1. **Multiple Means of Engagement:** This principle acknowledges that learners differ markedly in the ways in which they can be engaged or motivated to learn. Varied engagement styles among students on the spectrum can spring from differences related to spontaneity and repetition, novelty and routine, personal relevance, generalization, comfort level, and more.

2. **Multiple Means of Representation:** This principle acknowledges that all learners have different ways of approaching content and guides educators to present content in multiple ways. Varied learning styles among students on the spectrum can spring from challenges related to sensation, processing, organizational skills, and more.

3. **Multiple Means of Action and Expression:** This principle acknowledges that learners have different ways of navigating a learning environment and expressing what they know. Variations of action and expression among students on the spectrum can spring from language differences (affecting speech, expressive and receptive language, and writing) motor differences (affecting handwriting, speech, and manipulation), executive function differences (affecting planning, practice, organization), and more.

In this chapter, we'll take a closer look at why high-level academic skills are particularly challenging for students on the spectrum. Then you'll find a fleet of practical strategies to help you navigate this daunting landscape as smoothly as you possibly can. Using UDL principles as a guide, we will explore ways to help get information *in* through multiple means of representation and engagement, and to help get information *out* through multiple means of action and expression.

Still, the hard fact is that not all students will be able to go the distance. In your inclusion class, whether your state follows the Common Core or other rigorous standards, know that your role is about doing all you can to empower your students to be able to reach their highest potential and access every opportunity within their reach, whatever it may be, in their postsecondary lives.

Getting Information In: Challenges

Even after you have eased anxiety, adapted the sensory environment, and supported engagement, students on the autism spectrum may have very different ways of understanding and engaging in the curriculum. Several major obstacles stand in the way along the learning process for students on the spectrum.

Forest? What Forest?

Central coherence is the way in which our minds interpret and organize information. Strong *global* central coherence is the ability to see the big picture. It's being able to look at an endless expanse of trees and see a forest. Strong *local* coherence, on the other hand, means looking at an endless expanse of trees and seeing, well, an endless expanse of individual trees.

Today's challenging standards of learning expect all students to rely heavily on global coherence. Students need global coherence in order to meet English Language Arts (ELA) standards that involve critical thinking, getting the gist or main idea, summarizing, recognizing broad themes, comparing and contrasting concepts, creating core concepts, and supporting ideas with evidence. Math standards also rely on global coherence as students are expected to contextualize and decontextualize algorithms, recognize and utilize repeated reasoning, evaluate equivalencies and proportions, and understand the essential variability of variables.

Students on the spectrum, however, reside more in the realm of local coherence, gathering knowledge via a visual-perceptual system through which they see and process information in the smallest possible parts. The whole is not a sum of its parts. Each small part is a whole, in and of itself.

Uta Frith, professor emeritus at the Institute of Cognitive Neuroscience at the University College London and the originator of the concept of central coherence, describes someone with strong local coherence as being able to name the pitch of the pop as a cork comes out of the bottle, or identify a dozen brands of vacuum cleaner by their sound alone. At times, this highly circumscribed focus can lead to stunning discoveries that would not be possible if distracted by bigger-picture concepts (Happé & Frith, 2006). But the limitations of local coherence leave a lot of kids lost in the forest.

Embedded in Concrete

Typically functioning learners develop abstraction skills naturally across the elementary years. As they move through third grade and beyond, they begin to notice patterns and make spontaneous associations that facilitate generalization. In their work and their play, they subconsciously test their assumptions and continually modify the categories that are emerging in their consciousness.

Grounded as students on the spectrum are in concrete and discrete bits of information, they struggle to make the enormous leap from concrete questions like *Who, What, When,* and *Where,* to the more nebulous *How,* and ultimately, *Why.*

Be Hypervigilant for Hyperlexia

Be aware that some students exhibit extraordinary decoding skills that can mask very poor comprehension skills. There can be as much as a four-grade discrepancy between decoding and comprehension skills. This disparity, known as hyperlexia, can affect up to 10% of the autism spectrum population. Examine reading strengths and challenges very closely. Consult with your school's reading specialist to find assessments that will isolate reading comprehension issues. Work together to determine interventions to address those needs (Grigorenko, Klin, & Volkmar, 2003).

Smooth or Chunky?

Typically functioning learners organize their thoughts intuitively into fluid categories. New information flows in and is automatically sorted by category. It is then subconsciously assimilated into what students already knew, deepening and broadening their prior knowledge and supporting the development of an abstract or generalized concept.

But students on the spectrum tend to learn new information in concrete chunks that remain discrete in their minds. Imagine chunks of actual solid concrete. They are fixed and immutable. This inability to meld the pieces or connect the dots makes it very difficult for these students to amass a meaningful picture from isolated bits of information; instead they end up with a randomly arranged collection of dots. Therefore, the development of higher level skills, such as generalization, meaningful rule generation, complex problem solving, inferring, and extrapolating, is exceedingly difficult. And learning from mistakes does not happen readily because students may make no mental connection between their erroneous action and its consequence, no correlation between the *cause* and its *effect.*

As we encourage these students to generalize, they may struggle to understand the very concept of generalizing, let alone apply it appropriately, often undergeneralizing and sometimes overgeneralizing. For example, as author Ellen Notbohm describes, "If you teach [a student] to safely cross the street at the intersection of Main and Smith Streets, that 'learning' does not automatically apply to the situation that has him standing at the intersection of 23rd

Avenue and Johnson Drive. To his way of thinking, it's not the same" (2006, p. 28). He does not generalize this piece of learned information unless he is specifically told to.

At other times, a student on the spectrum may overgeneralize. For example, a student has learned, by rote, that it is polite to greet others with *Hi! How are you?* Now she uses that greeting with everyone she sees, all day long, even when she just saw the person a moment before. Figuring out when and how much to generalize is a nuanced skill that takes time to develop.

Learning to Learn

Students on the spectrum need to learn how to mentally sort, merge, label, categorize, file, and cross reference isolated bits of information into open-ended categories and then synthesize those categories into a fluid body of knowledge. They need to learn to learn from their mistakes.

> *"If children do not learn the way we teach them, then we must teach them the way they learn."*
>
> —Dr. Kenneth Dunn

Temple Grandin says that when she saw her first dog and her first cat, she memorized that the difference between a dog and a cat is that "a dog is large and a cat is small." She noted only the one specific difference and overgeneralized it. That worked for her until she saw a dachshund. Now nothing made sense. How could this tiny creature be a dog? Any other categorical differences between a dog and a cat had gone unnoticed.

Grandin had to study pictures of all kinds of dogs and cats to create a new schema in her head to redefine dogs. Now, even to this day, as an adult, she has a list of features she must scroll through in her mind any time she sees a new four-legged animal. First she examines the nose—she has memorized that cats' noses tend to be pink or otherwise light-colored, whereas dogs' noses tend to be black. If, after the nose analysis, she's still not sure, then she'll examine the sound the animal makes and even the smell of the animal. Even with these carefully constructed sorting systems, Grandin is still mired in the details; she has never been able to assimilate a generalized sense to allow her to know immediately whether she is looking at a dog or a cat.

Putting It All Together

In order to move through current learning standards, students are expected to utilize high-level cognitive skills such as critical and inferential thinking, information assimilation, deep knowledge in the disciplines, writing from sources, arguing based on evidence, incorporation of academic vocabulary, and through it all, metacognition. For students with ASD, the development of these skills is compromised by all of the challenges described throughout this book—i.e., anxiety, executive function, sensation, engagement, joint attention, socialization, mindblindness, language, communication, and behavioral regulation.

The strategies provided in all of the chapters preceding this one help you help your students become available for learning. But even once they are available, these students face a critical obstacle as they try to assimilate new information. *What do they do with the information they acquire?* The next section looks at the ways information is commonly filed in the minds of students on the spectrum, and then provides strategies for engagement and representation to help them organize their thinking, working from the outside in.

Getting Information In:
Strategies for Engagement and Representation

Because students on the autism spectrum generally assimilate new knowledge differently than their peers, in the inclusive setting they will need to be taught the conventional curriculum in unconventional ways. In Chapter 5, we looked at the unconventional strategy of using "the hook"—i.e., weaving a student's special interest into the curriculum in order to capture engagement and spark his interest and motivation. Now that you've got him hooked and ready to learn, this section will look at additional strategies for making the curriculum highly accessible in order to maintain engagement and maximize comprehension. Fortunately the routes toward effective engagement and representation have concrete pathways.

Strategies for Academic Engagement

After we have captured the attention and interest of students on the spectrum (which is, in itself, no easy feat), we need to guide their thinking. Because these students may resist new ideas, you may find yourself pushing up against resistance all the way through your lessons unless you present and represent content in ways that help them to file information in meaningful and retrievable ways. Here are some strategies for getting information in effectively:

✳ **Done!** Embed prompts to *stop and think* throughout lengthy tasks. Some students are more driven to get the job done, than to get it done well or meaningfully. They may breeze through decoding without ever giving a thought to engaging the higher-level tasks of comprehending, reflecting, making connections or predictions, and so on.

✳ **One Chunk at a Time:** Involve students in setting their own academic goals. Students on the spectrum are much more likely to be motivated to reach for goals that feel achievable. This may mean chunking your expectations so your students on the spectrum can have a personal celebration each time they complete a small task. Working with your students to determine together what feels manageable will go a long way toward boosting confidence, motivation, and success.

Engagement Through Contextual Connections

Imagine having a filing drawer in your desk, that has no file folders in it. Every time you get a new piece of information that you want to keep, you toss it randomly into that drawer, but it isn't filed anywhere. The drawer becomes cluttered with important information that is randomly strewn about. When you open that drawer again to retrieve a specific piece of information, you can't find it. This is often the case for students on the spectrum, so we have to let them know, overtly, where information must be filed. Here are some ways to help make that happen:

✳ **What Does That Have to Do With Anything?** Review scaffolding steps to help students understand how new information relates to previously learned concepts. Remember, students on the spectrum are not likely to spontaneously connect isolated pieces of information to bigger-picture ideas. Tell them exactly where each bit of information fits along the journey of deeper understanding.

✳ **News to Me:** Review prerequisite concepts before building on them. Don't assume that students on the spectrum will spontaneously or readily activate prior knowledge in order to move forward.

Person, Place, or Thing?

The game of Twenty Questions encourages the organization of facts into flexible categories. Suppose, for example, you begin the game with, *I'm thinking of a place that starts with* D. Immediately, students need to circumscribe their thinking and sort all the places they know into a new category: *What places do I know that start with* D?

As students ask questions, possibilities narrow.

Is it in our town?

No.

State aloud what kinds of places are being eliminated based on the answers: *So we know it can't be Davis Elementary School, even though that starts with* D, *because Davis is in our town.*

Record the questions in yes and no columns in front of the class, so students can keep track and visually add and subtract information.

Would we take a plane to get there?

Yes.

Now students have to generalize all the places they can think of that are far enough to fly to that also start with *D*. They are challenged to make new associations and create brand new categories. This is fluid thinking.

Is it fun there?

Yes!

The most valuable part of the game for these students will be continually revising, redefining, and assimilating new information all along the way. Once the correct answer has been revealed, write it at the top of the chart: *Disney World*. Then review aloud all the steps taken toward discovery and discuss specifically how each answer modified and narrowed your collective thought process.

✱ Cause and Effect: Make cause-and-effect connections overt, demonstrating that for every action there is a reaction. Point out these connections wherever you notice them and state the lesson to be generalized from the experience. *Whoops! We forgot to feed Coconut this morning. She must be hungry because we forgot to feed her. Let's put "Feeding Coconut" on our jobs schedule so we won't forget to feed her again.*

✱ Unpack Analogies: Analogies help students make connections by encouraging them to examine relationships between various concrete objects. *A square is to a quadrilateral as a violin is to an _____.* Help students build bridges between ideas. *How does a square relate to a quadrilateral? What is a violin an example of?* Making this process overt and conscious for students on the spectrum gives them the thinking tools they need in order to compare and contrast higher-level concepts, such as *The House of Representatives is to the U.S. Congress as the House of Commons is to _____.*

✱ Hashtag It: Always begin new topics by putting them in familiar and meaningful contexts. If you are about to discuss world explorers, start by pointing out what wonderful things can happen when we pursue our curiosities. Ask the students to discuss what they themselves have explored and discovered. Setting the scene in this way opens the familiar *curiosity* and *explorer* files in the minds of students on the spectrum, allowing the upcoming information to be filed practically and cross-referenced appropriately. Now they will be able to find it when they need it.

✱ What When? Since students on the spectrum are often number- and calendar-oriented, placing new information into explicit sequential or historical context can help them understand it in the context of what happened before and after.

At the end of the lesson, reiterate the context so that students walk away with a clear understanding of what this new information means to them. This whole-language approach, framing lessons in familiar and meaningful contexts, will support comprehension, retention, retrieval, generalization, and application.

✱ Create Continuity: Collaborate closely and regularly with team members (including parents or caregivers, resource room teachers, reading specialists, aides, counselors, occupational therapists, and so on) to ensure that you all use the same prompts and strategies. Because students on the spectrum will not generalize from person to person or moment to moment, seek to establish consistency and clarity of prompts and academic strategies across multiple contexts. (See more about collaboration with parents and colleagues in Chapters 6 and 7.)

For example, Ian, a third grader, worked intensively with his occupational therapist to improve his very poor printing. Over time, his handwriting in his occupational therapy workbook improved dramatically. When the occupational therapist told the classroom teacher that Ian had achieved his handwriting goal, the classroom teacher was astonished—she had seen no improvement in his handwriting at all. Ian had been returning to his classroom after each occupational therapy session and reverting immediately to his "old" handwriting!

Ian was then instructed specifically by the occupational therapist and teacher together that he should use his "new" handwriting *all the time now, everywhere.* Ian was happy to comply; it just had not occurred to him to generalize his new skill.

Engagement Through Technology

One of the smoothest implementations of UDL principles occurs through the integration of technology into classrooms. Not only is technology inherently appealing to most students, but it opens up an infinitely differentiateable galaxy of varied instruction techniques, actionable options, creative learning strategies, multisensory practice opportunities, high-interest topics and characters, information expression, and data collection. Moreover, digital technology has been a boon to students on the spectrum for a variety of compelling reasons, not the least of which is the fact that technology can make learning fun. Since motivation is one of the strongest predictors of success, don't underestimate the function of fun.

✳ **In the Driver's Seat:** Technology has a specific appeal to students on the spectrum because computers provide predictable, consistent responses. Every time we press a certain key, we get exactly the same result: on/off, open/quit, copy/paste, quieter/louder. This is in stark contrast to human interactions which can be maddeningly unpredictable and uncontrollable.

✳ **Level Completed!** Computers give instant feedback, which is encouraging and reinforcing to struggling learners. Computers also offer intuitive practice and gauges of fluency and mastery to ensure scaffolding of leveled content. So these students may be able to settle into a level of comfort and confidence when on the computer that we don't otherwise see in school. As defenses go down, engagement, motivation, comprehension, and concept assimilation go up.

From the Margins to the Mainstream

In the course of his research for his book *NeuroTribes* (2015), journalist and researcher Steve Silberman spent some relaxed time with a group of information technology (IT) experts. He observes that they were

> a tribe of digital natives with their own history, rituals, ethics, forms of play, and oral lore. While the central focus of their lives was the work they did in solitude, they clearly enjoyed being with others who are on the same frequency. They were a convivial society of loners.
>
> Their medieval predecessors might have spent their days copying manuscripts, keeping musical instruments in tune, weaving, or trying to transmute base metals into gold. Their equivalents in the mid-twentieth century aimed telescopes at the stars, built radios from mail-order kits, or blew up beakers in the garage. In the past forty years, some members of this tribe have migrated from the margins of society to the mainstream and currently work at companies with names like Facebook, Apple, and Google. Along the way, they have refashioned pop culture in their own image; now it's cool to be obsessed with dinosaurs, periodic tables, and Doctor Who—at any age. The kids formerly ridiculed as nerds and brainiacs have grown up to become the architects of our future (p. 3).

✳ Hey, Over Here! When reading and focus are challenging, on-screen highlighting draws focus and reduces distraction. Along similar lines, interactive books and magazines can bring an otherwise inaccessible page to life, helping to keep students alert and engaged. In many digital publications, optional "text to talk" audio support supplements visual reading comprehension.

Instructional Technology

The very same instructional technology you already use with your typically functioning students can go a long way toward engaging and supporting students on the spectrum. These include everyday 21st-century tools, such as iPads, laptops, file sharing, interactive whiteboards, document cameras, remote response systems, digital cameras, multimedia presentation programs, interactive books and magazines, interactive math programs, "makerspaces," and of course all of the vast content resources of the Internet. Some tools or programs are purchased in bulk for district-wide use. For other ideas, check with your school's special ed team and support personnel; search for instructional technology resources online; and exchange ideas with your colleagues. Build a library of tools so you will have options at the ready for your diverse group of students. Once you find a website, app, tool, program, or character your student on the spectrum connects with, stick with it! Keep these students hooked by collecting more programs of that type or that feature that same character. (See Finding the Hook in Chapter 5.)

Assistive Technology

In addition to the instructional technology you may already be using, many specialized tools are available to support a range of learning styles and challenges. Technology that is *mandated* for the support of students with special needs is known as assistive technology. When a student is unable to access the curriculum via conventional means, specific assistive technologies are listed on his or her IEP and must be provided. Whereas instructional technology is optional, assistive technology is mandated and required.

Just as students who are deaf cannot be asked to *listen harder*, students with recognized learning challenges need certain adaptations made to their learning environment in order to allow them access to it. Assistive technology supports for students on the spectrum include communication boards, highlighter strips, predictive word processors, and many, many others. When appropriately assigned, these devices augment students' ability to interact with the learning environment by facilitating independence, bolstering success, building confidence, reducing frustration, and improving behavior. Today a mind-boggling (but ultimately mind-organizing!) array of digital programs are available that support comprehension and engagement and serve as scaffolding tools to help move students forward. (See Chapter 9, which looks at a variety of ways of supporting interaction and communication, for more information on these interactive supports).

Strategies for Academic Representation

Since most students on the spectrum struggle with abstraction and generalization, they need ideas represented via multiple means and manifestations, topics placed in meaningful contexts, connections made transparent, and all of it organized into sensible categories and structures. While those learning skills may be intuitive for most of us, these students need direct practical guidance to sort, label, classify, and merge information. Because effective organization is key to meaningful comprehension and information scaffolding, retention, and retrieval, this section provides strategies for supporting students' organization of curriculum, both externally and internally. Your own scaffolding skills are more important than ever here, as you erect permanent thinking structures onto which your students will build a lifetime of knowledge.

Boosting External Organization

Some students on the spectrum are ultra-organized due to rigidity. They cling to organizational systems to maintain order and are intensely careful to keep their environment neat and predictable. But others are unable to create that kind of external order due to executive function challenges. Unfortunately, a disorganized *external* environment fuels a disorganized *internal* environment. And a disorganized internal environment gets in the way of basic functional needs, like staying calm, producing and processing language, and focusing. And when it comes to meeting lofty new standards in close reading, evidence analysis, or metacognition? *Fuggedaboutit.*

Where's My Stuff?

Today's students must establish different kinds of organizational skills than many of us did when we were young. Organizing digital files is not only necessary as a discrete school skill, but also as a life skill.

First, don't assume that your students on the spectrum have the same level of experience as their peers when it comes to using computers for practical purposes. Some students on the spectrum are exceptionally skilled with computers. Others play games on them, perhaps obsessively, but know nothing about using computers for schoolwork. While computer programs strive to be "user friendly," their designers presume that the "user" is astute at making inferences, generalizing information, learning from mistakes, and so on. Your students on the spectrum may need very basic tutorials in how to use computers for academic purposes.

Second, all students need to be taught to label and file documents in meaningful ways. Students tend to give their personal documents titles like "BestEssayIEverWrote" or "AnnoyingMathProperties." They need to be taught that labels must be straightforward; otherwise those documents will not be searchable . . . or findable. Titles like, "BookReport_TheBFG" or "Math-Properties" are much more useful. Along the same lines, meaningfully titled documents must be organized into meaningfully titled folders, e.g., "5thGrade_Reading" or "8thGrade-Math."

Representation of the Physical Environment

In Kamran Nazeer's *Send in the Idiots* (2006), Nazeer writes about his friend Craig, an adult on the autism spectrum. Craig had to travel as part of his work and sometimes found it difficult to stay in other people's homes overnight. Nazeer recounts that Craig found

> *there was always some idiosyncrasy to do with the shower ("pull the curtain all the way along to the left or the water'll drip on the floor"; "turn the knob on the left-hand side a couple of times—if you turn it three times, you've gone too far—and then turn the lever in the middle counterclockwise.") . . . Staying in other people's houses, interacting with a different set of personal effects and a wide range of objects all with stories behind them that he didn't know, remained difficult. . . . So he devised a strategy to help him manage. Every time he stayed with a friend, he reordered one thing. For example, if there was a pile of books on the coffee table, he might pick it up and alphabetize it. After he had done this one thing, introduced this coherence of his own, he came back to it every time he began to feel a little anxious (p. 123).*

In order to facilitate an organized cognitive environment, start from the outside in. Create a clear, comprehensive, and sensible spatial structure in the classroom to boost local coherence. Most students will feel calmer inside when they can find certain concrete elements of the classroom to rely on for clarity and order. So in order to set students up for learning, make the environment around them as clear and coherent as possible.

✱ **Define Space:** Incorporate small, visually defined areas within the large room to make the space feel manageable. Label these areas clearly with signs such as "Quiet Corner," "Writing Center," "Lab Equipment," and so on.

✱ **Sensible Set-Ups:** Place a Completed Homework bin just inside the classroom door, so students can drop off their homework as they arrive in the classroom.

✱ **Tell It Like It Is:** Do not rely on students on the spectrum to intuit or remember that what you call "the Mailbox" is actually not a box and does not contain mail, but is, in fact, a folder containing worksheets that will be due tomorrow. Replace or supplement the cutesy name with real information: *Tonight's Homework.*

Representation of Workflow

✱ **Subject Sets:** Color-code all folders, notebooks, even worksheets according to subject. Students will have a much easier time taking home the correct sets of books if their social studies textbook, workbook, notebook, and worksheet all match. Color-code them with tabs or

School-to-Home Checklist

☐ Did you copy your homework assignment off the board?

☐ Did you put your homework books into your backpack?

☐ Did you put your planner into your backpack?

☐ Do you have your lunch box?

☐ Do you have your coat?

☐ Do you have your backpack?

Have a nice afternoon!

with wide strips of brightly colored tape on the bindings. This is especially helpful for middle school students who have many different sets of books and expectations to track.

✻ **School-to-Home Checklists:** Laminate a school-to-home checklist. Attach it to students' binders or planners and have them check off items with a dry-erase marker as they are completed. Consider enhancing this chart with photographs or line drawings, as needed.

Always prompt students to check the chart before leaving your classroom or at the end of the day, or post a sign by the door asking, *Did you check your checklist?*

✻ **Home-to-School Checklists:** Suggest that parents or caregivers keep a home-to-school checklist, or other similar checklists for difficult times of day. Many families use checklists to help less organized children get through the fast-paced morning or reluctant bedtime routine.

✻ **Online Support:** Try to post each night's homework online, if possible, for students who may have recorded it incorrectly, recorded it correctly but didn't understand it, or cannot read their own handwriting in their planners. This is also an enormous support for parents and caregivers as they try to help with homework.

✻ **Forget Forgetting:** When possible, allow students to keep extra copies of textbooks at home if these important items tend to be forgotten. Or post digital versions of literature or textbooks online if you can.

On the flip side, suggest that parents send in an extra comfort anchor that can stay at school, so that the absence of a forgotten comfort object does not derail the school day. (See discussion of comfort anchors in Chapter 3.)

Representation of the Visual Field

✻ **Leave No Room for Doubt:** Keep worksheets plainly organized by labeling items clearly with numbers or by drawing boxes around separate elements.

✻ **Eschew the Curlicue:** Use a straightforward, highly readable font on worksheets, avoiding word art, outlines, shadows, elaborate curlicues, or other unnecessary frills on letters.

✻ **Curtail Clutter:** Be sure there isn't too much information on any one page. Leave plenty of blank space to give the eyes a place to rest.

✻ **Guide the Eyes:** Create a clear visual connection between each question and its answer space, by using ellipses, dashes, or other visual connectors. For example:

Magnets have positive and negative poles . . . . True or False?

Boosting Internal Organization

Once the external environment is clearly organized, students on the spectrum can make sense of it. Then they can begin to relax into the orderliness of their surroundings, recognizing that everything has its place. *Ahhh.*

But we still need to help students to make meaningful sense of what they've learned. By making expectations and concepts unequivocally clear and meaningfully accessible, we can boost comprehension to ensure that new knowledge gets in and stays put.

A Homework Staple

Supporting organization may require only very simple adjustments. For example, Daphne gets utterly tangled up when trying to work on a packet of double-sided pages that are stapled in one corner. She never knows whether she is on the front or back of any page, and loses track of which way to flip: *Is it time to turn the whole packet over or just turn a page?* Inevitably, she either misses pages throughout or she does a couple of pages and then starts flipping backwards, coming to the erroneous conclusion that she has completed the entire packet when she hasn't at all.

Three staples down the left side of the packet, instead of only one in the corner, immediately turns an incomprehensible floppy mess into a neat booklet and eliminates this problem completely.

Representation of Expectations

As discussed in Chapter 3, setting clear, concrete, and consistent expectations is helpful and comforting for students on the spectrum. Following instructions and rules may be an area of strength for these students and a way they can set an example for the whole class. In fact, they may be your best rule followers.

But students on the spectrum may also be rule followers to a fault. The extent to which expectations can be generalized is not likely to be inferred by these students. And since expectations are often learned by rote, they are not memorized in a way that is meaningful. Worse, if the parameters of the rules or instructions are vague or unclear, this will raise anxiety and compromise compliance. When you say *Excuse me: There should be no talking when I'm talking,* your student may not be able to decipher whether that means only right now, or ever. Here are some ways to make parameters clear for your students:

✳ **Instructions:** Label instructions by name every time they appear: *Instructions.* Write out instructions succinctly and in clear, unequivocal language. Verify that your students truly understand what is expected of them by asking them to say it back in their own words to ensure accurate comprehension and assimilation.

✳ **Section by Section:** Use horizontal lines to separate sections before a new set of instructions is about to go into effect.

✳ **Why?** Help students to consider *why* rules and instructions are what they are. My son had been taught and had memorized that light- and dark-colored clothes must be sorted before being placed in the washing machine. At seventeen, he ran his first load of laundry all by himself. When the clothes came out of the washer, I saw that the light- and dark-colored clothes had been in the washer together. I pointed out, "Oh, I guess you forgot to sort the colors."

He replied, indignantly, "No! I *did* sort them! And then I put them in."

He had, apparently, sorted the lights from the darks, as instructed. But then he had summarily dumped them all into the washer together. The sorting instruction had been memorized by rote; he hadn't placed it into any context, and so it was not applied in a meaningful way. I should have explained to my son that we keep the light clothes away from the dark clothes in the washer because when dark-colored clothes are wet, the colors may seep out of the fabric and stain the light-colored clothes. And that's why, once we sort the clothes, they need to stay separate throughout the wash and dry cycles.

✳ **What's In and What's Out?** Set boundaries around expectations, including both what is included in the rule and what is not. For example, I should also have clarified for my son that after the clothes are washed, dried, and folded, it's okay to put them all together into the dresser! In fact, at that point, a new sorting system takes over: sorting by type of clothes—i.e., all socks in one drawer, all pants in another drawer, all shirts in another—regardless of their color.

Representation of Concepts

✳ **What Where?** When discussing broad or abstract concepts, support concept organization by using graphic categorizing tools, such as charts, columns, grids, cluster maps, concept webs, Venn diagrams, character trees, sequencing activities, and timelines. These visually delineate where categories begin and end, and organize what information fits where. Being able to see the parts that comprise the whole helps students recognize an abstract entity as a compilation of individual parts.

✳ **A Little Estimating:** The task of estimating draws students away from concrete details to try to get an overall sense about a situation. But students on the spectrum may be much more comfortable mired in the precision of the details, *thankyouverymuch*, and have a hard time stepping back to make an estimate. When you ask them to take a guess about how many people might be able to sit in the auditorium, they may find it much easier to count every seat or even to multiply by rows than to take an "educated" guess.

Affirm the value of counting, even as you present the value of estimating. Contrast situations that call for specific answers with others in which non-specific answers are more appropriate. The more students on the spectrum can recognize different ways to think, the more thinking strategies they will have at their disposal.

✳ **Modeling:** When you show a diagram or picture of a concept, you are expecting students to visualize what it would look like in reality. This is a leap students on the spectrum may not be able to make. Really, with all due respect, your diagram of a heart looks nothing like an actual heart. Provide real or physical models of concepts whenever possible to represent perspective and spatial relationships in full dimensions.

✳ **Switch It Up:** Consider that literacy and other skills can develop in nonlinear ways, facilitated by creative input. Know your students' sensitivities and learning styles and offer choices. Provide opportunities for looking, listening with headphones, touching, manipulating, interacting, performing, creating, even smelling and tasting. Expose students to lessons using varied approaches, always seeking one that flips the switch, makes a connection.

For example, in her book, *You're Going to Love This Kid!* (2003), Paula Kluth, a former special educator and professor of education, describes having students "walk" a sequence or timeline. She suggests writing the names of important events on individual pieces of paper and having students place events in order as they walk, hop, crawl, skip, or jump along the sequence. At each step they might call out a detail or fact about that event or name an important player or element related to it. In addition to the academic reinforcement, this kind of kinesthetic learning experience can awaken interest and reinforce retention for most of the students in your class. It also provides valuable proprioceptive and vestibular input to students who need it. (See Chapter 4 for more about various types of sensory input.)

But be aware that for some students on the spectrum, this same exercise could be an onslaught of too many expectations at once. Offer choices. Give students the option of simply placing the events along the timeline without speaking. Allow students to write the timeline on paper and draw pictures of the events. Appoint a fact-checker, who walks the timeline only after others have completed it and checks their work.

Vari-Sensory Instruction

Representing topics via numerous modalities at once, known as multisensory instruction, often helps students integrate new knowledge. For many students, having the opportunity to touch textured letters while simultaneously seeing their shapes and hearing their sounds enhances learning. Indeed, many students on the spectrum learn much better through some senses than through others.

However, due to sensory and other processing challenges, students on the spectrum may get overwhelmed by an abundance of sensory stimulation. For some, receiving input via multiple senses at the same time could be the worst approach. Rather than throw multiple stimuli at them all at once, try presenting different sensory approaches one at a time, serially. Consider conveying the same information numerous times, each time utilizing a different sensory experience. Instead of multisensory instruction, that's vari-sensory instruction.

Along the same lines, try not to require students to do two things at once, such as *Watch and take notes* or *Listen to this story while you finish cutting* or even, *Look at me when I'm talking to you*. (See more about eye contact in Chapter 5.)

Some teachers fade their use of visual and other extra supports toward the upper grades of elementary school and into middle school, believing them to be no longer necessary or "age appropriate." But students on the spectrum may continue to benefit from these supports to help compensate for their enduring challenges in other areas.

Getting Information Out: Strategies for Action and Expression

As described in the preceding pages, getting information into students on the spectrum depends largely upon effective representation of information, student engagement and motivation, and the organization of both the external and internal learning environments. But another challenge remains: Once that information gets in, how do we get it back out?

Supporting Output

You will probably find that getting students on the spectrum to demonstrate their knowledge is an uphill battle. To be in your inclusive classroom, they are pushing up against their challenges all day long. With obstacles emerging around every corner, these students may get impatient and frustrated just trying to get the words out. They may not dig in to or persist with difficult work. Their impulsivity and prior failure experiences may cause them to give up as soon as the going gets tough. They may actually hold impressive volumes of relevant knowledge in their heads but be unable to translate them into the verbal format you require. If you have students like these, any of the following strategies can help organize their efforts to help them hang in there long enough to get the job done. Here is where we incorporate the UDL principles of multiple means of action and expression.

✳ **Jot It Down:** Encourage students to make notes and keep lists. Many students on the spectrum have a fondness for lists. Lists are orderly, predictable, direct, and easily self-maintained. Notes and lists can serve two purposes for students on the spectrum. First, they can help compensate for working memory challenges. Second, they can help students put aside intrusive thoughts, confident in the knowledge that once those thoughts are committed to writing, they won't disappear and can be revisited later.

✳ **It's All About the Journey:** The more you incorporate graphic organizers into your students' work, the more access you will have to understanding and guiding their thought processes. Don't emphasize the final product; grade the *process*. This is a powerful intervention with struggling learners. By celebrating the value of effort over achievement, you will greatly bolster their willingness to *try*.

I Think I Can, I Think I Can . . .

Teach students on the spectrum the concept of trying when it's hard. Affirm that the work is indeed hard, but that only means we have to work even harder at it: *We don't give up when it's hard; we try harder when it's hard* (Baker, 2009).

✱ **Try Hand-Under-Hand:** Instead of the usual hand-over-hand support by which we help students manipulate materials, try *hand-under-hand*. Put your own hand directly on the material and let the student wrap his or her hand around yours. By having their own hands on top, students feel that they are making something happen, that they are in control of the action. This bolsters their confidence that they will ultimately be able do the activity themselves (Baker, 2009).

✱ **Any Which Way They Can:** The opportunity to demonstrate knowledge in a variety of ways can help students on the spectrum to demonstrate what they know and reinforce its assimilation into a body of cohesive knowledge. For example, when possible let students choose whether to use print or cursive, pen or pencil, laptop or desktop. Remember that for students with fine motor challenges, the effort required to form letters by hand may obstruct the expression of words and ideas. Typing may be a much smoother route of expression for letting words and ideas flow freely.

If writing paragraphs about a historical event, for example, is too challenging, offer the options of creating a magazine cover, drawing cartoon versions of the event, acting out the factions, rewriting the ending, writing a poem about the situation, comparing this event to another using a Venn diagram, participating in a (school-sanctioned) online discussion forum, and so on. Let them speak it, draw it, act it, sing it, dance it, paint it, videotape it, map it, collage it, montage it, podcast it, timeline it, PowerPoint it. All students may benefit from structured whole-class projects that allow for creative expression, such as performing a play for other classes, presenting projects to parents and caregivers, performing a rap song, staging a debate, videotaping a documentary, creating a brochure, filming a commercial, and more.

By encouraging your students on the spectrum to engage in alternative means of expression, you are also enhancing their comprehension of the topic by making it personally meaningful for them. Now they've got something to write about. If your students couldn't write about the intended topic in the abstract, maybe now they can write about their experience dancing or debating it. That's a step in the right direction. The more they write, the better they'll get.

Thinking Outside the Arteries

Linda, a fifth-grade teacher, collaborates with Keith, a physical education teacher, to set up a larger-than-life model of the circulatory system in the gym. Via four-wheeled scooters, students propel themselves across the floor, on their stomachs. Like individual blood cells, they glide along, circulating through veins, arteries, valves, ventricles, and atria, demonstrating their knowledge of the route on this sanguine journey they'll never forget.

Tech Support

In addition to the word processing programs and apps described in Chapter 9, tools and programs that support writing and the organization of ideas are available in abundance to help students demonstrate their knowledge. Your district may already have tools and programs available to support students. Additionally, check with the special ed team for tech recs. Ask reading, speech and language, occupational therapy, or other support personnel for ideas; search for instructional technology resources online; and exchange ideas with your colleagues.

✱ **Presto Chango:** Many students benefit from online tools that guide the transformation of ideas into sentences into paragraphs into essays, such as word banks, Wordle maps, pop-up word and picture dictionaries, and pronunciation guides.

✱ **Homework Is a Drag:** Interactive organizers allow students to drag ideas around the screen to help plan and edit essays, organize ideas into concept maps and flow charts, and integrate that information into outline form.

✱ **You're So Close:** Built-in prompts promote efficient use of time to support pacing and reduce anxiety.

✱ **File Folders!** Responsive digital filing cabinets guide students to organize their thoughts, providing essentially an external hard drive to compensate for those overflowing file drawers in students' heads.

✱ **Exponential Benefit:** Math programs offer supports that include digital graphing and charting; draggable numbers, symbols, and shapes; predictive symbols; talking calculators; organization and alignment of math problems; and multisensory number manipulation.

Accessing Assessments

Some of the state assessments that are administered digitally have gotten on board with "universal" design to offer "universal" access, embedding many features that make the tests easily accessible to all kinds of learners without sacrificing content validity. These include volume control, bookmarking, highlighting, and more.

Additional accessibility features and accommodations can be enabled based on documented individual need, as indicated on the IEP. These can include text-to-speech technology, use of a calculator, the ability for test directions to be read aloud and repeated as needed (on headphones), word prediction, extended time, and more. All of these supports provide students with adapted means of accessing the curriculum, while minimizing the stigma of receiving support. If you feel your student would strongly benefit from this kind of support, bring it up with the IEP team or special ed department, who can determine whether the need meets the accommodation criteria.

A 21st-Century Perspective

Consider the absolute value of certain skills. If a specific skill is not developing, despite longstanding and creative interventions, UDL guidelines, and IEP accommodations, and if the effort is causing the student intense stress and anxiety, consider carefully whether the attainment of that particular skill is worth the battle. Collaborate with parents and caregivers to keep perspective on the necessity of attaining certain skills. For example, psychologist Tony Attwood (2009) views handwriting as a passé 20th-century skill, much the way saddling up a horse to go from New York to Boston is a 19th-century skill. In this high-tech era, there may be reasonable ways to compensate for certain skill deficits. If not, in some cases, achievement expectations will need to be modified on the IEP.

Assess Your Assessments

What are your tests actually testing? Sometimes what looks like poor comprehension on the part of students on the spectrum may actually be a problem *expressing* comprehension through traditional means. Consider that responding on a written test requires focus and organization; manipulating materials requires hand-eye coordination; participating verbally in class requires verbal ability, language processing, and consistent engagement. In these cases, your assessments may not be assessing what the students know as much what they can produce. If you have students who struggle to process and produce information, try some of these strategies to create contexts in which all students can demonstrate their concept competence.

Consider the Physical Environment

✱ **Sounds of Silence:** When administering an assessment, implement some common-sense adjustments to the classroom environment. Shut down classroom computers to eliminate their distracting humming and hypnotic screensavers; turn off buzzing overhead lights; keep the classroom door closed. Choose another time to sharpen pencils, staple projects onto the bulletin board, eat your crunchy salad, and so on.

Consider Format

✱ **Read Between the Lines:** Just as you have learned to look beyond students' behaviors and reactions to see what they are really trying to communicate, examine your assessments through a similar lens. Read over your questions and instructions with the assumption that nothing is self-evident to students on the spectrum. They cannot read between the lines, but you can. Are you really saying what you mean? Are your expectations crystal clear? If you present information in simple, straightforward language, you just might get the same back.

✽ Start Their Engines: Since generating ideas and getting started can be a particular challenge for students on the spectrum, offer sample sentence starters.

✽ Cloze It Up: Use multiple choice, True/False, and matching column question formats, as opposed to open-ended questions that require students to jump inside your head and read your mind—an especially difficult leap for students on the spectrum who may be limited by mindblindness.

If you must use fill-in-the-blank formats, stick with cloze sentences, such as *Tropical rainforests are located near the _____, which is the 0° latitude line that circles the Earth* or *George Washington was the first _____ of the United States.* These are more specific in their expectations than wide-open questions like, *Where are rainforests located?* or *Who was George Washington?*

> ## A Relative Space
>
> One teacher recently shared with me that her sixth-grade student on the spectrum answered a written assessment question as follows: *The second step in the scientific method is the <u>at</u>, which is an educated guess about the outcome of an experiment.*
>
> When she asked the bright young man why he wrote the word *at* instead of *hypothesis,* he replied, "Well, the instructions said: *Choose the word that best fits in the blank space.* The blank space was so small that the only word I could think of that would fit in that space was *at.* The word *hypothesis* would never have fit."

✽ Put It in the Bank: Always accompany fill-in-the-blank questions with a small word bank. Word banks ensure that you are testing for word recognition and concept knowledge, rather than word retrieval.

✽ One Step at a Time: Many students on the spectrum have difficulty with working memory; this means that they cannot hold onto one concept while considering others. So by the time they figure out the value of y, the value of x has vanished from memory. Some students may benefit from writing down every step of each math problem, even the parts they do in their head, to prevent them from getting lost along the way.

On the other hand, for others, putting their mental math into writing presents a critical obstacle to effective numeracy. (See box, "Just Do It," on page 223.)

Consider Content

✽ Cut to the Chase: Be sure your content-area tests are testing only content, and are not dependent upon speed, vocabulary, working memory, word retrieval, organization, handwriting, or other isolated skills that could interfere with the demonstration of content knowledge.

Just Do It

It is widely known that many individuals on the autism spectrum excel in mathematics. There is a comfort to numbers: they maintain a fixed value; they interact with other numbers in predictable ways. In fact, many of the world's greatest scientists and mathematicians have gone to numerical places no one had gone before, largely because of their distinctively spectrum-y qualities of tenacious immersion in numeracy.

Katharine Beals, a professor of education, and Barry Garelick, a high school math teacher, suggest, however, that "mandatory demonstrations of 'mathematical understanding'. . . can impede the 'doing' of actual mathematics" (2015). It is true, indeed, that many children on the autism spectrum, even those who are mathematically gifted, struggle when asked to convert their numerical answers into words. Suddenly, the skill involved is no longer a mathematical one.

Beals and Garelick affirm their point by recalling that "back in 1944, Hans Asperger, the Austrian pediatrician who first studied the condition that now bears his name, famously cited one of his patients as saying, 'I can't do this orally, only headily.'"

The researchers consider this inability to be an unprecedented liability in Common Core America, where the standardized tests require children to explain how they reached their answers—and sometimes to explain why certain answers are wrong. Beals and Garelick propose that the ability to explain answers is only one marker of understanding. Another marker, they suggest, is "the answers themselves. If a student can consistently solve a variety of problems, that student likely has some level of mathematical understanding. . . . At best, verbal explanations beyond 'showing the work' may be superfluous; at worst, they shortchange certain students and encumber the mathematics for everyone" (2015).

Since demonstration of the problem-solving process may be necessary on standardized tests, look for classroom opportunities to sit alongside a student as she does her mental math, and provide a narrative, in real time, of the steps she is mentally leaping over. Gradually she may come to associate the words you attach to the process, even if they describe steps that are not occurring consciously or discretely in her mathematical process.

✷ **Focus on Fluency:** Since attention and engagement can be quite fleeting among students on the spectrum, information can seem to flow in and right back out of their minds. Work to teach and reteach discrete skills until your students are fluent in them. Once a particular skill is imprinted, it is much more likely to stay put. Encourage students to persist until they are masters at a skill and then challenge them to perform it even more quickly or in another context before moving on to something new.

For example, suppose you have taught multiplication, and now you expect your students to apply their multiplication facts to the next unit: division. Of course any students who are not fluent in multiplication facts will struggle with this transition. But students on the spectrum may actually lose their grip on multiplication facts as they move into the new concepts of division. Be sure to give students on the spectrum ample opportunity to practice, practice, practice a skill until it comes easily and expertly—until they are fully fluent in using that skill—before building on it.

✳ **Chew *and* Swallow:** Emphasize content meaning over content regurgitation. For example do students really need to memorize the precise longitude and latitude of the Amazon rain forest in order to understand the meaning of the word *tropical* and the relationship between tropical climates and the equator? Rather than test rote regurgitation of facts, reach for conceptual competence.

✳ **One Skill at a Time:** Try to test one skill at a time as skills are developing. If you are testing for structure, be flexible about length; if you are testing vocabulary, be flexible about punctuation; if you are testing for facts, be flexible about handwriting.

What's Not Standard About Standardized Assessments

Of course, as gentle as you make your own classroom assessments, your students will inevitably face sharper obstacles whenever they face standardized state assessments. Moreover, be aware that you have probably made reference to The Test many, many times before test day. Anxiety builds in every student each time you mention it, but without strong coping skills, students on the spectrum may not be able to regulate that escalating anxiety, especially if they don't know what to expect.

It doesn't help that on Test Day, they walk in to find the classroom rearranged. Or, if your students are granted a separate testing location on their IEP, they may be whisked away to a previously unknown location. Suddenly there are new rules about clearing books and devices off the desktops, and the usual schedule is nowhere to be found. In middle school, students may find their familiar teacher to be inexplicably replaced by a proctor they have never met before.

Find out from your administrator or state education office how the standardized test scores are used in terms of student placement or promotion. While the stakes may be high for your school or even for you as the teacher, they aren't necessarily high for individual students. If you learn that the test scores are not a major factor in these decisions, pass that enormously reassuring information along to your students. Don't worry about encouraging slacking: Not only are calm students happier students, but calm students are better test takers!

Once the test begins, your students' compromised engagement and academic capacities are stretched to their limits and beyond, all in the context of new sets of instructions, expectations, and answer formats, and all under an intense time pressure. Don't leave your students to muddle their way through those challenges uninitiated. Instead:

- Teach or review basic testing skills:

  We sit still, mouths closed, bodies quiet.

  We do our best.

  We read each question twice in our heads.

  We cross off answers one by one as we eliminate them.

  We circle the topic words in the sentence.

  The focus is not on getting it done but getting it done well.

- Unpack conceptual conundrums like *None of the above* and *All of the above.*

- Provide lots of practice with organizational hazards like bubble sheets.

- Let them experience what fifteen minutes of testing feels like . . . what twenty minutes of testing feels like.

- Give them a visual schedule for Test Day in advance.

- Let them know everything they can expect: *What will be different? What will be the same?*

- Remind them that all they need to do is their best and that will be good enough. And good enough is good enough.

● ● ● ●

This chapter has offered strategies for getting curricular skills and knowledge into and out of students on the autism spectrum. It's been a bumpy road and most likely you have fallen into a few potholes along the way. You may feel that it's taken an awful lot of effort for you to get to this chapter and for your students on the spectrum to become "ready to learn."

But as you think back over what you've read in this book, realize that you have been moving steadily forward, putting one foot in front of the other to teach your students on the spectrum, and that they have been learning from you *every step of the way.*

- ✔ You have taught these students that others see and admire their strengths, which has boosted their self-esteem and inspired their belief in their own potential.

- ✔ You have taught them to trust in the safety and predictability of your classroom environment, optimizing their independence and capacity for flexibility.

- ✔ You have taught them how to monitor their own anxiety and sensory reactions, giving them tools and strategies to self-regulate and self-soothe.

- ✔ You have met them on their own terms and taught them how to expand their narrow horizons and risk moving out of their comfort zones to tune into new experiences.

- ✔ You have talked to and learned from their families, opening and maintaining the vital link of school-home continuity and seamless support.

✔ You have shared your wisdom and cultivated a community of support throughout the building.

✔ You have taught your whole class life-lessons in diversity and acceptance by building a village that cultivates kindness and champions citizenship.

✔ You have created a responsive classroom, facilitating all kinds of communication and teaching students on the spectrum that their words and ideas are valuable and valued.

✔ You have shown these students that their team of supporters can capably sustain them through their most difficult moments and transform those moments into positive change.

✔ You have stood tall in the face of challenging new standards, and brought your students along as far as they can go.

✔ And, I hope, you have learned a thing or two along the way as well.

Best of all, the lessons you have taught your students on the spectrum are *skills for life* that they could not have learned on their own. These forever-lessons are now part of who they are and who they bring forth to the social world. You have imbued their futures with promise and their spirits with possibility.

Going forward, your students on the spectrum may always remember every single rule of grammar or the developments in musket construction in the Revolutionary War. They may be able to recite every single geometrical theorem from memory. They may remember the scent of your shampoo or the date and day of the week you were born. Or they may remember you as the teacher who gave out french fries during social studies. But you can be sure that all of your students, whether on or off the spectrum, will remember you as a teacher who listened, understood, accepted, and believed.

Supporting Students With Autism Spectrum Disorder

Facts and Tips for Special Area Teachers

The information on this sheet will help you create a positive learning environment for students on the autism spectrum while they are with you. Thanks for your willingness to learn about and support them!

Students with Autism Spectrum Disorder (ASD) are quirky, endearing kids who struggle with a wide range of challenges in any or all of the following areas:

Anxiety: Students with ASD often have limited coping skills, which can lead to extreme anxiety in unfamiliar situations. They depend heavily on routines and structure, and may cling to certain objects or repetitive interests to help them feel safe.

✔ Ask the teacher to help you prepare a visual schedule to create predictability and reduce anxiety.

Rigidity: Students with ASD tend to be rigid rule followers. Rules make life more manageable and predictable. *These students very much want to follow the rules, but may not understand exactly what the rules are.* This same rigidity means these students may get extremely agitated when rules are broken or when something unexpected happens.

✔ Use concrete and specific language. Try to make your expectations as clear as possible.

Communication: Many of these students express themselves in unusual ways or have a hard time making their thoughts and needs known. They may also have difficulty understanding your words.

✔ Remember that making conversation is a developing skill. Be patient and supportive.

Socialization: These students struggle socially. Interactions may be awkward, one-sided, or nonexistent. Be aware that social challenges make these students very vulnerable to being bullied.

✔ Keep a watchful and protective eye out for provocation, bullying, teasing, or other disrespectful treatment by peers.

Sensation: Most students with ASD take in far too much or far too little sensory input. Hand-flapping, rocking, and similar behaviors are related to sensory challenges.

✔ Adapt the sensory environment based on individual needs and teacher input. *Offer options* whenever possible.

Behavior: *All behavior is a form of communication.* Difficult behaviors indicate that something is wrong. Chances are, a behavioral problem is the result of one of the challenges described above.

✔ When students with ASD misbehave, they need help— not consequences.

Inside/Outside: Some students with ASD demonstrate obvious, *external* challenges: They may flick their fingers or talk endlessly about a single topic.

✔ Don't *underestimate* these students; they may have lots of clever, creative ideas going on inside.

Other students are primarily affected by *internal* challenges: They may appear typical.

✔ Don't *overestimate* these students; they may struggle intensely with many challenges that can't readily be seen.

Know Your Student

- Don't reinvent the wheel! Talk with the classroom teacher or case manager to find out what your student's special interests are, how best to engage her, what tends to set a student off, and what makes things better.

- Read the IEP to find out more about the challenges this student faces and what goals have been set.

- Attend team meetings to learn about current stressors and new strategies. If you can't get there, ask for a summary of the discussion and recommendations.

Flip the page to find ideas for your special area!

Perspectives on Art

Break the Mold: Sensory challenges abound in the art room, any of which may be unbearable: the *feel* of fingerpaint, glue, clay, charcoal, papier maché, or oil pastels; the *smell* of paints, markers, plaster, pottery dust; the *sound* of markers, Styrofoam, or wood sanders. Offer choices of medium.

Paint With a Broad Brush: Be aware that fine motor and visual-motor challenges may cause students to grip and press on art implements so hard that they tear the paper or so lightly that their work is illegible. Allow use of various implements and accept alternative outcomes.

Realism Versus Impressionism: Some students with ASD struggle to differentiate colors, shapes, and other detailed elements of pictures, such as subject versus shadow and figure versus ground. Accept general impressions if details are elusive.

Music Notes

Scale It Back: The sounds of some instruments may be painful to some kids—sometimes. Watch the volume. Headphones, earplugs, and area rugs are effective at making the sound and acoustics manageable for students with ASD.

Tune In: Sensory discrimination challenges may prevent some students from distinguishing among musical tones and rhyming sounds. Allow flexible types of musical interpretation.

Drum Up Alternatives: Consider fine motor, oral motor, and visual-motor challenges when students play or read music. Offer instruments that require less or different types of coordination.

Library Reference

Brave New World: Moving abruptly from the noisy hallway into the silent library can be very challenging for students with ASD. Help them shift gears by providing gentle support and allowing them time to make the adjustment.

Great Expectations: Among many students with ASD, decoding is far stronger than comprehension. Look for books that pair age-level content with simpler text. Graphic novels can be very accessible to students with ASD.

A Series of Fortunate Events: Engagement is one of the greatest obstacles in getting students with ASD to read. Take the time to introduce students to a series. Once your student is acquainted with Violet, Claude, Sunny, and Count Olaf (or with Harry, Ron, and Hermione), those characters provide a thread of familiarity that can open up whole new worlds.

Classroom Teacher Notes: _____

_____

_____

_____

For more information, touch base with the classroom teacher or principal (or browse through *Autism Spectrum Disorder in the Inclusive Classroom*).

Elaborating on Collaborating

Group work is a special challenge for students on the spectrum. Here's how you can maximize success:

- Give a whole-class lesson on group-work skills including flexibility, negotiation, compromise, tolerating mistakes, problem solving, and recognizing when and how to get help.

- Choose group-mates mindfully.

- Create structure by assigning roles that are suited to individual strengths. Consider positions like media manager, art critic, music critic, efficiency expert, or fact-checker.

Facts and Tips for Phys Ed Teachers and Coaches

The information on this sheet will help you create a positive learning environment for students on the autism spectrum while they are with you. Thanks for your willingness to learn about and support them!

Students with Autism Spectrum Disorder (ASD) are quirky, endearing kids who struggle with a wide range of challenges in any or all of the following areas:

Anxiety: Students with ASD often have limited coping skills, which can lead to extreme anxiety in unfamiliar situations. They depend heavily on routines and structure, and may cling to certain objects or repetitive interests to help them feel safe.

✔ Ask the teacher to help you prepare a visual schedule to create predictability and reduce anxiety.

Rigidity: Students with ASD tend to be rigid rule followers. Rules make life more manageable and predictable. *These students very much want to follow the rules, but may not understand exactly what the rules are.* This same rigidity means these students may get extremely agitated when rules are broken or when something unexpected happens.

✔ Use concrete and specific language to make your expectations as clear as possible.

Communication: Many of these students express themselves in unusual ways or have a hard time making their thoughts and needs known. They may also have difficulty understanding your words.

✔ Remember that making conversation is a developing skill. Be patient and supportive.

Socialization: These students struggle socially. Interactions may be awkward, one-sided, or nonexistent. Be aware that social challenges make these students very vulnerable to being bullied.

✔ Keep a watchful and protective eye out for provocation, bullying, teasing, or other disrespectful treatment by peers.

Sensation: Most students with ASD take in far too much or far too little sensory input. Hand-flapping, rocking, and similar behaviors are related to sensory challenges.

✔ Adapt the sensory environment based on individual needs and teacher input. Offer options whenever possible.

Behavior: *All behavior is a form of communication.* Difficult behaviors indicate that something is wrong. Chances are, a behavioral problem is the result of one of the challenges described above.

✔ When students with ASD misbehave, they need help—not consequences.

Inside/Outside: Some students with ASD demonstrate obvious, *external* challenges: They may flick their fingers or talk endlessly about a single topic.

✔ Don't *underestimate* these students; they may have lots of clever, creative ideas going on inside.

Other students are primarily affected by internal challenges: They may appear typical.

✔ Don't *overestimate* these students; they may struggle intensely with many challenges that can't readily be seen.

Flip the page for specific suggestions!

Overcoming Hurdles in Phys Ed

Take One for the Team: Being part of a team is a special challenge for students on the spectrum. Before breaking into teams, take a few minutes to conduct a whole-class lesson on teamwork. Review important skills like flexibility, patience, negotiation, compromise, tolerating mistakes, problem solving, and recognizing when and how to get help. Choose teammates kindly and mindfully. Create structure by offering positions that play to individual strengths, such as timekeeper, scorekeeper, equipment manager, efficiency expert, or sportscaster.

Run Interference: The sounds of pounding feet and skidding sneakers may be overwhelming to students on the spectrum. Look for signs of discomfort. Offer breaks or, *if necessary*, less intense ways of participating.

Par for the Course: Poor athletic performance may be due to challenges of gross motor, visual-motor, or hand-eye coordination; motor planning; focus; or auditory processing. Offer gentle guidance and optional activities that play to a student's skills.

Lay Out the Game Plan: Sit everyone down quietly to explain or review the rules of a new game. Comprehension will be up when noise and movement and other distractions are down. Also be aware that these students may not have been included in pick-up games in the neighborhood, so they may not know basic rules of common games.

Touch Base: In phys ed, adrenaline flows and aggressive instincts surge. This is a socially vulnerable time for students with ASD. You can't see or hear bullying from the pitcher's mound. Move around the field and dugout to listen and look closely for signs of trouble.

And They're Off: Some students with ASD have difficulty with balance and stability. Activities that require them to be off the ground or upside down, such as climbing, gymnastics, or yoga, may be dizzyingly disorienting. Be at the ready with extra support or alternative activities, if needed.

Foul! Students with ASD are rigid rule followers. They've been taught all their lives that it's never okay to push others or to grab a toy from someone else's hands. Suddenly, in competitive sports, *shoving, tackling,* and *stealing* are encouraged and celebrated. To these students, that's just WRONG. Teach them that here, in the gym, in specific games, it really is okay.

Classroom Teacher Notes: _____

_____

_____

_____

For more information, touch base with the classroom teacher or principal (or browse through *Autism Spectrum Disorder in the Inclusive Classroom*).

Know Your Student

- Don't reinvent the wheel! Talk with the classroom teacher or case manager to find out what tends to set her off and what makes things better.

- Read the IEP to find out more about the challenges this student faces and what goals have been set.

- Attend team meetings to learn about current stressors and new strategies. If you can't get there, ask for a summary of the discussion and recommendations.

Reproducible Fact and Tip Sheets

Facts and Tips for Building Staff and Bus Staff

The information on this sheet will help you play a positive role in the entire school experience of students on the autism spectrum. Thank you for your willingness to learn about and support these kids!

Students with Autism Spectrum Disorder (ASD) are quirky, endearing kids who struggle with a wide range of challenges in any or all of the following areas:

Anxiety: Students with ASD often have limited coping skills, which can lead to extreme anxiety in unfamiliar situations. They depend heavily on routines, structure, and repetitive interests to help them feel safe.

Rigidity: Students with ASD tend to be rigid rule followers. Rules help make life feel more manageable and predictable. *These students very much want to follow the rules, but may not understand exactly what the rules are.* This same rigidity means these students tend to get extremely agitated when rules are broken or when something unexpected happens.

Communication: Many of these students have a hard time making their thoughts and needs known clearly. They may also have difficulty understanding your words.

Socialization: These students rarely understand how to interact with others in socially expected ways. Conversation may be awkward, one-sided, or nonexistent. Be aware that social challenges make these students *very* vulnerable to bullying.

Sensation: Students with ASD often have sensory challenges. They may take in far too much or far too little sensory input. Hand-flapping, spinning, rocking, and similar behaviors are necessary to help students to cope with their sensory challenges.

Inside/Outside: Some students with ASD demonstrate many obvious external challenges: They may flick their fingers, have trouble speaking, or talk endlessly about a single obscure topic. Don't underestimate these students; they may have lots of clever, creative ideas going on inside. Other students are primarily affected by *internal* challenges: They may seem typical in appearance or in conversation. Don't overestimate these students; they may struggle intensely with cognitive, communicative, emotional, sensory, and other challenges that can't readily be seen.

Behavior: *All behavior is a form of communication.* Difficult behaviors tell you that something is wrong. When students with ASD misbehave, they need help—not consequences.

———————————————

Here are some simple ways you can support these kids in your everyday interactions with them:

- ✔ Use concrete and specific language. Try to make your expectations as clear as possible.

- ✔ Be calm and reassuring. Loud, angry voices will make things worse, not better.

- ✔ Remember that making conversation is a developing skill. Be patient and supportive.

- ✔ Praise them for the skills they are doing well and remember that manners may not be a priority—yet.

- ✔ Keep a watchful and protective eye out for bullying or other disrespectful treatment by peers.

- ✔ Above all, be mindful of the enormous challenges these students face at every turn and help them feel safe and supported in our school.

Flip the page for specific suggestions in your area of the school community!

Cafeteria Workers: The cafeteria is sensory chaos: Kids are shouting, chairs are scraping, smells are stewing. The lunch line presents new challenges every day, requiring quick thinking and decision making. The social pressure is intense. And it's all without the support of the teacher and the comfort of the classroom! Be patient and help students through this unrelentingly stressful experience.

Recess Monitors: The playground, which is supposed to be fun, can be a sensory and social nightmare for students with ASD. They may need help taking turns with equipment and understanding the rules of games. They often get teased, left out, or bullied, so they need close supervision when they are out among their peers. Keep in mind that you cannot recognize bullying from a distance; keep a *close* eye and ear on peer interactions to be sure that everyone is okay.

School Nurse: The fragile equilibrium of students with ASD can be easily shattered. Some students have strong sensory reactions and feel discomfort very intensely, even if their symptoms may not seem so bad to you. They're not being hypochondriacs; trust that if they say something hurts, something hurts. But be aware that some students may find it very difficult to communicate clearly what hurts and in what way it hurts.

On the other hand, some students with ASD may be *less* aware of pain and discomfort than others. They can get badly injured but feel nothing. They need to be watched for fever, nausea, dizziness, internal bleeding, and other internal problems, especially following a fall or collision.

Office Staff: Know that it may be a significant achievement for students with ASD simply to leave the classroom on their own. Remembering the route to the office, and figuring out what to do when they get to you, may be all they can handle now. Congratulate them on a job well done, even if they don't greet you with a proper "Good morning."

Custodians: You are often the first-responders when drinks spill or when vomit happens. These incidents are extremely upsetting to students with ASD because their rigid rules and expectations may have been accidentally and dramatically broken. Also keep in mind that some students have difficulty with motor coordination, which may make them especially clumsy. No matter what happened, be gentle and reassuring and know that the incident is far more troubling to them than it is to you.

Bus Staff: The bus ride poses endless challenges for students with ASD. It's loud, it's crowded, it's a social minefield, and it's an anxious transitional time between one comfort zone (home) and another (school). You cannot be available to support sensory challenges and social skills while you're driving, but you can encourage vulnerable students to sit near you and allow them to wear earplugs or headphones if it helps them feel better.

Keeping It on the D.L.

Be aware that any information you receive about specific students must, by law, be kept strictly confidential. You may not share any personal information about students with other building staff, bus drivers, students, or with your friends and family.

However, if you observe or are involved in an incident with a student, discuss it with the school personnel who work with a particular child—e.g., his or her teacher, the principal, or the student's aide. But take care that such conversations are not overheard by others.

Classroom Teacher Notes: _____

_____

For more information, touch base with the classroom teacher or principal (or browse through *Autism Spectrum Disorder in the Inclusive Classroom*).

Reproducible Fact and Tip Sheets

Facts and Tips for Classroom Paraprofessionals

The information on this sheet will help you play a positive role in the school experience of students on the autism spectrum. Thank you for your willingness to learn about and support these kids!

Students with Autism Spectrum Disorder (ASD) are quirky, endearing kids who struggle with a wide range of challenges in any or all of the following areas:

Anxiety: Students with ASD often have limited coping skills, which can lead to extreme anxiety in unfamiliar situations. Visual schedules, routines, structure, and repetitive interests help them feel safe. *Be patient and supportive.* Life on the autism spectrum can be overwhelming. That's why you're here.

Rigidity: Students with ASD tend to be rigid rule followers. Rules help make life feel more manageable and predictable. *These students very much want to follow the rules, but may not understand exactly what the rules are.* This same rigidity means these students may get extremely agitated when rules are broken or when something unexpected happens.

Communication: Many of these students express themselves in unusual ways or have a hard time making their thoughts and needs known. They may also have difficulty understanding your words. Use visual symbols and concrete, specific language to make communication as clear as possible.

Socialization: These students struggle to make friends. Interactions may be awkward, one-sided, or nonexistent. Be aware that social challenges make these students very vulnerable to bullying. Keep a watchful and protective eye out for provocation, teasing, or other disrespectful treatment by peers. Many people don't see past the challenges; help others recognize your student's fabulousness!

Sensation: Most students with ASD take in far too much or far too little sensory input. Hand-flapping, rocking, and similar behaviors are necessary to help students cope with their sensory challenges. When they feel overwhelmed, be calm and reassuring. Loud, angry voices will make things worse, not better.

Inside/Outside: Some students with ASD demonstrate obvious, *external* challenges: They may flick their fingers or talk endlessly about a single topic. Don't underestimate these students; they may have lots of clever, creative ideas going on inside. Other students are primarily affected by *internal* challenges: They may appear typical. Don't overestimate these students; they may struggle intensely with many challenges that can't readily be seen.

Behavior: *All behavior is a form of communication.* Difficult behaviors indicate that something is wrong. When students with ASD misbehave, they need help—not consequences. Be a detective. Look for patterns and warning signs so that you can ease the situations that trigger strong reactions *before* difficult behaviors erupt.

For guidance on offering meaningful one-on-one support in the classroom, flip the page.

Support for Supporters

On the Front Lines: You are on the front lines of challenging behavior. There will be moments when it is hard for you to stay calm and patient—but it's crucial that you remain professional. When a student loses control, try not to take her words or behaviors personally. She can't control herself or learn independently yet. Remember that impulsivity is *part of her disability*. Your student needs to be guided to learn more positive ways of functioning in the classroom and beyond. Be prepared to repeat yourself. This kind of learning takes time.

What's Up: While the teacher must attend to the needs of many students, you have a uniquely up-close-and-personal perspective to see details the teacher cannot. When you notice small signs of progress or new areas of concern, offer to share them with the classroom teacher.

Backing Off: *The best help you can provide is to gently guide your student toward independence.* Be on the lookout for hot spots—those times when he needs you to help him manage a challenging situation. But also look for times when you can fade your support and let him do his thing, independently.

Don't worry about "appearing" busy: The teacher and principal understand that you don't need to be interacting every moment in order to be doing your job well. This doesn't mean you can zone out. Instead, you need to remain fully engaged and attentive to your student, even from a distance.

Keeping It on the D.L.: Be aware that all personal information about specific students must, by law, be kept strictly confidential. You may not share *any* personal information about students with other building staff, bus drivers, students, other parents, or with your friends and family. Don't even share the *name* of the student to whom you are assigned.

You can discuss this student only with other school professionals who work with him or her, such as the classroom teacher, principal, or therapists. But take care that such conversations are not overheard by others.

The Rules of Cool: Needing a 1:1 aide can be a tremendous source of embarrassment, especially in upper elementary and middle school. Do your best not to make your student feel singled out and different. Keep your interventions discreet and low-key, give him a little space when possible, and offer help to other students when you are available.

Classroom Teacher Notes: _____

_____

_____

_____

_____

For more information, touch base with the classroom teacher or principal (or browse through *Autism Spectrum Disorder in the Inclusive Classroom*).

Reproducible Fact and Tip Sheets

References

American Psychiatric Association. (2013). *Diagnostic and statistical manual of mental disorders V Fifth Edition*. Washington, D.C.: American Psychiatric Association.

Asperger, H. Problems of infantile autism. *Communication: Journal of the National Autistic Society*. Vol. 13, 1979.

Attwood, T. (2009). *Making friends and managing feelings*. Presented at Autism/Asperger's Syndrome SuperConference. Guilford, CT: Future Horizons.

Baker, J. (2009). *No more meltdowns: Managing behavior in the home and classroom*. Presented at Autism/Asperger's Syndrome SuperConference. Guilford, CT: Future Horizons.

Baker, J. (2001). *The social skills picture book*. Arlington, TX: Future Horizons.

Baron-Cohen, S. (1995). *Mindblindness: An essay on autism and theory of mind*. Cambridge, MA: The Massachusetts Institute of Technology Press.

Baron-Cohen, S. (2001). Theory of mind in normal development and autism. *Prisme*, 34, 174–183.

Baron-Cohen, S., Johnson, D., Asher, J., Wheelwright, S., Fisher, S. E., Gregersen, P. K., & Allison, C. (2013). Is synaesthesia more common in autism? *Molecular Autism, 4*, 40. http://doi.org/10.1186/2040-2392-4-40.

Beals, K. (2014). The common core is tough on kids with special needs. *The Atlantic*. Retrieved from http://www.theatlantic.com/education/archive/2014/02/the-common-core-is-tough-on-kids-with-special-needs/283973.

Beals, K., & Garelick, B. (2015). Explaining your math: Unnecessary at best, encumbering at worst. *The Atlantic*. Retrieved from http://www.theatlantic.com/education/archive/2015/11/math-showing-work/414924.

Bergland, C. (2013). The size and connectivity of the amygdala predicts anxiety. *Psychology Today*, November.

Blanco, J. (2008). *Please stop laughing at us*. Dallas, TX: BenBella Books.

Bollick, T. (2009). Seeing the forest and the trees: Teaching concepts, principles, and higher-order thinking. *Autism Spectrum Quarterly*, Summer, 24–27.

Canter, L. (2002). *Assertive discipline—new and revised: Positive behavior management for today's classroom*. Santa Monica, CA: Canter & Associates.

CAST. (2011). Universal design for learning guidelines. Version 2.0. Wakefield, MA.

Dunkley, V. L. (2014). Why CFLs aren't such a bright idea. *Psychology Today*. Retrieved from http://www.psychologytoday.com/blog/mental-wealth/201409/why-cfls-arent-such-bright-idea.

Eggertson, L. (2010). Lancet retracts 12-year-old article linking autism to MMR vaccines. *Canadian Medical Association Journal*. 182(4): E199–E200.

Ernsperger, L. (2003). Developing proactive strategies for managing problem behaviors. In *The Best of Autism Asperger's Digest Magazine* (Vol. 1). Arlington, TX: Future Horizons.

Exkorn, K. S. (2005). *The autism sourcebook: Everything you need to know about diagnosis, coping, treatment, and healing*. New York: HarperCollins.

Gerould, L. (1996). *Balancing the tray*. Schnecksville, PA: Carbon-Lehigh Right to Education Task Force.

Goehner, A. L. (2011). With autism, one size doesn't fit all. *The New York Times*. New York.

Grandin, T. (1992). An inside view of autism. In E. Schopler & G. B. Mesibov (Eds.), *High-functioning individuals with autism*. New York: Plenum.

Grandin, T. (2008). *The way I see it*. Arlington, TX: Future Horizons.

Gray, C. (2000). *The new social story book: (Illustrated Edition.)* Arlington, TX: Future Horizons.

Greenspan, S. I., & Wieder, S. (2006). *Engaging autism: The floortime approach to helping children relate, communicate and think*. New York: Perseus.

Grigorenko, E. L., Klin, A., & Volkmar, F. (2003). Annotation: Hyperlexia: disability or superability? *Journal of Child Psychology and Psychiatry*. 44(8), 1079–91.

Gutstein, S. E., & Sheely, R. K. (2002). *Relationship development intervention with children, adolescents, and adults*. London: Jessica Kingsley.

Happé, F., & Frith, U. (2006). The weak coherence account: Detail-focused cognitive style in autism spectrum disorders. *Journal of Autism and Developmental Disorders*. Vol 35, No. 1. DOI 10.1007/s10803-005-0039-0

Heaton, P., Williams, K., Cummins, O., & Happé, F. (2008). Autism and pitch processing splinter skills. *Autism, 12*(2), 203–219.

Howlin, P., & Asgharian, A. (1999). The diagnosis of autism and Asperger's syndrome: Findings from a survey of 770 families. *Developmental Medicine & Child Neurology. 41*, 834–839.

Kana, R. K., Uddin, L. Q., Kenet, T., Chugani, D., & Müller, R.-A. (2014). Brain connectivity in autism. *Frontiers in Human Neuroscience. 8*, 349. http://doi.org/10.3389/fnhum.2014.00349

Kaufmann, W.E., M.D. (2012). DSM-V: The new diagnostic criteria for autism spectrum disorders. Presented at 2012 Research Symposium. Boston, MA: Autism Consortium.

Kennedy Krieger Institute. (2014). Educational and behavioral therapies. Interactive Autism Network.

Khazan, O. (2015). Autism's hidden gifts. *The Atlantic*. Retrieved from http://www.theatlantic.com/health/archive/2015/09/autism-hidden-advantages/406180.

Kluth, P. (2003). *You're going to love this kid!* Baltimore, MD: Brookes.

Koegel, R. L., & Koegel, L. K. (2006). *Pivotal response treatments for autism: Communication, social, and academic development*. Baltimore, MD: Brookes.

Kranowitz, C. (2016). *The out-of-sync child grows up: coping with sensory processing disorder in the adolescent years*. New York: Perigee.

Kübler-Ross, Elizabeth. (1997). *On death and dying*. New York: Touchstone.

Kuder, S. J. (2003). *Teaching students with language and communication disabilities*. New York: Pearson Education.

Kutscher, M. L. (2004). *ADHD book: Living right now!* White Plains, NY: Neurology Press.

Lavoie, R. (2005). *It's so much work to be your friend: Helping the child with learning disabilities find social success*. New York: Simon & Schuster.

Mandell, D. S., Novak, M. M., & Zubritsky, C. D. (2005). Factors associated with age of diagnosis among children with autism spectrum disorders. *Pediatrics. 116*, 1480–1486.

Mehrabian, A. (1980). *Silent messages: Implicit communications of emotions and attitudes*. Belmont, CA: Wadsworth Publishing.

Miller, L. J. (2006). *Sensational kids: Hope and help for children with sensory processing disorder*. New York: Putnam.

Molloy, C. A., & Manning-Courtney, P. (2003). Prevalence of chronic gastrointestinal symptoms in children with autism and Autism Spectrum Disorder. *Autism. 7*(2) 165–171.

Nazeer, K. (2006). *Send in the idiots: Stories from the other side of autism*. New York: Bloomsbury.

Norris, J. A., & Hoffman, P. R. (1990). Language intervention within naturalistic environments. *Language, Speech, and Hearing Services in Schools*, Vol. 21, 72–84.

Notbohm, E. (2006). *Ten things your student with autism wishes you knew*. Arlington, TX: Future Horizons.

Owens, R. E. (2009). *Language disorders: A functional approach to assessment and intervention (5th ed.)*. Boston: Allyn and Bacon.

Padawer, R. (2014). The recovered. *The New York Times*. August 3.

Polimeni, M. A., Richdale, A. L., & Francis, A. J. (2005). A survey of sleep problems in autism: Asperger's disorder and typically developing children. *Journal of Intellectual Disability Research, 49*(4), 260-268.

Peale, N. V. (1996). *Have a great day*. New York: Ballantine Books.

Polyak A., Kubina, R. M., & Girirajan, S. (2015). Comorbidity of intellectual disability confounds ascertainment of autism: implications for genetic diagnosis. *American Journal of Medical Genetics*, Part B, 168B:600–608.

Pychyl, T. (2009, March 5). Perseveration: The deep rut of change procrastination, [blog post]. Retrieved from http://www.psychologytoday.com/blog/dont-delay/200903/perseveration-the-deep-rut-change-procrastination.

RTI Action Network. (2015). What is RTI? National Center for Learning Disabilities. Retrieved from http://www.rtinetwork.org/learn/what/whatisrti.

Reade, D., & Mears, H. (2015). What is defense mode? Asperger experts. Retrieved from http://www.aspergerexperts.com/defense-mode/what-is-defense-mode/asperger Experts:

Robison, J. E. (2007). *Look me in the eye: My life with Asperger's*. New York: Crown.

Saulny, S. (2009). Students stand when called upon, and when not. *The New York Times*. New York.

Schlieder, M. (2007). *With open arms: Creating school communities of support for kids with social challenges using circle of friends, extracurricular activities, and learning teams.* Shawnee Mission, KS: Autism Asperger Publishing.

Schoen, S. A., Miller, L. J., Brett-Green, B. A., & Nielsen, D. M. (2009). Physiological and behavioral differences in sensory processing: a comparison of children with Autism Spectrum Disorder and Sensory Modulation Disorder. *Frontiers in Integrative Neuroscience.* Vol. 3; Article 29.

Sensory Processing Foundation, 2016. *About SPD.* Greenwood Village, CO. http://www.spdfoundation.net/about-sensory-processing-disorder/otherdisorders/

Smagorinsky, P. (2011). Confessions of a mad professor: An autoethnographic consideration of neuroatypicality, extranormativity, and education. *Teachers College Record.* 113:8, pp. 1700–1732.

Solomon, A. (2013). *Far from the tree: parents, children, and the search for identity.* New York: Scribner.

South, M., Van Hecke, A., & McVey, A. (2015). Anxiety in autism: Mechanisms, measurement, and treatment. Presented at International Meeting for Autism Research. Salt Lake City, UT: International Society for Autism Research.

South, M., Newton, T., & Chamberlain, P. D. (2012). Delayed reversal learning and association with repetitive behavior in autism spectrum disorders. *International Society for Autism Research*, Wiley Periodicals. Vol. 5, Issue 6, pp. 398-406.

Sundberg, M. L. (2008). *VB-MAPP: Verbal behavior milestones assessment and placement program.* Concord, CA: AVB Press.

Tammet, D. (2007). *Born on a blue day.* New York: Free Press.

Thompson, S. J., Morse, A. B., Sharpe, M., & Hall, S. (2005). *Accommodations manual: How to select, administer, and evaluate use of accommodations for instruction and assessment of students with disabilities (2nd ed.).* Washington, D.C.: The Council of Chief State School Officers.

Tordjman, S., Somogyi, E., Coulon, N., Kermarrec, S., Cohen, D., Bronsard, G., Bonnot, O., Weismann-Arcache, C. Botbol, M., Lauth, B., Ginchat, V., Roubertoux, P., Barburoth, M., Kovess, V., Geoffray, M., & Xavier. J. (2014). Gene x environment interactions in autism spectrum disorders: role of epigenetic mechanisms. *Frontiers in Psychiatry, 5*, 53.

Trafton, A. MIT 10/7/14. Autism as a disorder of prediction. MIT News Office Massachusetts Institute of Technology–Cambridge, MA

Treffert, D. A. (2009). The savant syndrome: an extraordinary condition. A synopsis: past, present, future. *Philosophical Transactions of the Royal Society B: Biological Sciences, 364*(1522), 1351–1357. Accessed at http://www.ncbi.nlm.nih.gov/

U.S. Centers for Disease Control and Prevention (2016). Prevalence and characteristics of autism spectrum disorder: autism and developmental disabilities monitoring network, United States, 2012. MMWR Surveillance Summaries, 65(3);1–23.

U.S. Centers for Disease Control and Prevention (2014). Prevalence of autism spectrum disorders: Autism and developmental disabilities monitoring network, United States, 2010. MMWR Surveillance Summaries, 63(SS02);1–21.

U.S. Department of Education, Office of Special Education Programs, Individuals with Disabilities Education Act (IDEA) database. (2014). Digest of Education Statistics. Table 204.60.

Watson, T. S., & Skinner, C. H. (2004). *Encyclopedia of School Psychology.* Springer: NY.

Wetherby, A. (1986). Ontogeny of communicative functions in autism. *Journal of Autism and Developmental Disorders, 16*, 295–316.

Whalen, J., & McKay, B. (2013). Fifteen years after autism panic, a plague of measles erupts. *The Wall Street Journal.* July 20–21; A11–A12.

White, R. (2005). Autism first-hand: An expert interview with Temple Grandin, Ph.D. *Medscape Psychiatry & Mental Health 10*(1).

Zablotsky, B., Ph.D., Black, L. I., Maenner, M. J., Ph.D., Schieve, L. A., Ph.D., & Blumberg, S. J., Ph.D. (2015). Estimated prevalence of autism and other developmental disabilities following questionnaire changes in the 2014 National Health Interview Survey. *National Health Statistics Reports*, [2015(87):1-20]. US CDC Division of Health Interview Statistics, Hyattsville, MD.

Ziv, S. (2015). Andrew Wakefield, father of the anti-vaccine movement, responds to the current measles outbreak for the first time. *Newsweek.* February 20, New York.

Index